RED ARCTIC

RED ARCTIC

★ RUSSIAN STRATEGY ★
UNDER PUTIN

ELIZABETH BUCHANAN

BROOKINGS INSTITUTION PRESS
Washington, D.C.

Published by Brookings Institution Press
1775 Massachusetts Avenue, NW
Washington, DC 20036
www.brookings.edu/bipress

Co-published by Rowman & Littlefield
An imprint of The Rowman & Littlefield Publishing Group, Inc.
4501 Forbes Boulevard, Suite 200, Lanham, Maryland 20706
www.rowman.com

86-90 Paul Street, London EC2A 4NE

The Brookings Institution is a nonprofit organi zation devoted to research, education, and publication on important issues of domestic and
foreign policy. Its principal purpose is to bring the highest quality independent research and analys is to bear on current and emerging
policyp roblems.

Composition by Westchester Publishing Services
Typeset in Sabon

British Library Cataloguing in Publication Information Available

Library of Congress Cataloging-in-Publication Data Is Available

ISBN 978-0-8157-4004-9 (cloth)
ISBN 978-0-8157-3888-6 (pbk.)
ISBN 978-0-8157-3889-3 (ebook)

CONTENTS

Contents

PREFACE

In 2007, a Russian expedition planted a titanium flag on the seabed of the Arctic Ocean. It was a move that effectively claimed the North Pole in the name of Russia. However, more than fifteen years since Russia's flag stunt, the Arctic remains a zone of international cooperation. In this time, Russia has gone to war with Georgia, wrapped a second battle with Chechnya, fought insurgents throughout the Northern Caucasus, and intervened militarily in Syria. And while Moscow may have absorbed Crimea and sustained military aggression toward Ukraine, since 2014, it has yet to annex the North Pole. Why not?

This book delves into Russian Arctic strategy under Vladimir Putin to illustrate how Moscow, as the largest Arctic actor, approaches the region through a largely cooperative agenda. This contention will naturally raise eyebrows (if not calls to investigate the origin of funding for this work). Nonetheless, I argue the strategic basis for Russia's Arctic agenda is more or less cooperative. This concept deviates significantly from Russian security strategy outside the Arctic region.

This apparent divergence in strategy highlights the necessity to better understand Russian Arctic policy. After all, understanding Russia's rationale would allow other nations to understand and perhaps preempt Russian strategic calculations in the Arctic well into the future.

Generally, the Arctic narrative is framed by competitive and con-flictual connotations. In international media coverage, three key elements of the Arctic story have become constant features: the Arctic is warming due to climate change (with extra points for the awkward inclusion of heating-up state-to-state tensions as the causal factor for a warming Arctic); the Arctic melt process in turn unlocks the region's rich oil and gas bounty; and the final element, realists rejoice as great power competition spills over into the Arctic and states scrap for primacy.

Sure, the Arctic is a potential flashpoint for international war. So is the moon. But the Arctic as a theater for great power competition is no new reality. The Arctic has played a feature role in both World Wars, as well as the Cold War. Of course, Russia's assertive foreign and military policies since 2014 have accentuated the popular perception that the Arctic is characterized by conflict, tense ties, and unprecedented competition. Simply, Arctic geopolitical realities became a work of fiction. The zone became a Tom Clancy eighties novel, on steroids.

In an age of globalized communication and the unabated 24-hour news cycle, compounded by a proliferation of social media platforms, it becomes difficult to put the "Arctic war" genie back in the bottle. And yet, this is the task of my book. In the following pages, I methodically develop the rationale for Russia's Arctic interest and strategy under President Vladimir Putin. In doing so, I arrive at the conclusion that Russia largely requires a cooperative Arctic environment to achieve its strategic objectives and deliver on Moscow's critical economic interests. The foundational starting point for this book is the notion that Putin's Russia seeks to regain great power status on the back of its energy wealth. Of course, many of these energy deposits are in the Russian Far North— well within Russia's Arctic zone.

What follows is a succinct examination of Russian Arctic strategy under Putin in terms of how it is formulated, what is currently driving it, and where it is likely going. Russia's recent foreign policy actions on the Crimean Peninsula and in Ukraine since February 2022 under-score that an assertive Moscow plans to remain a relevant (albeit dis-ruptive) actor on the West's radar. Yet, Moscow's Arctic strategy relies upon continued cooperation via commercial partnerships and Eastern injections of capital to realize Putin's Arctic aspirations. How can one reconcile these two divergent strategic appetites of Putin's Russia?

In a sense, this book is the antithesis of the popular narratives of a looming Arctic war or a Russian plot to "take" the Arctic. It illustrates how Arctic cooperation results from Russia's technological and investment requirements from abroad; Russia's solid legal case in the Arctic with regard to the continental shelf debate, given Moscow's sheer geographical stake in the Arctic zone; and finally, the strong precedent of cooperation over Arctic matters throughout the contracted period of worsening Russia-West ties. Even if these tensions persist in the Russia-West relationship, the "new cold war" paradigm will not apply to the Arctic.

I craft this case across seven chapters. Chapter 1 surveys the Arctic "great game," delving into the current geopolitical situation in the Arctic by unpacking popular assessments of Russian Arctic strategy. I use this chapter to contextualize the broader notion of Russian resurgence and aggression in the Arctic. The chapter reviews the key contenders in the Arctic game, as well as the resource and shipping prizes at stake. Then I head back to the drawing board, back to the basics of what Russia would want in the Arctic. To do this, chapter 2 explores the role of energy in Putin's Russia. The primacy of energy for Moscow's economic bottom line is an important aspect of the cooperative agenda Russia seeks in the Arctic. Russia's natural resource base is central to its future economic plans, and realizing this potential has been a personal quest under Putin. Chapter 2 examines the relationship between Putin and energy across four key phases between since 2000: recentralization; renationalization; the modernization agenda; and the revival of great power strategy. From this baseline, I chart the development of Russian Arctic strategy under Putin. Building from the primacy of energy to Putin's Russia, chapter 3 then presents Russia's Arctic playbook.

Chapter 4 moves to examine the notion of "conquering" the Arctic. Here I illustrate the processes of Arctic stakeholder engagement through the region's governance structure, the Arctic Council, and the Arctic powers' continued adherence to international legal norms in the region.

This chapter includes a discussion on Arctic challenges and opportunities, aspects of which serve to shape the basis for state engagement in the region. Taken as a whole, whether they are Arctic rim or "near Arctic," states operating within the region are viewed as partaking in a process of conquering the Arctic. Chapter 4 serves to demystify Arctic engagement and reject popular connotations of an Arctic carve-up. Fact-checking the narratives of resource clashes in the Arctic, along with illustrating that Arctic geopolitics today is far from the throes of Arctic warfare, is an important correction sorely needed in contemporary Arctic debate.

Building on a clear understanding of Russian Arctic strategy, chapter 5 illustrates the cooperative nature in which the strategy is employed in the region. Using two case studies, I demonstrate the cooperative nature of Russian Arctic policy. I chart various state-state engagements in the Arctic under Putin, including the decades-old maritime dispute over the Barents Sea and the resolution between Norway and Russia. The second case study illustrates Russia's engagement with foreign energy corporations in the Russian Arctic. Russian state energy firm Rosneft and private energy firm Novatek account for the lion's share of Russia's current Arctic energy projects. Further, these firms' engagement with foreign corporations by way of joint energy ventures is examined. In both its state-state Arctic engagement and joint venture Arctic energy partnerships, Moscow has pursued cooperative agendas.

With the Arctic great game correctly contextualized, notions of a new cold war in the region and of Russian Arctic aggression become unsubstantiated. From this more realistic starting point, I reengage with the current Arctic gloom and doom narrative of a looming Arctic war. Throughout chapter 6, I consider the viable elements that may yet drive the Arctic region toward actual conflict, perhaps even war, starting with the assumption of Russia-West tensions spilling over into the Arctic zone. Here, the 2022 iteration of the Russia-Ukraine war, is an interesting litmus test to illustrate the foreign policy anomaly that is Arctic cooperation under Putin.

Some fallout of Russia's Ukraine policy since 2014 is still felt in the Arctic—particularly the Western sanctions that affected much of Russia's Arctic energy ventures since 2014. Furthermore, in March 2022,

Western Arctic states suspended engagement with Russia in the context of the Arctic Council. While cooperation via this particular avenue has indeed been curtailed, conflict has not replaced it nor should we expect it to.

While the global oil price dive in 2014 exacerbated the pressure on Moscow, Russia still managed to source alternative pools of capital and technology for energy ventures. The entry of nontraditional Arctic players to the region, including China, and a revived US Arctic interest under President Donald Trump (and thus far maintained under President Joe Biden) are considered potential variables that might yet garner an aggressive Russian response.

In the final chapter of this book, I lay out the case that counters the popular narrative of a looming Arctic war. Chapter 7 ties together the threads and rejects the notion that Russian Arctic strategy is geared to plunging the Arctic into conflict. At the heart of this notion is the reemerging debate over whether to expect conflict or cooperation over access to, and control of, Arctic energy reserves. Chapter 7 makes a strong case that it is unlikely Arctic rim powers will engage in armed warfare over access to the Arctic's riches. Rather, the chapter outlines the ways in which the Arctic is a natural conduit for Russia-West cooperation—something increasingly difficult to sustain elsewhere as the two enter an era of prolonged tension not seen since the Cold War.

Finally, I consider the idea that the Arctic provides the Kremlin with a potential exit ramp, an alternative to Russia-West tensions as seen elsewhere. From a purely commercial standpoint, Russian joint ventures in the Arctic are enduring, with China ramping up its investment and market demand. In recent years, the Arctic has hosted unprecedented industrialization, with much of the activity occurring in the Russian Arctic region. The Arctic is no short-term play for Putin's Russia. Rather, it is the future resource base of the Russian Federation, and as such, a high degree of Russia's national security interests are assigned to this region. As this book highlights, low tension in the Arctic is a consistent facet of Putin's Arctic strategy.

What follows is a semirevisionist reading of Russian Arctic strategy under Putin. More broadly, this book aims to fill a gap within existing Arctic studies, in which the bulk of the literature positions the Arctic as an emerging theater for conflict. Certainly, the military-security angle garners the most international attention and serves a clickbait function.

While this book frames and views the Kremlin's approaches through the lens of cooperation, this is no attempt to obscure assertive or aggressive elements of Russian posturing in the region. Cooperation does not necessarily mean acquiescence nor dereference to another. Robert Keohane's definition of cooperation is apt when considering Russia's interpretation and use of cooperation in the Arctic context. Keohane notes that powers adjust their behavior to the anticipated or actual preferences of other powers, and this affects the beliefs, rules, and practices that form the context for future action.[1] Crucially, cooperation does not necessarily mean the absence of conflict. After all, cooperation itself is only possible in situations where powers are potentially in conflict. As such, this book defines *conflict* as simply a disagreement or dispute that is typically protracted. Similarly, this text uses *war* to describe situations when a military is deployed in a state-state conflict.

When using the word *energy*, I am referring primarily to oil and natural gas. References to *resources* or *resource wealth* signify the oil and natural gas assets of the Arctic. These two commodities are inherently political. Access to, transport of, and control over both energy sources are increasingly significant on the international energy security agenda. They are a determining facet of relations between the energy rich and the energy poor. Throughout this book, I use the Brent Crude trading classification when discussing oil prices and express monetary values in US dollars unless otherwise specified.

This book is crafted upon a primary source document-based study that includes a number of semistructured interviews. It draws upon various pools of reference—the commercial petroleum industry, formal government reportage, academia, and think tank papers—with the ultimate aim of forming a nexus between them. I owe a great deal of gratitude to those individuals who agreed to provide insights and private assessments on Russian Arctic strategy. Given the commercial sensitivity of Arctic dealings and national security implications of internal defense positions, interviewees are not identified.

I also consulted government research bodies of Arctic rim nations—particularly those based in Scandinavia—as they provide strong insights into Arctic geopolitics. These research units have expansive research budgets, which allow for insights on topics of national security interest not widely considered by other agencies. I acknowledge the support of The Centre for Borders Research (IBRU) at the University of Durham for their permission to use maps from their fabulous Arctic series. I encourage readers to head to their website to read the briefing notes and associated research briefs. This book also incorporates primary sources in the form of in-house publications of major energy firms. I am eternally grateful to my network within resource firms that made various internal modeling and scenario publications readily available. Incorporating these diverse pools of reference into this book is important because, drawn together, they provide real-time assessments of the current climate in the Arctic, beyond merely politics. Geoeconomics and commercial strategic cultures of oil majors within the Arctic great game are indeed worthy of some of the limelight.

ACKNOWLEDGMENTS

Publishing a book is eerily like parenthood, and in many ways *Red Arctic* is my first child. This project began in 2013 with my candidacy at the Center for European Studies at the Australian National University, Canberra. Several fieldwork trips from Australia to Russia always began with the amusing (and at times, frustrating) assumption I had arrived in Moscow to discuss Antarctic strategy. While this book was born out of my Ph.D., which was awarded in mid-2018, it was only possible (as with parenting) thanks to a village. Thanks first to my publication village, the wonderful team at the Brookings Institution Press (Bill Finan and Yelba Quinn in particular). Thanks also to Mary Ribesky at Westchester for her sharp eye (and patience). I've also hassled much of my academic village for years now, on all things Russia, energy, and geostrategy. Unfailingly, my academic village continues to support, mentor, and challenge me. Thanks here to Fiona Hill, Angela Stent, Andrew Monaghan, and Andrei Zagorski in particular. The peer review village provided robust feedback and review of this book, and I am extremely grateful for the readers' time and care in constructively enhancing the manuscript. Of course, any errors or oversights in this book are entirely on me. Finally, to my personal village, the people who stepped in (and up) on the parenting front, enabling my career and publishing dreams: thank you. We did it, and here's to the next book.

1

THE ARCTIC GREAT GAME

"IF THE ENEMY LEAVES A DOOR OPEN YOU MUST RUSH IN."

—SUN TZU

Great power rivalry has long facilitated "great games." These great games involve political and strategic competition, often leading to military conflict, over control of or influence over foreign soil and the resource wealth it possesses. Textbook great game examples include historical great power competition within (and over) Central Asia and Africa. The Arctic has, on face value, many of the hallmarks of a looming twenty-first century great game. There is the energy bounty and rising international interest. The irony in the contemporary Arctic great game is, quite simply, there is not much to really scrap over.

Arctic great game and Arctic war narratives are becoming even more alluring for the general public thanks to clickbait, including "The Arctic is melting due to rising tensions" and "Great power competition has reignited a battle over the Arctic." Add "Russia will invade the US via its Alaskan Arctic frontier" to the mix, for good measure. The lengths that news media platforms will go to get the reader to consume outrageous and erroneous Arctic analysis by way of "clickbait" headlines is impressive. Of course, one could argue this book's doomsday-alluding title and marvelous cover art do something similar, luring readers into this book.

In a sense, the "looming Arctic war" assessment has been mainstreamed to the point it is now normalized and often accepted as fact. The increasingly popular "new cold war" narrative of the Arctic is merely a misreading of contemporary Arctic geopolitics. This narrative is a rather prickly work of fiction. Perhaps the real Arctic great game is the enduring effort undertaken by subject matter experts to correct and fact-check the inundation of hot takes on Arctic affairs. Before delving into Russian Arctic strategy, I provide much-needed context for the current state of affairs in the Arctic region.

What is one referring to when one speaks of the Arctic? While a rather simplistic question, it is an important one that is often overlooked. Clear operational boundaries and definitions are crucial to any strategy, and this is also true of any serious geopolitical assessment. The lack of consensus in defining "the Arctic" has served to further cultivate the region's air of uncertainty and mystery. There are numerous definitions of the Arctic region—some determined by political considerations and others to scientific ones. Contrasting the Arctic with its southern polar sister, the Antarctic, is a useful starting point. The Arctic is essentially characterized by the Arctic Ocean, which extends from the numerous territorial seas of sovereign states circling the ocean, whereas the Antarctic is a continental landmass surrounded by ocean. The Antarctic is protected as an international park of sorts, assigned to scientific endeavor and global cooperation as enshrined by the Antarctic Treaty.

There is no Arctic Treaty because the region, unlike the Antarctic, is no *terra nullius*. The Arctic is home to long-delineated maritime borders, and while some overlapping claims to the Arctic Ocean's continental shelf exist, there is still minimal basis for dispute in the region. These claims, as well as the international legal norms and principles along with the overall governance aspects of the Arctic, are further developed in the next chapter. Of course, understanding the existing legal architecture is an important starting point, which should, in practice, deny popular attempts to sell the Arctic as a region of lawlessness and arena for territorial conquest. This Arctic simply does not exist: There is no sovereignty vacuum in this zone.

This book defines the Arctic according to the political definition utilized by Arctic states and their key governance forum, the Arctic Council, whereby the Arctic is the region north of the Arctic Circle, as shown in figure 1-1. It is a zone that includes the states with territory north of the Arctic Circle—otherwise known as the Arctic Eight (Russia, US, Canada, Denmark, Iceland, Finland, Sweden, and Norway). However, most geopolitical Arctic definitions focus on the so-called Arctic Five (Russia, US, Canada, Denmark—by way of Greenland—and Norway). These five states have maritime boundaries fronting the Arctic Ocean via their territorial seas.

Narrowing down the focus to the Arctic Five for geopolitical Arctic analysis is apt, given the mechanics of international law at play. These five states have both territorial sovereignty above the Arctic Circle and various maritime claims extending out into the Arctic Ocean. The UN Convention on the Law of the Sea (UNCLOS) is the rather effectively implemented maritime governance approach for the Arctic. While states have jurisdiction over inland waterways and rights in their territorial seas, UNCLOS further allocates each state's exclusive economic zone (EEZ) and special rights over the resources within it. The complexity of Arctic applications of UNCLOS are further examined in chapter 2, particularly in terms of the Arctic continental shelf debate (the whole "who owns the North Pole" conundrum).

This notion of who "owns" the Arctic is an important one, if not solely because it is a widely misunderstood concept. The Arctic Ocean has only small maritime areas that may be viewed as international commons, referenced as the high seas in accordance with UNCLOS. Most of the Arctic is well delineated and not contested. Nonetheless, this reality is clouded by the allure of the Arctic great game—connotations of a global race to claim the riches of Arctic resources. This resource prize is often referred to in terms of the 2008 US Geological Survey findings, which concluded that 30 percent of the world's remaining natural gas and 18 percent of the remaining oil were located in the

Figure 1-1. The Arctic

Source: UNEP/GRID-Arendal, 2008. https://www.grida.no/resources/8353.

Arctic. It is important to note two things here. First, any review of the survey's methodology would indicate these findings are entirely estimative. The hydrocarbon (natural gas and oil) prize in the Arctic might prove to be significantly lower. Further, producing energy in the offshore Arctic is simply not viable in the current, and likely mid-long term, global commercial energy market. Globally, there are known reserves of hydrocarbons elsewhere that will be tapped before energy firms broach the technically challenging and financially prohibitive advent of offshore Arctic oil. The second point worth noting is these deposits are largely located in parts of the Arctic Ocean and onshore

Arctic regions that are not contested. These resources are mostly located well within the exclusive economic zones (EEZs) of Arctic states. Therefore, while the resource bounty of the Arctic might make for a catchy news item and simplistic explanation of increased state interest in the Arctic, the notion of a race for riches is more or less hot air.

The Arctic great game narrative is further cultivated by imagery of melting ice caps. Tensions are rising, conflicts are heating up between Russia and the West in the Arctic—and the ice is melting. Or at least this is the not unique play on words that 90 percent of published analysis online is using to deal with a serious Arctic security challenge: climate change. It is most apparent in the polar regions, with various studies concluding the Arctic is warming at rates two times that of the rest of the world. The Arctic is the canary in the coal mine for global warming. The Arctic Ocean ice cap is at its minimum in September, and with each year that passes the ice cap extent is growing thinner and thinner. NASA satellites log Arctic sea ice extent and indicate the rate of ice sheet decline in the Arctic is about 13 percent every decade, as illustrated in figure 1-2. If this trend continues, the world should expect ice-free summers in much of the Arctic Ocean by 2050.

In theory, these statistics should be alarming. However, facilitated by climate change, the Arctic is opening both economically and in terms of access. Indeed, much of the literature tends to focus on the opportunities that arise from an opening Arctic. Coupled with advances in offshore drilling technology, there is an increasingly popular narrative that a warmer Arctic equals ease of access to resources once locked beneath the ice. As noted above, said resources largely fall well within EEZs and therefore the notion of an "Arctic free-for-all" over oil and gas is rather implausible. Beyond the resource wealth of the Arctic, climate change is facilitating easier access to Arctic transportation routes. The Arctic includes three central routes: the Transpolar Sea Route (TSR), the Northwest Passage (NWP), and the Northeast Passage (NEP). The transpolar route treks through the heart of the Arctic Ocean and through the North Pole remaining largely in international waters. The NEP is more commonly referred to as the Northern Sea Route (NSR), which is merely one component of the NEP, and hugs

Figure 1-2. Average Arctic Minimum Sea Ice Extent (September)

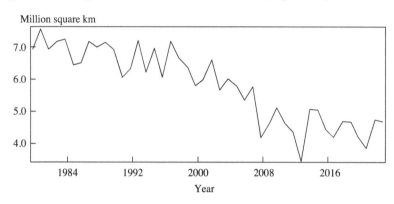

Million square km

Source: https://climate.nasa.gov/vital-signs/arctic-sea-ice/.

the Russian Arctic coastline linking Asia to Europe. Under Vladimir Putin, as chapter 3 examines, the NSR has increasingly become securitized by the Kremlin and is at the heart of Russian Arctic strategy. The NWP runs between the US and Canadian Arctic zones, skirting Greenland into Europe.

With climate change "opening up" these routes, they become viable international alternatives to the Suez Canal and may be treated as new international "superhighways," at least in theory. However, the Transpolar Route is unlikely to be entirely ice-free, and the sheer remoteness and operational challenges are not going to be muted by climate change. Whereas the NSR and NEP might "open up" in terms of reduced ice extent, or thinner ice, climate change will not alter the international legal norms applied to these two routes. Russia treats the NSR as an internal waterway, and Canada views the NEP as internal waters. Easier access to Arctic energy and transport or shipping routes does not necessarily mean either will become commercially viable overnight. A Suez Canal blockage in early 2021, in which a ship ran aground and stymied global shipping for six days, did not result in any real "bump" in Arctic shipping. While 10 percent of the world's shipping was disrupted, few turned toward the Arctic and considered the contingency of the northern passages. Insurance premiums for Arctic shipping are increasing due to the sharpening of operational hazards of the remote polar environment. Indeed, climate-induced melting of Arctic ice does not make Arctic transport passage easier or safer. Fast ice formation, ever-shifting ice movement, and inability to predict passage through the Arctic Ocean are further curtailments to the commercial bottom line considerations of any Arctic shipping superhighway coming online.

Climate change does not deliver an "unlocked" Arctic; instead, it supercharges ecodisasters and socioeconomic threats. Permafrost melting throughout the Russian Arctic has already resulted in environmental disaster. Just look to the 2020 Norilsk oil spill, where the erosion of permafrost due to a warming climate had left a mining firm's oil storage infrastructure (tanks) sitting on a ticking time bomb, environmentally speaking.

Against the backdrop of an Arctic that is opening up and anticipation of looming resource races, there is also a Russia problem. A resurgent Russia under Vladimir Putin has been busy modernizing its military hardware, flexing its muscles in neighboring countries and interfering in the far abroad. Lines of communication between the Kremlin and the West are largely fractured, and it is increasingly apparent that Russia seeks no "warming" of relations beyond issues of mutual interest. The problem, of course, is there appears to be very little that Russia and the West have by way of mutual interests. Russia has failed to shake its Cold War reputation of "other" in Washington's worldview. It does not help that Moscow seeks an entirely new world order in which the US-unipolar system is dismantled and a multipolar system is erected in its place. Ideally, this multipolar system would see Russia assigned a seat at all decisionmaking tables, as a pole of acknowledged equal power with the US. While it is true this is Russia's goal, it can also be true that Russia is a cooperative, collaborative actor in the Arctic. Duality of foreign policy, and the ability for states to pursue multipronged strategies across various theaters throughout the globe, is a difficult notion to grasp at the best of times. It is even more so with the addition of the Russian element.

Russia's Arctic strategy is largely perceived by the global community as aggressive and expansionist. Yet, the strategy in its very essence is pragmatic, in line with international law in the region, and not dissimilar to the strategies of the other Arctic rim powers.

Literature on Russia's Arctic ambitions appears concentrated at either end of the Arctic "carve up" spectrum, with a new cold war camp at one end and an arena for international cooperation camp at the other. Proponents of the new cold war view frame Russia's Arctic strategy in terms of Moscow's efforts to stoke regional competition.[1] Harking back to the Cold War–era struggle between the Soviet Union and the US, this group relies on a simplified rebranding to stoke connotations of revived "bloc" competition between Moscow and Washington. Useful in this new cold war narrative and framing is the geographical proximity of the Arctic—a frontier at which both Russia and the US indeed meet. The irony here is during the actual Cold War, the Arctic was a heavily militarized theater in which the two states monitored continually for the other to strike first—after all, this Arctic is the shortest distance for missiles to travel from Russian to American soil (or back the other way, depending on one's ideological leaning). This group continues to perpetuate the myth that the Arctic will descend into a new scramble for territory and control of Arctic resource wealth.[2] For some, the Arctic will become a battlefront for the looming resource war that will result from global energy supply failing to meet global energy demands.[3] Proponents of the new cold war theory argue that military clashes are most likely to occur in regions where energy resources are to be won or lost—and that the Arctic qualifies as such a region.[4] Generally, this group tends to label Russia's Arctic strategy as neoimperialist. Ariel Cohen notes that a key feature of Russia's neoimperialist approach to the Arctic is the way in which Russia views the region as a "mega project" for the twenty-first century.[5] Cohen also argues that Russian Arctic strategy under Putin represents a throwback to the 1930s Stalinist attempts to conquer the Arctic. Taken together, these elements further cultivate the notion of a mad dash for the North Pole, with the Arctic emerging once more as an ideal field for expression of great power ambitions.[6]

Some Arctic conflict proponents tend to point to odd sources within Russia to legitimize their hot take on what is driving Russia in the region. Useful idiots largely discredited by serious Russian scholars are trotted out as evidence of Moscow's neoimperialist Arctic endgame. Take, for example, sounds bites taken as gospel and afforded far too much attention from Russia's Aleksandr Dugin. The concept of Dugin having the ear of Putin or a place in the inner decisionmaking circles of the Kremlin is one of those relentless untruths that folks in the Russian field use to sort pundits from scholars. True, Dugin incites nationalist fervor and actively trumpets a neoimperialist agenda. For example, when addressing the Russian public on Arctic matters, Dugin declared, "The purpose of our being lies in the expansion of our space. . . . Polar bears live there, Russian polar bears."[7] This statement was then weaponized by news media to apparently represent the unveiling of aggressive expansionist plans for the Arctic.

Nonetheless, this Arctic strategic panic group can be contrasted with those who identify Russian Arctic strategy as paving the way for, and encouraging, healthy competition in the region.[8] Proponents of this camp at the other end of the Arctic spectrum assert that competition, but not necessarily to the extent of conflict, will result from looming global energy security challenges. This group accepts the concept of growing global demand for scarce energy supplies but refutes the notion that armed warfare will ensue as a result.[9] For Brenda Shaffer, the rise in unconventional energy sources[10] will continue to ensure that the global energy market stays ahead of global energy demands.[11]

The notion that Arctic competition may not necessarily result in Arctic confrontation is also supported by Marlene Laruelle.[12] She examines contemporary Arctic geopolitics as evidence of the return of nationalist rhetoric, something not unique to Russia. Laruelle makes the point that such rhetoric is largely an identity-building project for Putin. She plots the changes in Russian strategic thinking about the Arctic and concludes that Russia does not have "sufficient capability to dominate" the Arctic. On this point, I would argue domination is not the end goal of Putin's Russia in the Arctic; it may be the goal for the Russian Arctic, but it is not for the Arctic zone writ large. Russia has modernized its Arctic military capabilities and outposts, revamped the Northern Sea Fleet, and added many naval vessels to its maritime toolbox, with more on the way. So, why has Russia not simply claimed the North Pole by military might? Why has Putin's Russia opted to follow the agreed international channels in its ongoing claim to an extended continental shelf, all the way up to and just beyond the North Pole?

Some have already put in the hard work to disprove the new cold war theses by way of unpacking common misconceptions of Arctic geopolitics. Lawson Brigham notes the oversimplification in the news media of the Arctic's resource wealth, arguing the Arctic is unlikely to experience any kind of "twenty-first century gold rush."[13] The realities of extracting resources in the harsh, largely inoperable offshore Arctic environment, as well as the rapid uptick in alternative energy sources, will no doubt stymy any race to offshore Arctic oil. In tackling common misconceptions of Russian Arctic strategy, Ekaterina Klimenko has also exhaustively examined the Arctic security climate.[14] While flagging the potential for tensions outside the region to spill into the Arctic, Klimenko makes the important point that Russia's growing military capabilities may be taking place in the Arctic but are not necessarily targeted toward the Arctic.

Valery Konyshev and Alexander Sergunin also argue against the notion of a looming Arctic conflict.[15] For these Russian scholars, Moscow's military ambitions serve three major goals: to demonstrate Russia's sovereignty over the continental shelf; to protect economic interests; and to demonstrate that Russia remains a great power through its military capabilities. At first glance, this argument reinforces the notion of Russia gearing up to take on enemies in the Arctic. Under Putin, the world has witnessed the introduction of new military capabilities, not just revived Soviet capabilities, in the Russian Arctic—new command posts, hardware, and frequent exercises. To arrive at the same reading of militarization of the Russian Arctic, it is necessary to consider the idea that state-state competition can indeed have both cooperative and conflictual facings. Of course, Russian Arctic military presence today is still a shell of its Arctic capability from the Soviet Cold War era.

Farther along the cooperation end of the Arctic geopolitical conflict-cooperation spectrum are Christian Le Mière and Jeffrey Mazo. They argue the opening of the Arctic should be viewed in terms of the vast opportunities for global cooperation the region presents.[16]

Cooperation in the Arctic is the means by which Arctic stakeholders will access the required financial capital and the foreign technologies necessary to explore and exploit the stakeholders' Arctic resource sectors. Energy security demands that major energy exporters, like Russia, can deliver supply security to their customers. Maintaining conflict-free Arctic transit routes such as the NSR is crucial to delivering energy exports to Asian and European markets. This is a key component of Russian foreign energy strategy—secure supply routes and trustworthiness to deliver contracted energy security. Indra Øverland further points out that, to date, Russia has adhered to all legal frameworks governing the Arctic.[17] Of course, in terms of geography, Russia is in a strong position legally (basic geography affords Moscow the majority share of the Arctic) and can therefore afford to be magnanimous.

This variety of assessments along the conflict-cooperation spectrum is also apparent in literature on Russian Arctic strategy. Little analysis falls in the balanced middle ground when it comes to drivers of Putin's Russia in the Arctic. This book aims to fill that middle ground territory. Ideally, any pragmatic assessment of Russian Arctic strategy would include the following foundations: a statement identifying Russia as the region's largest legitimate stakeholder; an acknowledgement that the outstanding overlapping claims to the Arctic Ocean continental shelf are dealt with through agreed international legal channels; and recognition of the role that rising international significance and interest in the Arctic plays in shaping global views of Russian legitimacy in the region. An ideal assessment of Russian Arctic strategy would then downplay narratives of arms build-ups in favor of promoting the requirement for regional cooperation in the Arctic, given the litany of shared challenges.[18]

It is far too simplistic to merely state Russia is a legitimate Arctic stakeholder and is pursuing a cooperative Arctic agenda. One must go deeper. What is driving Arctic strategy within Russia? Why is it geared toward cooperation in the Arctic, while elsewhere a conflictual foreign policy is followed? Peering into the black box of Russian strategy is Pavel Baev, a leading expert on Russian Arctic matters. He suggests that Russian Arctic strategy represents an identity-building project for Russia. The Russian Arctic represents a new front on which to express its self-assertion and promote "strength." Yet, Baev notes at the same time, significant domestic constraints exist on Russian capability to deliver fully on its Arctic agenda.[19] These questions of what is driving Russia's Arctic strategy, as well as the concerns around constraints upon Moscow delivering on its strategy, are further explored in the coming chapters.

2

THE RUSSIANS ARE COMING (HOME)

"THE ARCTIC IS OURS AND WE SHOULD MANIFEST OUR PRESENCE."

—A. CHILINGAROV

No question, the quote above reads as imperialistic. However, here context matters. Often these words are attributed to Vladimir Putin, but they were in fact spoken by Artur Chilingarov, Russian polar explorer extraordinaire, Russia's special envoy to the Arctic, and former deputy chairman of the Duma. Chilingarov is responsible for the infamous 2007 Russian flag stunt on the Arctic Ocean seabed. Note that Russian scientific research led by Chilingarov into the outer limits of the Russian continental shelf predated the scientific research "rush" from Denmark and Canada with regard to the Arctic continental shelf. While in hindsight the geological origins of the underwater Arctic ridge do indeed connect all claimants, during the first decade of the 2000s Russian Arctic exploration was by default neoimperialist, with Moscow extremely active in the North Pole scientific space.

Building upon an understanding of the current state of the Arctic and Russian Arctic strategy, this chapter delves into Russia's Arctic stake: Where does the strategy come from? The chapter begins with an illustration of the link between energy and Putin's Russia, and the role energy rents play in assuring great power ambitions. It provides a brief discussion of the Soviet Arctic identity and the role of the Arctic in a historical sense, particularly as a point of tension during the Cold War, as well as Stalin's Arctic legacy. This chapter then explores Russia's partial Arctic continental shelf claim via an international legal avenue, the Commission on the Limits of the Continental Shelf (CLCS)—examining Moscow's original claim submitted to the CLCS in 2001, its subsequent submission in 2015, and the revised submission in 2021. Using open source UN Convention on the Law of the Sea (UNCLOS) submissions made by the Kremlin, this chapter illustrates the realities of a legitimate, legally sound Russian Arctic claim. This evidence further refutes the popular new cold war thesis involving an Arctic-grab by Putin.

So, what is Russia up to in the Arctic? There is a simple answer: legitimate state business. But that makes for an extremely short book. Generally, efforts to pragmatically explain Russia's legitimate Arctic stake are criticized largely as a result of colored perceptions crafted from events far beyond the Arctic. Unfortunately, not even the use of visual tools—like a map—assist in crafting the case in support of Russia's Arctic legitimacy.

Borrowing from the words of Robert Kaplan, Russia's Arctic stake is best framed as "the revenge of geography." Russia is the largest geographical stakeholder in terms of territory above the Arctic Circle. It follows that basic geography hands Russia an Arctic coastline of almost 25,000 kilometers. A territory so vast that it spans eleven time zones, this region accounts for over 85 percent of Russia's natural gas production. With this starting point and the application of agreed international law principles regarding the law of the sea, Russia has an irrefutable, legitimate claim to most of the Arctic region.

Any real debate of whether to expect Russian cooperation or conflict in the Arctic is moot if the foundation of the narrative continues to include the notion that Russia lacks a legitimate majority stake in the Arctic. Driving Putin's Russian Arctic agenda is a range of forces that can be broadly divided between economic and military-security interests. Taken together, they constitute components of the Russian Arctic national interest under Putin.

ENERGY AND PUTIN'S RUSSIA

Russia's importance to global energy security derives from the country's vast resource base, its geographical position, and its attempts to leverage those energy resources to build and exert influence. In 2020, Russia was the largest natural gas supplier to the European Union (EU). While it has spent decades arguing for the need to reduce dependency on Moscow for energy, in mid-2022 the EU still imported about 40 percent of its gas from Russia. Of course, EU plans to wean off Russian gas appear to have turbo-charged in late 2022, with new bans on importing Russian energy. Russia ranks among the world's leading countries in reserves and production in all three categories of global primary energy sources: natural gas, oil, and coal. Moscow controls a third of global natural gas reserves and ranks alongside the US as the world's largest gas producers. Holding the second-largest coal reserves is less relevant in the increasingly post-coal era, but Moscow is nonetheless moving coal to China in response to bilateral tensions between Australia and China, in which Canberra's coal exports have continued to suffer. In the age of liquified natural gas (LNG), Russia is one of the leading exporters. Russia also jostles with Saudi Arabia to claim the top spot in oil production.

Central to Russia's foreign energy strategy are two national energy firms: Gazprom and Rosneft. When Putin first came to power in 2000, his plan for Russian resurgence called for the creation of "national energy champions," and Gazprom and Rosneft would soon fit the bill. For Putin, a national champion is an energy corporation that would ultimately place state interests before profit maximization.[1] Soon after coming to power, Putin removed Viktor Chernomyrdin—Boris Yeltsin's former prime minister—from his position as Gazprom's chairman and replaced him with Dmitry Medvedev, a long-time associate of Putin's. In addition, Putin removed Chernomyrdin's protégé and Gazprom CEO, Rem Vyakhirev, replacing him with Alexei Miller, another former associate of Putin's from his KGB days in St. Petersburg. The overall aim was to merge state interests with private sector capabilities.[2] Putin recognized the strategic value inherent in the natural gas sector and acted swiftly to bring Gazprom into the hands of government. Indeed, by early 2004, the Russian government had secured a majority stake in the gas company.[3]

Rosneft is Russia's oil giant. In 2014, the Russian government announced it was selling 19.5 percent of Rosneft's shares. The sale aimed to net the Kremlin $11 billion, with Putin stating, "We need the money." The guidelines for privatization were announced in July 2016 to include that the shares must be held for at least three years; shareholders must sign an agreement stipulating they will vote in favor of any government member who applies for a seat on the board of directors; and finally, investors must be free from corruption charges.[4]

Despite the creation of his national champions in the energy space, Putin is limited by the fact that only one resource is easily "weaponized" for foreign policy: natural gas.

The concept of Putin's Russia using its energy reserves as a foreign policy "weapon" is certainly not a new one.[5] While no longer a superpower, Russia remains a major world power thanks to some 17 million square kilometers of landmass, its nuclear weapons arsenal, and its standing army headcount, as well as its permanent member status on the UN Security Council. Russia's increased assertiveness has resulted largely from the influx of "petrodollars" filling government coffers, which has increased room for maneuvering within its foreign policy. Since coming to power, Vladimir Putin has, in effect, worked to nationalize the energy sector and demonstrate the Kremlin's willingness to use energy as a political weapon. Putin's Russia has often employed its energy wealth to pressure or influence other countries—especially former Soviet states and other neighbors. Notably, Russia has long employed energy as a coercive tool in its dealings with Ukraine, as demonstrated in the 2006 and 2009 gas "wars" that severely disrupted EU natural gas supplies. Given that energy is a central driver of Russian Arctic strategy under Putin, it is essential to trace the primacy of energy within Russia's strategic outlook. To do this, I track the unique phases of Putin since 2000 to capture the role energy has played in Russia's great power quest.

Phase One: Recentralization

Putin was elected in 2000 with over 50 percent of the vote. For Simon Pirani, Putin was "elevated to the presidency not by a KGB plot, but by Yeltsin's corrupt entourage."[6] From 1991 to 1996, Putin was based in St. Petersburg, working closely with then mayor Anatoly Sobchak before moving in 1996 to Moscow with the help of his old Petersburg friend and senior Yeltsin official Alexei Kudrin.[7] In Moscow, Putin rose rapidly appointed as Pavel Borodin's deputy in a key department of the Yeltsin presidential administration by May 1996 and then director of the Federal Security Service (FSB) by July 1998.[8] The "Yeltsin clique" was looking for its 2000 presidential candidate, and the consensus among Kremlin watchers was that Putin had the full support of Yeltsin's most powerful cronies: that is, support from former oligarch (a powerful person who controls a country or an industry) Boris Berezovsky, Yeltsin's daughter Tatiana Dyachenko and future son-in-law Valentin Yumashev, and Putin's former chief of staff Aleksandr Voloshin. For some time, former finance minister Kudrin remained in Putin's circle, Borodin lost favor with Putin and was removed from office, as was Yeltsin's daughter, in an effort to rid the administration of the potentially challenging Yeltsin "family" remnants.

Putin's career in the Russian political apparatus had begun in the KGB, where he worked from 1975 to 1991, including a formative stint in Dresden, East Germany, leading up to the collapse of communism there. Putin left the KGB with the rank of lieutenant colonel and went to work for his former law professor and reformist politician, Mayor Anatoly Sobchak, in his St. Petersburg office. It was there that Putin became known as a "smooth but capable enforcer."[9] Certainly, Yeltsin appreciated such a trait, and he made Putin the deputy chief of the Russian President's Business Management Department in 1996 and then the deputy chief of the Russian Presidential Administration, as well as the chief of the President's Main Control Directorate in 1997. A year

later, in 1998, Yeltsin promoted Putin to the directorship of the FSB
and, in 1999, to the role of secretary of the Security Council of the Russian
Federation (SCRF).[10] In August 1999, Yeltsin appointed Putin as Russia's
prime minister, with observers noting that Yeltsin felt he could rely on
the loyalty of Putin, who appeared to be a "professional and unassuming
employee of the state that lacked political ambitions of his own."[11]

Later, as president, Putin inherited from Yeltsin an embattled Russia that had been losing respect and significance in the global arena.
However, the restoration of high energy prices on the back of an
increase in global energy demand made Putin's pursuit of Russia's economic and political resurgence much easier. When Putin came to power,
he also immediately worked to strengthen the control of the state over
public life.[12] This meant a series of "democratic rollbacks" for Russian
independent media. Putin's efforts to reassert state power over the press,
Russian civil society, and state political structures were all facets of his
grand domestic strategy of *derzhavnost*, which translates roughly to "authoritarian statism."[13] The president saw *derzhavnost* as the means by
which Russia could once more behave like a great power.

Putin's authoritarian statist approach can be seen as the restoration
of a paternalist state marked by "a return to a traditional Russian form
of legitimacy characteristic of the tsarist and Soviet periods, in which
the idea of a strong state replaces that of a nation."[14] Putin's principal
aim during his first presidential term was to reassert centralized authority over the Russian state. He implemented a "managed democracy"
style of leadership, built around top-down control,[15] with the re-creation
of Russian federal districts that represented "super regions" to which
individuals directly linked to Putin were appointed.[16] Putin's efforts to
reestablish central authority within the energy sector during his first
term included important taxation reforms.[17] In January 2002, Putin in-
troduced the mineral resource extraction tax, which had a recentral-
izing effect, shifting energy revenues from regional coffers to the federal
government.[18] These reforms strengthened Russia's fiscal health, as
earnings from key resource sectors were no longer sitting in oligarch
bank accounts but rather were returning to the state. Russian tax revenues as a percentage of gross domestic product (GDP) during Putin's

first term rose from 9.2 percent of GDP in 1998 to around 20 percent by 2004. Such increases in fiscal budgetary strength in this period would not have been possible had the oligarchs continued to personally reap the benefits of increases in global energy prices. As a result of Putin's domestic reforms, namely the selective curtailment of oligarchs, there was an influx of petrodollars into state coffers.

The political and economic reforms implemented by Putin in his first term highlight an important point. Although people often credit the "oil boom" that started in the late 1990s and lasted (with fluctuation) through Putin's first two terms in office as the reason for Russia's resurgence, it is crucial not to overlook Putin's role in Russia's fiscal resurgence. If Putin's tax reforms had not occurred, or if the oligarchs had continued to control Russia's vast resource sectors, it is likely that the economy would not have benefited as much as it did from the increase in global energy prices. The inclusion of St. Petersburg economists such as Alexei Kudrin and German Gref in Putin's trusted circle of advisors also contributed to Russian fiscal resurgence in the early Putin years, through sensible reform and wise fiscal management. But Putin's recentralization of power in the natural resource sector was vital to the state reaping the benefits of high energy prices and increasing global demand. Indeed, the oil price rose from around $25 per barrel in 1999 to $65 by 2004.

Russia's economic resurgence relied heavily upon Putin's ability to ensure the petrodollars from Russian natural resources were returned to the state. The oligarchs, extremely wealthy Russians who "fuse power and capital," proved to be a significant roadblock to Putin's grand strategy for Russian resurgence.[19] They emerged from the economic reforms executed under Yeltsin, namely his "shock therapy" and the associated privatization processes. Yegor Gaidar and Anatoly Chubais were two important figures in creating Russia's new economic system under Yeltsin. In significant measure, the "chaos" they unleashed was essential to the spurts of growth that later occurred under Putin.

Gaidar's most important contribution was to free market pricing from state control, as state control had "cripple[d] the centrally planned economy" that Russia inherited from the Soviet Union. However, the effect of freeing market pricing was to cause hyperinflation across Russia.[20] Chubais sought to break the monopoly of the state in property, which allowed for "the enormous industrial wealth of the country [to fall] into private hands."[21] Gaidar's free pricing initiative all but "eroded the life savings of the population," and Chubais did not seem to mind where the riches of the resource sector fell, so long as it was not in the hands of the state.[22] The Yeltsin-era reformers were motivated not just by the desire to unleash the economic force of private enterprise, but also by efforts to put an end to the Soviet state by delinking it as far as possible from the commanding heights of the national economy.

The resulting jolt to the system, which came to be known as shock therapy, allowed oligarchs to amass their wealth by purchasing strategic assets cheaply. This was evident in widespread oligarch purchases of property from the state's resource sector. Yeltsin continued to support the process of privatization via what was known as voucher privatization, which involved the state giving away some 148 million "vouchers" (one for every child, man, and woman of the Russian Federation) that could be traded for shares in companies.[23] However, the vouchers were "less an economic tool than a political gambit . . . to make people feel they were getting a piece of the pie."[24] In reality, it was a select few individuals, the oligarchs, who managed to purchase entire assets at prices far below their actual value. As a result, widespread public unrest stemming from Yeltsin's "shock therapy" and economic reforms threatened his reelection as president. So, to secure victory in 1996, Yeltsin relied heavily upon the oligarchs, such as Berezovsky, to support his re-election bid. Through financing Yeltsin's campaign, the oligarchs' political influence increased. Yeltsin won with the aid of oligarch funding that bought "advertising to drown out the voices of the opposition."[25]

In line with his authoritarian statist approach, Putin set about stripping Russia's oligarchs of their power. He regarded the oligarchs as business "owners who had acquired their wealth in the 1990s [and] had done so illegitimately."[26] Many were removed from corporations and replaced with individuals favored by Putin. Given that his aim of regaining control over the economic flows associated with the rise in global energy prices was at odds with the continued power of unruly oligarchs, systematic attacks on their power and wealth began. Early in his first term, Putin met with these oligarchs and "laid out the new rules of the game," whereby the oligarchs were warned to invest back into the economy, pay taxes, and above all, stay out of politics.[27] The highly publicized 2003–2005 "Yukos case"—essentially, Putin's political attack on an oligarch (Yukos oil company owner Mikhail Khodorkovsky)—was a further grim warning to Russia's wealthiest businessmen that failure to respond to Kremlin demands would be punished severely.

The *siloviki*, who were likewise "wedded to the concept of a strong Russia," were important allies for Putin in his efforts to establish power during his first term.[28] The *siloviki* are individuals in influential positions with military or KGB backgrounds. Generally, *siloviki* have a worldview and foreign policy outlook in conflict with the West, informed by a mix of "patriotism, anti-Westernism, imperialism, orthodox clericalism, militarism, authoritarianism, cultural uniformity, [and] xenophobia."[29] Putin's appointment of *siloviki* to head five of the seven federal administrative districts created in 2000 was widely viewed as "evidence for the fact that what [was] . . . happening [was] the insertion of a police-state mechanism into a . . . declarative democratic state."[30] Under Putin, there was an increase of *siloviki* within Russian elite groups, although the presence of *siloviki* in key positions in post-Soviet politics was not a wholly new phenomenon. Yeltsin incorporated *siloviki* into numerous high-level political or administrative posts, with, for example, Yevgeny Primakov serving as foreign minister and prime minister, Sergei Stepashin serving as federal security minister, Vladimir Putin serving as prime minister, and Alexander Korzhakov heading the Presidential Security Service.[31]

Yeltsin also surrounded himself with a group known as the family, who have been described as a "fluid group of favored Kremlin insiders."[32] Putin systematically replaced remaining members of Yeltsin's inner circle, the family, with close associates from Putin's former St. Petersburg and KGB/FSB years.[33] Putin had a favored group of individuals with whom he had previously worked, and they soon became known as Putin's men. Although they were often categorised as *siloviki*, "Putin's men" came from a range of business, economic, and technocrat backgrounds. So, "Putin's men" represented a "new" *siloviki* who were equipped with business or economic backgrounds and placed on the boards of most Russian energy corporations.

Phase Two: Renationalization

By his second term, beginning in 2004, Putin's inner circle had consolidated to include *siloviki*, like former deputy prime minister (and current CEO of Rosneft) Igor Sechin and former minister of defense and chief of staff Sergei Ivanov, as well as groups such as St. Petersburg lawyers Medvedev and Kozak, and St. Petersburg economists Gref and Kudrin.[34] And so began the second phase for Putin: renationalization. On March 14, 2004, Putin was reelected in a "landslide," with 71.31 percent of the presidential vote. However, 2004 was largely remembered for the trial of Russia's richest man, Mikhail Khodorkovsky.[35] For Putin, Khodorkovsky represented an oligarch refusing to toe the line and stay out of politics. As Putin has done with many anticorruption campaigners, he accused Khodorkovsky himself of corruption and initiated show-trial proceedings against him. Putin also set his sights on Khodorkovsky's multibillion-dollar oil company, Yukos.[36] Most Western observers believed the 2004 trial illustrated the increasingly antidemocratic nature of Putin's Russia, and that it was driven essentially by "political considerations, political grievances, and political rivalries."[37] Putin, meanwhile, continued efforts to consolidate presidential power and exert state control over the energy sector.

In early 2008, the Duma passed a law slightly altering the stringent restrictions on foreign investments within Russia's energy sector. The new law allowed foreign capital investments of up to 49 percent in Russian energy sector operations. Putin also inserted high-profile foreigners to take the helm of strategic energy corporations. The appointment of former German chancellor Gerhard Schröder to head the pipeline consortium Nord Stream was one highly dubious example.

More broadly, despite these selective overtures to foreign business interest, Putin's second term saw the emergence of an increasingly assertive, and at times aggressive, Russia. Throughout Putin's second term, he consolidated the domestic reforms he established in his first term. Putin's men were largely running the state's energy sector and also reinforcing the state apparatus Putin had built up. Significantly, Putin's second term fostered a closer merger between energy and politics in Russia.[38] The consolidation of presidential power over this strategic resource sector and the Russian political system more broadly was Putin's central objective.

Gazprom emerged (and perhaps peaked) in Putin's second presidential term as a key strategic corporation for Russia. Throughout Putin's first term, the Kremlin had made efforts to control the corporation by placing Putin's men at its helm. However, Putin's second term saw a move in 2005 to state ownership of the gas behemoth, with the state becoming the majority shareholder of Gazprom. In doing so, the Russian state increased its ownership stake in Gazprom from 38 percent to 51 percent.

This incorporation of Gazprom into the Russian state apparatus came at an important time. The Kremlin was concerned about increasing resistance to Moscow in neighboring countries because of rising nationalist sentiment, leading to color revolutions (political changes in post-communist countries) in Georgia in 2003 and Ukraine in 2004. In an attempt to bring unruly states back into Russia's orbit, Gazprom began deploying arbitrary price hikes under a veil of "market price" rhetoric. *Market price rhetoric* refers to Russia's demands (implemented by Gazprom) that former Soviet Union (FSU) republics begin paying "market prices" for natural gas, essentially putting an end to the large discounts the republics had historically enjoyed as part of the USSR.[39] Gazprom's demands ultimately reflected the reality that the state-owned corporation was acting as a coercive foreign policy tool.

With the state now the majority shareholder of Gazprom, the corporation began to act increasingly as an arm of Russian foreign policy. Gazprom's strategic purchasing of domestic energy infrastructure abroad is a good example. By the end of Putin's second term, Gazprom had purchased energy assets in approximately twenty European countries. However, particularly aggressive ownership takeovers of strategic energy assets took place within the FSU. The use of Gazprom as an arm of foreign policy was well illustrated by the 2007 Kovykta gas field incident. The joint venture TNK-BP held a 63 percent stake in the Kovykta gas field in Eastern Siberia until the Kremlin directed Russia's Natural Resource Ministry to withdraw TNK-BP's license to develop the field.[40] As a result, BP was excluded and Gazprom acquired the field—home to some 1.9 trillion cubic meters of gas, equal to roughly the entire amount held by the world's (then) third largest gas producer, Canada.

Another example of political motives prevailing in the Russian energy sphere is that of the Shtokman field.[41] Shtokman, located in the Barents Sea, holds 3.2 trillion cubic meters of gas, and in 2005, in line with Putin's foreign investment law passed by the Duma, 49 percent of the field was opened to foreign investment. It is considered one of the world's largest natural gas fields. Foreign investment interest in the field came from five main corporations: Norsk Hydro, Statoil, Chevron, ConocoPhillips, and TotalEnergies (formally known as Total S.A.). Yet, in 2006, Gazprom announced that it would develop the field itself because none of the five interested parties offered assets of values "that would correspond in terms of quality and volume to Shtokman's reserves."[42] Evidently, Gazprom was after more than foreign investment; Gazprom was seeking substantial asset swaps from the five interested parties. Shtokman is the phantom Russian Arctic project. It is online one year and off the next, and was formally postponed in 2019.

Phase Three: Modernization

By 2008, a new phase in Putin's "energy inc." emerged. This era was marked by a modernization agenda. Putin assumed the role of prime minister, placing his handpicked successor, Medvedev, in the presidency.[43] This "tandemocracy," as it soon became known, sought to represent Russia's democratic progression, with Putin seemingly stepping back from power as required (at the time) by the Russian constitution. In reality, Putin retained the political power and influence once assured by the presidential title, and Medvedev became known as a "puppet president."[44] During Putin's stint as prime minister, he had the constitution amended to increase the Russian presidential term from four to six years, just in time for Medvedev to cede the presidency back to Putin, as planned, in May 2012.

Despite the puppet presidency label, Medvedev was responsible for a broad economic modernization agenda. It included a slight warming in Russia's relationship with the West, accession to the World Trade Organization in 2011, and a significant focus on developing Russia's technological expertise in the resource sector. Crucially, this period included the mammoth task of modernizing the Russian military machine. This military reform and the modernization agenda were major achievements of the Medvedev presidency.[45] Further, Russia's bilateral relationship with China strengthened on matters of natural gas.[46] Russia's energy ties with Latin America also deepened. Overall, Medvedev's modernization agenda centered around technological innovation in all areas for Russia—a so-called intelligent economy shift.[47]

Phase Four: Great Power Redux

Come 2012, Putin reassumed the Russian presidency and kicked off phase four: the reintroduction of the great power agenda. International challenges have been plentiful since Putin assumed the presidency for his third official term. In early 2012 the US signaled the end of the costly Iraq War. The departure of US forces rippled across the Middle East, plunging the post-Arab Spring region deeper into chaos. Coupled with the global rise in terrorism and the rapid emergence of decentralized terror cells, securitization was back on the global agenda. The emergence of a mutual enemy had allowed for the development, under Barack Obama, of warmer Russia-US ties and even attempts of a "reset" in Russian-US relations. However, the competitive hunt to secure individual energy futures soon came to the forefront of the relationship.

Spurred by intensifying of focus on climate change since 2012, the global energy mix started to change as it shifted away from coal-intensive economies. Notably, China's public shift from high-intensity coal power to natural gas caused gas-producing nations to jostle for China's business. For Russia, this was an opportunity to diversify its customer base away from Europe, putting Europe in a difficult position, given it has no short-term alternative to Russian gas. In 2014, after a decade of negotiation, Russia signed a thirty-year gas supply partnership with China.[48] But some key components of that deal remain unclear, and it appears that in its desire to demonstrate to the West that Russia had other options, Moscow allowed Beijing to push through a very tough deal, largely in Beijing's favor.

In similar fashion to its 2008 Georgian invasion, Russia showed its defiance of international laws and norms by annexing Crimea in 2014 and actively destabilizing the Ukrainian region of Donbas. Effectively plunging Ukraine into a lengthy civil conflict, Russia has continued to probe farther into Ukraine, seeking to divide the nation and culminating in a February 2022 full Russian invasion. Certainly, this causes concerns for European security more generally. Russia has reintroduced an assertive foreign policy in Europe and the West more broadly. Since Putin's third term, the reemergence of Russia's great power quest has been obvious.

Russia's 2014 annexation of Crimea was punished by an array of Western sanctions.[49] Beginning in April of that year, sanctions targeted Russia's Arctic energy market and were sharpened considerably after the downing of Malaysian Airlines flight MH17 in June. These sanctions crippled Russia's ability to explore new regions for hydrocarbon potential, blocking Western transfer of exploration technology and funding. Given the Kremlin's reliance upon technology and investment from the West, the sanctions have effectively delayed the production by new Russian fields in the offshore Russian Arctic. However, some joint ventures between Russian energy firms and Western counterparts were protected from the sanctions because they did not apply retroactively.

Oil and natural gas (both piped and liquid versions) are the hydrocarbon jewels in Russia's energy crown. Yet, emerging energy sources—shale gas and renewables—are certainly areas in which Putin's Russia is weak.[50] The head of Gazprom, Alexei Miller, asserted publicly that the shale gas revolution is a "bubble that will burst soon."[51] But he was wrong. The value of Gazprom has plummeted from $350 billion in 2008 to around $50 billion in 2023. Many think that shale gas constitutes the "next big thing" in energy.[52] Not only are reserves thought to be plentiful, but also shale gas is environmentally friendlier than coal and oil. Further, proponents of shale gas believe it is key to diversifying the global energy mix—allowing for the reduction of unilateral dependency on "petrostates" such as Russia. Shale gas is natural gas produced via a hydraulic fracking process—essentially the process blasts water into the earth (shale rock areas) to release gas deposits. Shale gas has been dubbed a revolution, given the impact on US energy markets. In 2000, shale gas in the US constituted 1 percent of domestic gas production, and by 2010 it constituted some 20 percent. The US predicts that by 2035, nearly 50 percent of its domestic gas supply will come from shale.[53]

Although Russia is aware of its shale gas potential in the eastern region above the Arctic Circle, Moscow has opted to put this energy source on the back burner. Russia largely ignores the potential of shale gas in its energy mix, but it is also the case that the country does not require access to its shale wealth, at least in the short term.[54] Russia's existing and readily accessible hydrocarbon resource base provides ample product for the global market. Shale does, however, pose a threat to Russia's foreign energy strategy, through the growing capacity of shale gas producers to muscle in on Russia's customer base.

I discuss the development of the relationship between energy and Putin's Russia to illustrate two points. First, energy was relaunched under Putin as a strategic lever in Russian foreign policy and viewed as the ticket to reattaining great power status. It would, in theory, follow that Moscow would securitize its Arctic energy resources and employ them as a strategic weapon. Yet, Russia has done the opposite. While Moscow has secured its economic stake in the Russian Arctic, it does not use its energy resources as political levers. It does not cut or withhold supplies, and foreign investment is welcomed. This leads to the second point. Moscow's cooperative approach to the Arctic, and indeed the absence of conflict in Russia's Arctic agenda itself, deviates from the way in which Russia views energy and uses it as a weapon elsewhere. Why is this the case? As the following pages argue, the Kremlin requires Arctic

cooperation and an air of low tension across the region to achieve
Russian strategic interests related to Russia's Arctic resource wealth.

ENERGY, THE ARCTIC, AND RUSSIA'S GREAT POWER AGENDA: PUTIN'S TRINITY

Putin's quest to recapture Russia's great power status stemmed from the
desire to return Russia to a standing reminiscent of the Soviet era. Great
power status was not just an objective of Kremlin policymakers; it was
also a nostalgic desire of the Russian people. Dmitri Trenin supports
this by citing a series of polls conducted in Russia that indicated the
majority of Moscow high school students would "like to see the return
of the Soviet Union or at least something approximating the empire of
the Czars."[55] For Putin, re-creating this empire may require not only
expanding Russian territory into the FSU, but also building Russia's international standing into that of an energy superpower.

Russia was once a great power, as the czarist and Soviet periods of
history demonstrate. Looking to the Soviet period, it was evident that
by 1980 the USSR was a superpower. For Stephen White:

> [The USSR had] acquired an international influence that
> accorded . . . with the country's enormous territory, population and
> natural resources. . . . The USSR has acquired a strategic capability
> which gave it an approximate parity with the USA. . . . The Soviet
> Union had one of the world's largest armies and one of its largest navies,
> and it stood at the head of the world's two major military alliances. It
> was the centre of one of the world's major trading blocs . . . and an in-
> fluential member of the United Nations.[56]

Furthermore, Soviet foreign policy boasted that the Soviet Union was
one of the greatest world powers, and although perhaps such rhetoric
was an exaggeration, it was nonetheless a key feature of Moscow's international identity.[57] Today, Russia considers energy to be a power-
house of economic growth and the basis of the nation's claim to great
power status. Certainly, Russia's importance as "Eurasia's leading en-

ergy power" along with its seat on the UN Security Council and its arsenal of nuclear weapons situate Russia as a "key regional player with global ambitions."[58] With the collapse of the Soviet Union in 1991, it appeared that Russia had lost its superpower status and thus, lost great power. Putin sought to regain Russia's great power status by positioning it as a key global energy player. He voiced general concern in stating the following:

> Russia is in the midst of one of the most difficult periods in its history. . . . [For] the first time in the past 200–300 years, it is facing a real threat of falling into the second, and possibly even third echelon of world states.[59]

Essentially, there were four driving factors behind the notion that Russia had lost significant political standing in world affairs. First, the breakup of the Soviet empire resulted in vast territorial loss as well as a significant dispersion of the Russian population, with some 25 million Russians finding themselves within the confines of newly independent states. Second, the economic collapse of the 1990s, culminating in the 1998 financial crisis, crippled Russian economic power. Third, as a result of the economic collapse and years of lack of funding, the crippling of Russia's military potential contributed significantly to the loss of great power status. Fourth, Russia's demographic issues such as decreased life expectancy and a shrinking birth rate no longer allowed Russia to lay claim to great power, because the state was crumbling from within.[60]

Those domestic issues are still roadblocks on Russia's path to reattaining great power status. For instance, despite influxes of petrodollars into state coffers, Russia has not been able to improve individual life expectancy. In 1960, Russia's life expectancy was more or less on par with that of developed countries at the time. However, today the average life expectancy in Russia for the population is seventy-two years.[61] This poses a risk for the future of Russia and its ability to populate the workforce, particularly in the labor-intensive energy sector. Furthermore, Russia's shrinking birth rate has an impact of the future of the nation's workforce.

Despite these challenges to Russian great power status, Putin continues to see energy and the military as key, while comparatively neglecting urgently needed budgetary outlays for education and health. The notion of regaining great power status also demonstrates Russia's desire to regain an identity in the international political arena.[62] Peter Shearman notes the importance of Russia's search for identity in the context of contemporary Russian foreign policy.[63] For instance, he argues that Russia's consistent opposition toward North Atlantic Treaty Organization (NATO) expansion within the near abroad[64] demonstrates the "psychological factor linked to questions of prestige and identity" within Russian foreign policy.[65] Under Putin, a reinvigorated sense of Russian national identity has emerged, based on the notion of a strong state, no longer being a "junior partner" of the US but an equal one, and being a key player in the global energy market. By 2007, Russia had made headway in its great power ambitions, with 66 percent of Russians believing that there had been a definite improvement in global respect for Russia.[66] This figure has increased further in recent years with Russia's increasing assertiveness within in its foreign policy.

Putin's concern for Russia's fall from great power status predates his presidency. His plan for recovering that status can be found in his 1997 St. Petersburg Mining Institute doctoral dissertation.[67] Whether Putin actually wrote the dissertation is up for debate, the fact that he put his name to it in effect supports the study. In it, the strategic significance of Russia's vast natural resource wealth was honed in on and molded into somewhat of a "Putin plan" for economic revival. Marshall Goldman notes that Putin's plan encompasses the following tenets: the Russian government should reassert control over natural resources; oligarch control within the energy sector should be eliminated, as "regardless of who is the legal owner of the country's natural resources . . . the state has the right to regulate the process of their development and use"; Russia should welcome international foreign investments, so long as the state remains in majority control; and only increased state control over the energy sector will allow Russia "to emerge from its deep crisis and restore its former might."[68] Note that eliminating oligarch control in the energy sector was more or less a process undertaken by Putin to substitute state-favored owners for the existing ones.

Putin's vision for righting what he viewed as historical wrongs saw energy ushered in as the key to returning Russia to great power status. A central feature of Russian energy diplomacy is that it employs its energy wealth as a foreign policy weapon when it deems it necessary. For Joseph Stanislaw, "Russia is an energy superpower that uses its vast resources as the basis of economic development and as an instrument for carrying out domestic and foreign policy."[69] Ariel Cohen goes farther, noting that what has developed in Russia is a comprehensive energy strategy that "masterfully integrates geopolitics and geo-economics."[70] Likewise for Michael Klare, Putin's belief in the crucial role of the state in the management of Russia's natural resource base has resulted in the emergence of a foreign energy strategy that employs oil and natural gas as the guarantors of the nation's international position.[71]

Certainly, the assertive nature of Russia's energy diplomacy under Putin is evident in its foreign energy strategy toward the FSU. Within Russian energy diplomacy literature, there appears to be a disagreement over whether economic or political ends drive the strategy.[72] For Brenda Shaffer, energy is the currency of power in contemporary international relations, whereby climate change is now a security threat and energy security has become a nation's leading security imperative.[73] Upon this basis, it is evident that Russian energy strategy is driven by both economic and political ambitions. For example, efforts to gain a foothold in the domestic energy markets of neighboring states indicate how Russian energy diplomacy is driven by a desire to use energy both as a political weapon and as a means on which to capitalize and, where possible, monopolize commercial opportunities. Under Putin, Russia has increasingly tied resurgent great power ambitions to its energy wealth. However, Russia's ability to effectively utilize its natural resource endowment to such ends is challenged by changes in the global energy mix and the move toward renewables, as well as domestic issues around lack of investment in new technology and exploration efforts.

Immediate challenges to Russia's foreign energy strategy are Russia's failure (to date) to diversify its economic base away from resources, as along with deep levels of sector corruption. The fact that Russia's "energy weapon" has lost some of its bite further compounds these issues. Europe, Russia's traditional key energy customer, is strategically planning to secure its energy future with a reduced reliance upon Russian gas. Indeed, since late 2022, Brussels has signaled its ambition to completely pivot away from Russian energy.

The oil price dive of June 2014, coupled with Western sanctions, delivered a severe blow to Russia's energy strategies and by extension, Moscow's Arctic agenda. Regarding the unsuspected nature of the 2014 price dive, an international oil company (IOC) representative commented:

> Firstly, no one saw this coming. Then again, we (in the industry) all say that, we have to or else we look terrible at our one job—prediction. But no one can accurately predict when these falls occur, and likewise we can't truly predict when prices will rise. Those who claim to have the magic to do that are flat-out lying. At best we can talk about a $10–$20 range when predicting oil prices. I would think Brent would sit at no more than $60 for 2016 and potentially even out till 2017, and then it could hit $130 again in 2018 and sit above $100 for another 5 years.[74]

Despite the $100 per barrel expectations of industry executives in 2015, oil prices never reached those heights; indeed, the 2020s began without witnessing oil prices above $80. This is important when considering the feasibility and commercial viability of Russian Arctic offshore oil projects. For the moment, Russia is quite resilient despite its economy's overreliance on energy rents. Russia's sovereign wealth reserves are healthy, and it holds the world's largest gold reserves. Given sanctions and the global economic slump, many thought Moscow would scale back spending—particularly in the defense sector—but this has not happened. This is probably partly due to the Kremlin assuming the oil price will inevitably bounce back and the growing demand for increasingly scarce supplies will leave Russia well placed to cash in sooner rather than later.

An important aspect to the study of Russia's Arctic strategy is this consolidation of the relationship between power and money under Putin.[75] Indeed, the incorporation of Putin's men and an increased presence of *siloviki* within Russia's energy sector are key facets of Putin's plan for Russia. Putin's "attack" against particular oligarchs was a necessary precondition to diverting Russia's resource revenue back to the state rather than the pockets of a select few individuals. Those pockets are still lined; it is just that a few of the *dramatis personae* have changed.

RUSSIA'S ARCTIC LEGACY

In 1926, the Soviet Union claimed the entire Arctic area adjoining the polar coast, as shown in figure 2-1. Under the Soviet sectoral approach (drawing a straight line from the North Pole to Russian territory), the claimed territory was a large triangular area beginning at the western border of the USSR and stretching to the center of the Bering Strait, with its apex at the North Pole.[76] No other country recognized the Soviet delineation. In addition, the Soviets acknowledged four other sectors belonging to Canada, Denmark, Norway, and the US. When it came to the North Pole, the intersecting point of all five sectors, the leading Soviet authority on Arctic matters noted:[77]

> As to the ownership of the North Pole, it should be remarked that the Pole is an intersection of meridian lines of the said five sectors. Neither legally nor in fact does it belong to anyone. It might be represented as a hexahedral frontier post on the sides of which might be painted the national colours of the State of the corresponding sector.

The US, Denmark, and Norway did not recognize the 1926 claim or the sectoral claim principle in general. In 1925, Canada made a sector claim in the Arctic extending to the North Pole. Critics of the sector principle claim it has "no basis in international law," whereas proponents of the principle claim their theory is simple to apply and follow.[78]

As in other policy domains, Stalin was the most important figure in the evolution of official Soviet attitudes to the Arctic; arguably the

Figure 2-1. Soviet Arctic Claim

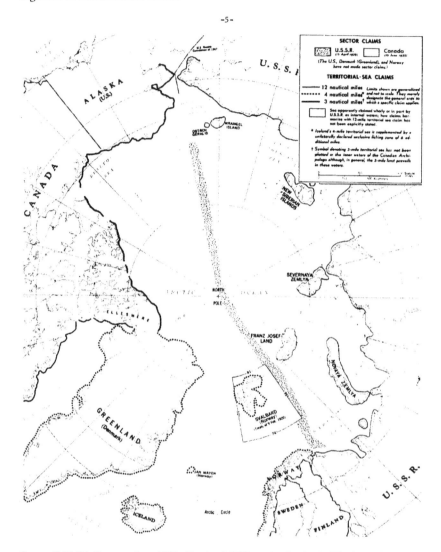

Source: RAND Corporation, 1972. *Territorial Waters in the Arctic: The Soviet Position,* rand.org/content/dam/rand/pubs/reports/2009/R907.pdf.

Arctic received more attention from Stalin than from any other Soviet leader. Stalin saw clearly the strategic potential of the Arctic and personally involved himself in three signature Arctic projects during the 1930s—construction of the White Sea Canal, development of Arctic aviation, and establishment of the Northern Sea Route (NSR).[79] When the Soviet Union navigated the NSR in 1932, it was an event that "transformed the Arctic and the state proved more than eager to take advantage of the public's enthusiasm for things polar."[80] Infamously, the Soviet Arctic also became home to extensive parts of Stalin's vast prison system, the Gulag.

In a process that has been dubbed the "Stalinization" of Arctic exploration, Stalin greatly increased global attention to the Arctic region.[81] Two key themes illustrate the centrality of the Arctic Soviet policies and ideology under Stalin: first, the Arctic's place in the modernization and industrialization agenda, and second, the significance of the Arctic for Stalin's propaganda campaign. The resource wealth of the Russian Arctic promised to fund Stalin's industrialization dreams, and the harshness of the Arctic environment coupled with humanity's battle to conquer it was a neat fit for communist propaganda.[82] The Soviet Union's wide array of successful explorations into the Arctic region with limited means could be repackaged to celebrate the Soviet system's unique capabilities. The Arctic became an important focus for propelling Soviet communist ideals. What emerged was the concept of the "Red Arctic"—a myth of popular Soviet culture epitomizing the leadership of the Soviet Union in all matters Arctic. For Marlene Laruelle, the Arctic was presented as "the forepost of Soviet civilization" that celebrated Stalin's core values of patriotism, heroism, and the exceptional industrial capacities of socialism, as the Soviet Union appeared to conquer the world's harshest environment.[83]

The year 1932 saw the end of the first five-year plan, whose primary focus was the establishment of heavy industry and the collectivization of agriculture.[84] Starting in 1933, the NSR underwent significant development sparked by the extensive Soviet Arctic expansion plan. For Stalin, the Arctic was of crucial significance to the future economic bottom line of the Soviet Union:

> The Arctic and our northern regions contain colossal wealth. We must
> create a Soviet organization which can, in the shortest period possible,
> include this wealth in the general resources of our socialist economic
> structure.[85]

After Stalin's death, Soviet interest in the Arctic faded. The Far East
presented itself as a more viable propaganda frontier and focus for the
Soviet economy, and by the 1960s, the West Siberian oilfields were of
central importance. But while in the post-Stalin period the Russia's
Arctic region lost some of its allure, at the same time it was "neither
rejected, nor exalted."[86] After Stalin, Soviet Arctic policy was driven
primarily by security needs. At the height of the Cold War, the Arctic
was transformed into a strategic and military space marked by East-
West tensions. Since the Arctic is the shortest distance between the
two superpowers, and with the development of ballistic missile technology, the Arctic became a Cold War front. Both superpowers built
and deployed missile defense systems, further entrenching the region
as a potential theater for conflict. Toward the end of the 1980s, the
Arctic was viewed as the strategic frontier in US-Soviet relations.

   Mikhail Gorbachev did much to shape Russia's contemporary Arctic policy in his October 1, 1987, speech in Murmansk, outlining the
Soviet Union's Arctic strategy.[87] The "Murmansk Initiative" was part
of Gorbachev's wider strategy to warm ties with the US.[88] The Murmansk Initiative was a key component of Gorbachev's overall *perestroika*
and *glasnost* reform programs. The Murmansk Initiative aimed at reducing the arms race and, specifically, the armed presence of both superpowers in the Arctic. Gorbachev envisioned the Arctic as a space for
cooperation and as the first step in implementing a wider peace initiative. He called for a nuclear-free zone, restrictions on naval military
activities, cooperative resource development, coordinated scientific research, environmental cooperation, and the opening of the Northern
Sea Route.

   Gorbachev argued that although the "international situation was
still complicated," there had been "some change."[89] Western leaders
were continually branding Soviet Arctic policy as "communist expan-

sion," and yet in reality, that sentiment was often "forgotten" when it came to "businesslike political negotiations and contracts" in the Arctic.[90] In the Murmansk speech, Gorbachev particularly focused on the dangers of rapid militarization of the Arctic:

> The militarization of this part of the world is assuming threatening dimensions. One cannot but feel concern over the fact that NATO, anticipating an agreement on medium- and shorter-range missiles being reached, is preparing to train military personnel in the use of sea- and air-based cruise missiles from the North Atlantic. This would mean an additional threat to us and to all the countries of Northern Europe. A new radar station, one of the Star Wars elements, has been made operational in Greenland in violation of the ABM Treaty. US cruise missiles are being tested in the north of Canada. The Canadian government has recently developed a vast programme for a build-up of forces in the Arctic. The US and NATO military activity in areas adjoining the Soviet Polar Region is being stepped up. The level of NATO's military presence in Norway and Denmark is being built up. Therefore, while in Murmansk, and standing on the threshold of the Arctic and the North Atlantic, I would like to invite, first of all, the countries of the region to a discussion on the burning security issues.[91]

Western distrust, even scepticism, initially made Gorbachev's cooperation objective difficult to realize.[92] However, Gorbachev's policy encouraged Canadian prime minister Brian Mulroney's government to engage with Russia in Canada's first multilateral negotiations since the formation of the Soviet Union.[93] Gorbachev's cooperative stance on the Arctic continued with Soviet prime minister Nikolai Ryzhkov visiting Norway and Sweden in 1988 to suggest reducing military exercises in the Arctic. Soviet foreign minister Eduard Shevardnadze's Arctic arms control proposals at the 1989 conference on Arctic cooperation, in which he stated a "willingness to negotiate an agreement with the US on limiting the areas of test and combat" in the Arctic, was further evidence of the Soviet Union's cooperative approach to the Arctic.[94] As Gorbachev's domestic and external reform programs gathered momentum, Western scepticism was replaced by a growing recognition that Gorbachev was a man the West could "do business with."[95] Essentially, Gorbachev's Murmansk Initiative was an attempt to desecuritize state-to-state relations in the Arctic.

Surprisingly, the fall of the Soviet Union did not reduce the cooperative atmosphere. Despite his personal rivalry with Gorbachev, the reformist leader of the Russian Federation, Boris Yeltsin continued his Soviet predecessor's cooperative approach to the Arctic, at least in the early years. Against the backdrop of the fall of the Soviet Union and coupled with the severe economic issues of the 1990s, Russia's northern regions became largely forgotten. This posed issues for the inherited armed forces of the Soviet Union posted in Russia's High North. During the early 1990s, "Russia [did] not intend to eliminate entirely its armed forces in the North, but it [didn't] know how many troops to keep." Moscow's inattention also affected the over 1 million military-related civilians living in Russia's Arctic region (areas north of the Arctic Circle).

However, the economic difficulties did not affect multilateral cooperation in the Arctic. Given the economic limitations, Yeltsin allocated a bare minimum of resources to the Arctic. This inevitably favored the maintenance of a cooperative approach. Under Yeltsin, Canadian-Russian relations in the Arctic warmed, as evidenced by the two countries' joint 1992 Declaration of Friendship and formal Arctic Cooperation Agreement. For Yeltsin, as he told a joint sitting of both houses of the Canadian parliament, it was the case that "only together can we solve all of the problems involving the Arctic."[96] Thus, aspects of Gorbachev's Murmansk Initiative survived the Soviet Union's fall and helped Russia bring about the establishment of the Arctic Council in 1996.

A range of committees and working groups emerged in the years that followed the Murmansk Initiative. The International Arctic Science Committee (IASC) was founded in 1990 by the Moscow, US, Canada, Norway, Iceland, Finland, Denmark, and Sweden; today the IASC also includes some fifteen non-Arctic states.[97] Likewise, in 1990, the International Arctic Social Sciences Association (IASSA) was founded following a meeting in Leningrad in 1988 on the coordination of research in the Arctic.[98] The 1991 Finnish Initiative resulted in the Arctic Environmental Protection Strategy (AEPS) signed by Moscow, US, Canada, Denmark, Finland, Iceland, Norway, and Sweden. The initiative aimed to "monitor, protect, and promote sustainable development in the Arctic region and recognize the rights of indigenous peoples in relation to environmental issues."[99] This was the forerunner of the Arctic Council, which was established five years later through the Ottawa Declaration.[100]

Gorbachev's Arctic legacy was, above all, to advance the cause of the region's potential for cooperation. Certainly, if it were possible "to assign a date marking the beginning of the current era of circumpolar cooperation, October 1st 1987, is it."[101] Yet, despite Gorbachev seeking a "radical lowering of the level of military confrontation in the region," the Soviets maintained their Arctic hardware at Cold War levels throughout Gorbachev's leadership.[102] Substantive Arctic demilitarization was ushered in by Yeltsin largely as a direct result of the fall of the USSR in 1991. For Russia, the military presence was too costly to maintain, while for the US the threat of the Soviet Union was no more.

A hangover of Soviet Arctic policy, with lasting effects for the contemporary Arctic, is the method by which the USSR decommissioned radioactive hazards. Utilized as a nuclear testing site, the Soviet Arctic was also routinely treated as a nuclear waste-dumping site.[103] Russia's state nuclear organization, Rosatom, reported to then president Medvedev in 2011 a catalog of Soviet-dumped waste. According to the report, there were some 17,000 containers of radioactive waste, nineteen ships containing radioactive waste, fourteen nuclear reactors, including five that still contained spent nuclear fuel, 735 other pieces of radioactively contaminated heavy machinery, and a K-27 nuclear submarine with its two reactors loaded with nuclear fuel, all dumped in the offshore Russian Arctic region.[104] The cleanup task has been tackled by a joint Russian-Norwegian task force, given that the majority of Soviet waste is in the nearby Kara and Barents Sea regions. Operations in 1992, 1993, and 1994 set a precedent for bilateral cooperation between Norway and Russia in this domain, and the cleanup is ongoing.

RUSSIA'S CONTEMPORARY ARCTIC CLAIMS

Russia's 2001 Bid

Russia's partial claim to the Arctic in 2001 sparked international concern over the future trajectory of the region. The claim centers on the extent to which the Siberian continental shelf extends up to the North Pole by way of an underwater mountain ridge—the Lomonosov Ridge—that also connects to Russia's continental shelf. Russia's claim to the Lomonosov Ridge was later reinforced in part by Chilingarov's 2007 Arktika expedition. The mission goals were to collect deep-sea soil samples to substantiate Russia's extended continental shelf claim and to plant the Russian flag on the seabed. It was the latter objective that gained global attention. The expedition's scientific value was "negligible compared with its political value."[105] This claim is supported by Russia's own Arctic and Antarctic Research Institute, which noted that "samples taken from the surface of the seabed are not very reliable ... besides we already know the geology of the Arctic Ocean's seabed and have been collecting samples for many years."[106]

Chilingarov announced "the Arctic is Russian" to onlookers on the expedition and declared that "the North Pole is an extension of the Russian coastal shelf."[107] The expedition was viewed largely by the West as an exercise in Kremlin public relations propaganda.[108] At the time, Chilingarov was not only an Arctic explorer, but also deputy speaker of the Russian parliament. Canada's foreign minister, Peter MacKay, signaled Canadian anger over the symbolic flag planting, stating, "This isn't the 15th century, you can't go around the world and just plant flags and say: 'we're claiming this territory.'"[109] Russian foreign minister Sergey Lavrov responded to criticism of the 2007 expedition by saying that "the aim of this expedition [was] not to stake Russia's claim but to show that our continental shelf reaches to the North Pole."[110] The symbolic planting of Russia's flag on the seabed of the North Pole sparked new debate surrounding a resurgent Russia. However, Arctic expeditions are not a new phenomenon in Russia, as established earlier in this chapter. Stalin's conquest of the north (*pokorenie severa*) initiatives between 1936 and 1939 set the historical precedent for post-Soviet Russian Arctic interest.[111]

Putin called all members of the Arktika expedition to thank them personally, a clear sign of the high importance of the operation to the Kremlin.[112] A Russian academic commented on the controversial nature of the expedition:

> The 2007 flag plant and mission resulted in an element of surprise among the Arctic neighbours. This was something Russia did not account for, we thought our objectives in the north were much clearer and didn't require a titanium flag to confirm. Chilingarov's team just used the flag to highlight Russia as a leading scientific Arctic power; they had no orders to carve out the North Pole as Russian. The US planted a flag on the moon and why didn't the world have issues with this? The US was not at any point claiming the moon! Just as Russia was not using the flag to claim the North Pole per se—we leave that up to international law. This is already in our favour.[113]

In retrospect, concerns were largely unwarranted as "Russian rhetoric [has] quieted down and its leaders [are] focusing on negotiated solutions to territorial disputes in the region."[114] In the years since the Arktika flag planting, the idea of Russia staking its Arctic claim by force has lost currency as Russia continues to seek confirmation of its extended continental shelf claim based on international law, by adhering to UNCLOS and utilizing the CLCS. Figure 2-2 shows the primary source document that Russia submitted to the CLCS to extend the outer limits of its Arctic continental shelf.

In providing evidence of an extended continental shelf beyond the 200 nautical mile exclusive economic zone (EEZ), the map offers various markers at the bottom left of the map translated into English as follows:

1. provisional line of delimitation of the continental shelf of the Russian Federation with neighboring states; subject to more precise determination through negotiations
2. 200 nautical mile zone from the baselines

Figure 2-2. Russia's 2001 Extended Arctic Continental Shelf Submission

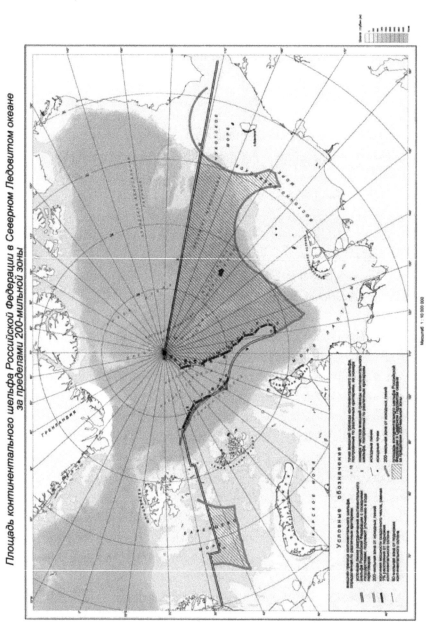

Площадь континентального шельфа Российской Федерации в Северном Ледовитом океане за пределами 200-мильной зоны

Source: Government of the Russian Federation, 2001. "Submission to the CLCS on the Outer Limits of the Russian Federation's Continental Shelf," un.org/depts/los/clcsnew/submissionsfiles/rus01/RUSpage5Legend.pdf.

3. line showing the thickness of the sedimentary rocks equal to 1 percent of the distance from the foot of the continental slope
4. 60 nautical mile zone from the foot of the continental slope
5. points of the outer limits of the continental shelf determined
6. numbers of segments of the outer limits of the continental shelf determined according to various criteria
7. baselines
8. basepoints
9. 200 nautical mile zone from the baselines
10. the area of the continental shelf of the Russian Federation in the Arctic Ocean beyond the 200 nautical mile zone

The CLCS circulates all submission materials and encourages UNCLOS signatory states to communicate their reactions to submissions. In 2002, Canada responded to Russia's 2001 claim by stating the following:

> [Canada] is not in a position to determine whether it agrees with the Russian Federation's Arctic continental shelf submission and that its inability to comment should not be interpreted as either agreement or acquiescence by Canada to the Russian Federation's submission.[115]

Denmark also responded in 2002 to Russia's submission, stating it, too, was "not able to form an opinion on the Russian submission." Denmark declared it would also make an Arctic claim in the coming years, although, not having ratified the UNCLOS until 2004, at the time Denmark was not pressured by the ten-year submission rule. Denmark also communicated "its reservation to the Government of the Russian Federation" about the claim extending Russia's continental shelf to that adjacent to Greenland.[116]

Norway also responded in 2002, citing the unresolved delimitation issue between Russia and Norway in the Barents Sea. Norway urged the CLCS to treat the Barents Sea issue as a "maritime dispute" and argued that as an area under dispute, it needed to be shielded from "prejudice" related to Russia's 2001 partial claim.[117] Finally, the US responded, stating that "the submission has major flaws as it relates to the continental shelf claim in the Arctic," and attaching a brief paper for circulation to all members of the UN convention.[118] The paper questioned the legal architecture of UNCLOS, noting "the United States of America is of the view that, while the commission has no competence over questions of baselines from which the breadth of the territorial sea is measured, it should not be perceived as endorsing particular baselines."[119] Further, the US argued that the Lomonosov Ridge "is a freestanding feature in the deep, oceanic part of the Arctic Ocean Basin, and not a natural component of the continental margins of either Russia or any other state."[120] The US response pushed for the Russian claim to be "considered in a deliberate manner . . . insofar as no applications to explore or exploit the Area have been made or are likely to be made in the Arctic for the foreseeable future, no prejudice is likely to result from a deliberate process."[121]

The CLCS ruled that Russia needed to provide further detailed scientific data to substantiate its extended continental shelf claim. The commission recommended "that the Russian Federation make a revised submission in respect of its extended continental shelf in the Central Arctic Ocean" and suggested that Russia "follow the scientific and technical advice as indicated."[122] Moreover, the commission ruled that "according to the materials provided in the submission, the Ridge cannot be considered."[123]

Russia's 2015 Revised Submission

In August 2015, Russia submitted a revised extended continental shelf claim to the CLCS. Based largely on its 2001 submission, the new claim was bolstered by additional scientific information that allowed for an additional extension via the continental shelf. The 2015 submission added over 100,000 square kilometers to Russia's extended continental shelf claim from 2001. The objective was to uncover enough evidence to prove that a state's continental shelf extends beyond the 200 nautical mile EEZ. The outer extension limit is 150 nautical miles; however, this merely ensures sovereign rights to resources on and beneath the sea-

Figure 2-3. Lomonosov Ridge as Continuation of Russia's Siberian Shelf

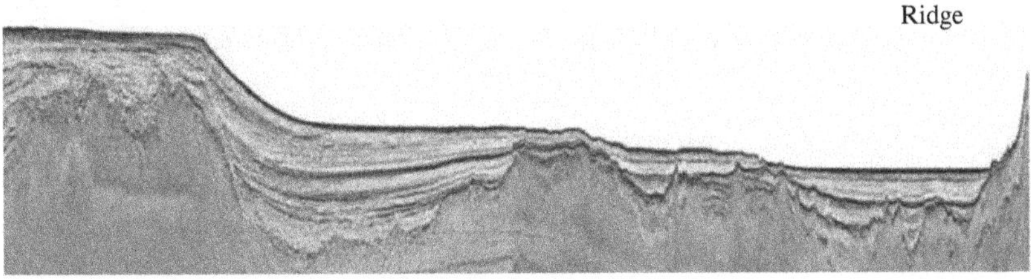

East Siberian
shelf   Podvodnikov Basin   Lomonosov
                                                                            Ridge

Source: Government of the Russian Federation, 2001. "Submission to the CLCS on the Outer Limits of the Russian Federation's Continental Shelf," un.org/depts/los /clcs_new/submissions_files/rus01/RUS_page5_Legend.pdf.

bed, not an extended 150 nautical miles of EEZ. Based on the 2015 extended continental shelf claim, given the estimated resources beneath the seabed, if unchallenged it would have extended Russian control to about 60 percent of all hydrocarbons found in the Arctic.

The Russian Federation's 2015 partially revised submission to the CLCS was prepared by a wide array of Russian federal authorities: the Ministry of Natural Resources and Environment; the Federal Agency on Mineral Resources; the Ministry of Foreign Affairs; the Ministry of Defense; the Department of Navigation and Oceanography; and the Russian Academy of Social Sciences.[124] Coordinating the large number of authorities on the revised Arctic bid accounts for the prolonged revision period.

Between 2002 and 2014, a range of geological expeditions were carried out in the Russian Arctic beyond the Arktika mission. Significantly, Russia was the first state to embark on deep-water drilling in the Arctic, first in 2004 and again in 2007 on the Lomonosov Ridge.[125] Seismic data was utilized to support Russia's claim that the Lomonosov Ridge was a natural prolongation of the Siberian shelf. Figure 2-3, which Russia provided formally as evidence in the 2015 revised submission, illustrates the claim that the Lomonosov Ridge is a natural progression of the Siberian continental shelf.

In anticipation of submissions from Denmark and Canada with regard to overlapping continental shelf claims, Russia held consultations in 2014 with both countries. All three reached an understanding on subsequent submissions to the CLCS, a summary of which is as follows.

When one State makes (a) Submission to the Commission, the other State shall immediately forward to the Secretary-General of the UN a diplomatic note that exactly says:

- A State does not object to the Commission considering the Submission of the other State and make recommendations thereon;
- The recommendations made by the Commission in respect of the Submission of one State shall be without prejudice to the rights of the other State in the course of the Commission's consideration of its own Submission;
- The above recommendations with respect to any State shall not prejudice the delimitation of the continental shelf between the two States.
- Each Party refers to this agreement in its Submission to the Commission; requests the Commission to make recommendations based on this agreement; and requests the Secretary-General of the United Nations to declare the content of the above-mentioned diplomatic note to Member States of the United Nations and the States parties to the Convention.[126]

Denmark responded to the CLCS in October 2015 in accordance with the agreement with Russia, drawing attention to the claim's "potential overlap with the continental shelf of the Kingdom of Denmark."[127] Denmark did not object to the CLCS "considering or making recommendations on the Russian submission" but requested that "the commission make recommendations taking [into] account" Denmark's formal submission in 2014.[128] The US also responded in October 2015, this time opting for a relaxed response compared to its 2001 approach. Besides supporting Russia's claim that both Washington and Moscow have adhered to the 1990 agreement regarding the delineation of the Chukchi and Bering Seas, the US confirmed that "it does not object to" Russia's revised submission.[129] Canada responded in November 2015 in line with its agreement with Russia, advising that Canada had "taken note of the potential overlap" of the continental shelves of Canada and the Russian Federation.[130] Further, Canada requested its response be made public to UN members.

The 2015 Russian claim added two new areas and subtracted one from the original 2001 claim. This renewed submission was deemed "neither surprising nor threatening," with the Arctic Five powers (Canada, Denmark, Norway, Russia, and the US) well aware of the negotiations that still lay ahead.[131] The 2015 Russian claim crossed into the Canadian and Danish sides of the North Pole for the first time. However, the Russian view is that while this may have symbolic impact (especially for Canada and Denmark), it is up to the CLCS to rule on the data validity.[132] An interview with a Russian government official confirmed Russia's commitment to cooperation in the Arctic:

> Russia's position is along the lines of "international law precedent does not define action." Georgia, Ukraine and the Arctic are all very separate areas of conduct. Russia might be seen to have breached norms in the first two regions—although that is a separate discussion entirely—however, we have shown adherence to UNCLOS in the Arctic and will continue to do so. The issue becomes one of our counterparts—and I am talking about the US primarily—not being able to accept our claim in line with international law. Arctic nations agreed to the regime of UNCLOS and our Arctic claim should not be seen as anything other than what it is: legal in the eyes of international law. Perhaps other precedent demonstrates otherwise, but there too are individual readings of international law.[133]

Russia's 2021 Addendum

In March 2021, Russia submitted two addenda to the 2015 partially revised submission to the CLCS. These two additional data sets related to the Gakkel Ridge, Nansen, and Amundsen Basins, and to the Lomonosov and Alpha Ridges, the Mendeleev Rise, the Amundsen and Makarov Basins, and the Canadian Basin. In effect, this revised extended continental shelf claim handed Russia 70 percent of the Arctic Ocean seabed. In practice however, Moscow has an uphill battle to satisfy overlapping claimant concerns over the seabed of the North Pole. Figure 2-4 illustrates the evolving size of Russia's submission to the CLCS in the Central Arctic Ocean.

Stimulated by variables partly beyond political control throughout the early 2000s—including climate change, energy security, and rising oil prices—the Arctic was thrust back onto the international agenda. Despite renewed tensions between Russia and the West under Putin, Arctic cooperation is surviving, if only by way of continued communication over Arctic matters. The Arctic represents one of the few spheres, besides space, in which Russia-West cooperation is continuing. Russia has a strong case for the extension of its (already vast) Arctic continental shelf and is following international law and engaging with the CLCS to make its case. Admittedly, it does so because upholding these particular rules and norms is well within Moscow's interest.

Russia's securitization of its Arctic border is, as this chapter has argued, an unsurprising behavior. Putin is invoking the Stalinist propaganda of "conquering the Arctic" not simply to mobilize domestic support. Drawing on the historical romanticism and national pride associated with the Arctic, Putin seeks to demonstrate his efforts to reinstate Russia's international prestige. Putin's prestige narrative is aimed at the domestic population yet is also often picked up by the West and translated into evidence of Russia's conflict-seeking agenda in the Arctic. Still, this chapter has provided evidence of Russia's commitment to observing rule of law and avoiding conflict in the Arctic.

Arctic conflict would not be in the interest of any of the Arctic Ocean rim powers, the Arctic Five. It would render hydrocarbon resources untouchable in the midst of warfare and severely complicate transit passage of goods—the two key touted gains of developing the Arctic. The Arctic Five nations are simply not interested in conflict

Figure 2-4. Russia's Evolving CLCS Arctic Submission (2001, 2015, 2021)

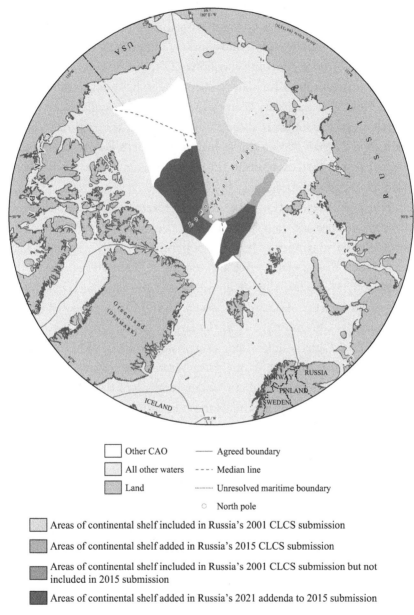

	Other CAO	—— Agreed boundary
	All other waters	- - - - Median line
	Land	·········· Unresolved maritime boundary
		○ North pole

Areas of continental shelf included in Russia's 2001 CLCS submission

Areas of continental shelf added in Russia's 2015 CLCS submission

Areas of continental shelf included in Russia's 2001 CLCS submission but not included in 2015 submission

Areas of continental shelf added in Russia's 2021 addenda to 2015 submission

Source: https://www.durham.ac.uk/media/durham-university/research-/research
-centres/ibru-centre-for-borders-research/maps-and-databases/arctic-maps-2021
/updated-maps-and-notes/Map-5-IBRU-Arctic-map-07-04-21-(Russias-evolving
-submission-in-the-CAO).pdf.

within the region, and this is evident in the consistent efforts to maintain multilateral dialogue. The March 2022 decision by western Arctic states was merely to pause dialogue with Russia—not to sever the relationship or plunge the region into conflict. The coming chapters further explore the broader geopolitical context of the Arctic Five.

The misreading of Russian Arctic strategy has a lot to do with residual Cold War geopolitical story lines, but it also stems from mixed signals from Russia itself about its intentions in the region.[134] From planting a Russian flag on the seabed of the North Pole to conducting large-scale military exercises in the region, Russia has certainly advertised its Arctic ambitions.

However, these actions are, first and foremost, propaganda tools directed at Russia's domestic audience. Beyond the public show of force, Russia continues to rely on cooperation with the West in Arctic matters. Russia's adherence and touting of international law in the Arctic reflects the fact that geography puts international law squarely in Russia's interest. The application of UNCLOS is expected by the international community, and as the largest Arctic Ocean rim power, Russia's larger Arctic stake is not a surprising outcome. The next chapter delves deeper into the Arctic great game—the contenders and the prizes at stake. Given a realistic understanding of the foundations of Russian Arctic strategy as well as the central role of energy to Putin's Russia, it now falls on the reader to evaluate the "hot air" surrounding Arctic geopolitics.

3

PUTIN'S ARCTIC PLAYBOOK

"ONE COMES ACROSS ALL SORTS OF FANTASTICAL
PREDICTIONS ABOUT A COMING BATTLE FOR THE ARCTIC."

—V. PUTIN

The Russian Arctic is by "no means a peripheral pursuit" for Vladimir Putin's Russia, with the region accounting for roughly 10 percent of Russia's gross domestic product (GDP) and 20 percent of all Russian exports. For any geopolitical study, definitions and boundaries are central to adequate strategic assessments. This, too, is the case for the Arctic, because the reality is there are many "Arctics." There is a North American Arctic, a European Arctic, and naturally, given this study, a Russian Arctic. Delineating the Russian Arctic area is perhaps the most important, and most overlooked, aspect to understanding what Russia wants in the Arctic. As Marlene Laruelle notes, for Russia, *the Arctic* traditionally referred to the off-shore Arctic Ocean and territorial seas in the region, with *Far North* used to reference the on-land northern territories of Russia north of the Arctic Circle. Today, based on the Putin's 2014 decree, the region delineated as the Arctic zone of the Russian Federation is arrived at by way of administrative districts.[1]

Russia's Arctic stake is about much more than the Northern Sea Route (NSR) and the tantalizing question of who "owns" the North Pole. Framing Russian Arctic interests with this in mind reduces the scope for ideologically charged assessments of a neoimperialist Russian Arctic agenda. For Putin, the Arctic offers a throwback to Soviet times in which he grew up and about which he is strongly nostalgic. The Arctic provides a new avenue for reinstating Soviet symbols in contemporary Russia.[2] Reinstating Soviet symbols, particularly those of Stalin, is a deliberate by-product of Putinism.[3] There are parallels between Stalin's "cult of the hero" Arctic propaganda and Putin's Arctic agenda. This is evident in the fact that Putin is the face of Russia's Arctic stake, demonstrated by his staged photo shoots in the region as well as his role in personally announcing most Arctic commercial dealings.

Russia was one of the first Arctic states to develop an Arctic strategy. Since Putin, Russian Arctic strategy has served two purposes: to outline Russia's national interests in the Russian Arctic zone, and to articulate the threats or challenges posed in the region to Russian national security. Of course, national security and national interests under Putin have become much broader than military might. Economic security, energy security, and resilience of Arctic investments in the face of external (man-made and natural) threats are often overlooked when western scholars contemplate "what drives Putin" in the Arctic. To highlight the themes of continuity and change, it is helpful to take stock of developments in Russian Arctic strategy.

RUSSIAN ARCTIC POLICY (2000–2010)

Moscow's first Arctic policy document for the millennium was the 2000 "Basics of the Russian Federation State Policy in the Arctic" (or Draft State Policy).[4] Putin signed the Draft State Policy into law, and it served as the basis for Russia's Arctic zone military modernization program. Early on, Putin recognized and harnessed the economic potential of the zone by earmarking it as the future resource base for the nation. Next came the 2008 "Principles of the State Policy of the Russian Federation in the Arctic to 2020 and Beyond" (or State Policy), signed by then president Dmitry Medvedev. This spelled out further national interests including the role of the Arctic zone as a strategic resource base to assist socioeconomic development; the maintenance of the region as a peaceful sphere; and commitments to environmental preservation. The 2008 State Policy also framed the NSR as a strategic interest in terms of its role as a critical sea line of communication and transport route for Russia.

The Medvedev presidency ushered in a period of a slightly more "softly-softly" approach in foreign policy, and this was reflected in the 2008 Arctic policy document. Russia's 2008 strategy garnered global interest mainly because it followed the 2007 publicity stunt in which Russian explorers planted the Russian flag on the seabed of the North Pole. The 2008 State Policy was the first document to clearly outline and articulate the national security interests of Russia in the Arctic, which were as follows:

- the utilization of the Russian Federation's Arctic zone as a national strategic resource base capable of fulfilling the socio-economic tasks associated with national growth
- the preservation of the Arctic as a zone of peace and cooperation
- the protection of the Arctic's unique ecological system
- the use of the Northern Sea Route as a unified transportation link connecting Russia to the Arctic[5]

In 2008, the strategic priority in social and economic development objectives remained the "expansion of the resource base." In the sphere of military security, the "defence and protection of the state border of the Russian Federation" was the key priority in the Arctic. Further, the 2008 strategy flagged requirements for the "necessary grouping of the Armed Forces of the Russian Federation."[6] With regard to international cooperation, the strategy outlined the objective of "maintenance of a mutually advantageous bilateral and multilateral cooperation" area within the Arctic "on the basis of international treaties and agreements."[7] The policy's objectives also addressed environmental security, information technology, and communication, as well as scientific interests. The 2008 policy presented ten future priorities for Russia in the Arctic:

1. carrying out of an active interaction of the Russian Federation with the sub-Arctic states with a view of delimitation of maritime areas on the basis of norms of international law and also for tackling issues of an international legal substantiation of the external border of the Arctic zone of the Russian Federation;

2. building-up efforts of the sub-Arctic states for the creation of a uniform regional system of search and rescue, and also prevention of man-caused accidents and liquidation of their consequences, including coordination of activity of rescue forces;

3. strengthening, on a bilateral basis and within the framework of regional organizations, frontier cooperation, including in the field of effective natural resources management and environment preservation in the Arctic;

4. assistance in the organization and effective utilization of transit and cross-Polar air routes in the Arctic, and also in the use of the Northern Sea Route for international navigation under the jurisdiction of the Russian Federation and according to international treaties of the Russian Federation;

5. activation of the participation of Russian official agencies and public organizations in the work of international forums devoted to Arctic problems, including the inter-parliamentary interaction within the framework of the Russia-European Union partnership;

6. delimitation of maritime spaces in the Arctic Ocean and maintenance of a mutually advantageous presence of Russia on the Spitsbergen archipelago;

7. perfection of the system of state management of the social and economic development of the Arctic zone of the Russian Federation, including through expansion of fundamental and applied scientific research in the Arctic;

8. improvement of quality of life of the indigenous population and social conditions of economic activities in the Arctic;
9. development of the resource base of the Arctic zone of the Russian Federation through the use of cutting-edge technologies;
10. modernization and development of the infrastructure of the Arctic transport system and the fisheries complex in the Arctic zone of the Russian Federation.[8]

Russia's 2008 Arctic policy outlined three key stages for the realization of Russia's Arctic objectives. In the first stage (2008–2010), basic "geologic-geophysical, hydrographic, [and] cartographical" works were to be carried out in preparation for "substantiation of the external border of the Arctic zone of the Russian Federation."[9] This exploratory work was used in evidence for Russia's 2015 extended continental shelf claim to the CLCS. The first stage also called for the "expansion of possibilities of international cooperation" in the Arctic. The second stage (2011–2015) focused on securing the "international legal formation of the external border of the Arctic zone and the realization on this basis of competitive advantages for Russian exploitation and transportation of energy resources."[10]

The second stage of the 2008 Arctic policy also earmarked the NSR for development of its "infrastructure and control systems." However, investment is still lacking, and Russia has not yet realized this component of its 2008 policy. The third stage (2016–2020) of the policy envisioned the "transformation of the Arctic zone of the Russian Federation into a leading strategic resource base." While some liquified natural gas (LNG) projects in the Russian Arctic are online, economic conditions for Moscow since 2014 have been difficult. Most Western foreign investment has been curtailed, and the COVID-19 pandemic has added further uncertainty to energy markets. But perhaps the most significant external factor hampering Moscow's Arctic energy dreams was the 2014 oil price dive. The 2008 policy was formulated in the midst of sky-high oil prices—$145 per barrel—and while oil prices have indeed fluctuated, since 2014 the price of oil has struggled to move out of $60–$70 per barrel territory.

The sentiment of how important the Arctic is to Putin's Russia is captured succinctly in this statement by a Russian Arctic policymaker:

> Mother Nature's gift to the Soviet Union was the Arctic. She placed it geographically in our care, but our caretaker role has changed as time has passed. There is still a strong security role for Russia, protecting our border and protecting customers who will use our Arctic region for passage, as well as producing energy with great care not to affect the ecosystem. Russia has a caretaker role now related to the Arctic as a future resource base to look after the Russian population. You asked about great power status and whether the Arctic will help lift us to this position—this is a pointless question for Russia was ensured great power from the start. The Arctic is Russian and will be developed when we decide to develop, just look to how many others are pushing to be included on our journey. I am talking about the states with no Arctic proximity—Singapore, Japan, China—they need access to our region and they know who to talk to, they communicate with the Arctic leader, they communicate with us.[11]

RUSSIAN ARCTIC POLICY (2010–2020)

Putin updated Russia's Arctic strategic planning again in the 2013 "Strategy for the Development of the Arctic Zone of the Russian Federation and Provision of National Security to 2020" (or Development Strategy). The Development Strategy added key priority areas to Moscow's agenda and repositioned the NSR to better reflect its strategic value as an economic corridor (a Blue Silk Road of sorts) for Russian Arctic LNG. Science and technology, as well as modernized information and telecommunication infrastructure interests, were added to Russia's Arctic agenda. The 2013 Development Strategy further illustrated the reemergence of Putin's military-security priorities in the Russian Arctic zone with the inclusion of efforts to protect and defend the state border of Russia in the Arctic. Overall, it was this iteration of the strategy that highlighted the military and national security vector of the Russian Arctic zone.

Note that the priorities outlined in the 2008 policy reflect some-what of a Gorbachev-Yeltsin liberal and cooperative approach to the Arctic by Medvedev. Of course, under the Putin-Medvedev tande-mocracy, it is unlikely the 2008 Arctic policy consisted of material Putin himself did not in effect approve. Putin's priorities for Russia's 2013 Arctic strategy refocused efforts across four spheres. First, the social sphere listed "negative demographic trends in most of the Arctic regions of the Russian Federation and the outflow of labour (espe-cially skilled)" as key issues. Second, the economic sphere identified the "lack of Russian modern equipment and technologies for exploration and development of offshore hydrocarbon fields in the Arctic" as well as "underdevelopment of basic transport infrastructure" as problems. Third, the scientific sphere regarded "scarce technical resources and capabilities" within the Arctic as issues for Russia. Fourth, the envi-ronmental sphere listed "potential sources of contamination and high levels of accumulated environmental damage" as threats to the Russian Arctic.[12]

In comparison to the 2008 policy, the 2013 strategy reordered the priority areas of the Arctic zone for Russia and presented them in a way that was more oriented to nationalist objectives. The 2013 Arctic strat-egy priorities now read as follows:

- integrated socioeconomic development of the Arctic zone of the Russian Federation
- the development of science and technology
- the establishment of a modern information and telecommunica-tions infrastructure
- environmental security
- international cooperation in the Arctic
- provision of military security, and protection of the state border of the Russian Federation in the Arctic[13]

The 2013 Arctic policy reflected a more determined, pointed Arctic strategy that was to be implemented in two stages. The first stage (2015) called for the groundwork to be laid for the "necessary conditions for strengthening national security through the integrated development of the Arctic zone, including coordination of all stakeholders of state policy." Further, this stage envisaged the "international legal registration of [the] outer limit of the continental shelf." It also mentions the "establishment and development of the Coast Guard of the Federal Security Service of the Russian Federation." The second stage (2020) focused more on reaping the rewards of stage one's groundwork. Stage two aimed to access "the competitive advantages" of "mineral resources in the continental shelf." This stage also called for the "retooling of federal border security" and the "protection of territory, population and critical facilities" in the Russian Arctic. The 2013 policy served to "strengthen the position of the Russian Federation in the Arctic and greater international security, peace and stability, as well as increased international cooperation."[14] Of course, with hindsight it is clear that the extended continental shelf debate has not been resolved in the Arctic, nor has the commercial extraction of mineral resources in this offshore Arctic Ocean region begun.

In 2014, during an extended meeting of Russia's Security Council, Putin articulated Moscow's lasting approach to the Arctic:

> This region has traditionally been a sphere of our special interest. It is a concentration of practically all aspects of national security— military, political, economic, technological, environmental and that of resources. . . . We are aware of the growing interest in the Arctic on the part of the international community. Ever more frequently, we see the collision of interests of Arctic nations, and not only them: countries far removed from this area are showing a growing interest as well. We should also bear in mind the dynamic and ever-changing political and socioeconomic situation in the world, which is fraught with new risks and challenges to Russia's national interests, including

those in the Arctic. We need to take additional measures so as not to fall behind our partners, to maintain Russia's influence in the region and maybe, in some areas, to be ahead of our partners.[15]

The key message here was a warning shot to non-Arctic actors—read China—to respect the sovereignty and existing arrangements in the region. Putin went on to outline six key tasks for Russia in the Arctic, flagging for the first time the leadership role Russia seeks in the Arctic zone. First, per Putin's implementation of the power vertical (the re-centralization of Russian governance), he outlined plans for a single center of responsibility for the Arctic. Overcoming decentralized Arctic policy planning processes and better coordinating ministry portfolios in the Arctic were also crucial parts of Putin's vision for straightforward and organized Arctic strategy. Second, socioeconomic development became a priority under Putin in the Arctic region. Charging agencies with prioritizing measures to ensure socioeconomic development of Russia's Arctic communities has remained an important component of Russian Arctic strategy. The third task outlined by Putin back in 2014 was the resolution of Russia's extended Arctic continental shelf limits. Consistently, Putin's Russia has worked within the remit of international law (UNCLOS) in resolving the overlapping extended continental shelf claims with Denmark and Canada.

Putin's Russia has consistently prioritized the Northern Sea Route (NSR). While often framed in terms of securing the Russian Arctic open border, for Putin the development of the NSR has always been first and foremost an economic project. This fourth task—the modernization of the NSR—was necessary as the route became more popular and the tonnage increased. Development of ports, communication, and navigation infrastructure, as well as adequate and effective search and rescue capabilities, became key tasks for Russia. Security agencies like the FSB and the Russian military took the lead in much of this modernization and management of the NSR and the Russian Arctic frontier. Of course, this is continually misrepresented as a signal of Russian "militarization" in the Arctic. Conflicting ideologies and existing preconceptions of Putin's Russia (often not far off the mark, given Moscow's activities beyond the Arctic) shape the militarization assumption.

For Putin, the fifth task of Russian Arctic policy is environmental security. While the Kremlin alluded to fragility of the Arctic ecosystem, in practice Russia had treated Arctic environmental matters as an afterthought. This appeared to shift in 2020 with increased references to environmental security and the perils of climate change upon Russian Arctic investments and programs. As permafrost melts in the Russian onshore Arctic region, causing immediate threat to existing military and energy infrastructure, Russia is likely to prioritize environmental mitigation strategies in the Arctic. The sixth task of Russian Arctic strategy since Putin involves the ability of the state to secure the Russian Arctic zone. While energy facilities and infrastructure, including export routes such as the NSR, are the priority sector to be "secured" by Moscow, Western coverage tends to illustrate the Russian Arctic zone as a launching base for Russian expansion into the Arctic Ocean. These external assessments of Russian Arctic security methods and policies tend to exclude the applicability of international law to the Arctic region—which clearly assigns the lion's share of the Arctic region to Russia.

Implementing these key tasks of Russian Arctic strategy since Putin involves a range of actors. Ekaterina Klimenko has studied the decisionmaking processes in Putin's Russia largely in terms of the energy sector. I have expanded on her findings to present an all-inclusive table of Russia's Arctic policy establishment (table 3-1).

In Arctic policymaking, individuals are also powerful forces in Putin's Russia. Bobo Lo captures this sentiment in stating, "Decisions, rarely if ever, reflect an 'objective' national interest, but are made by individuals with their own particular biases, prejudices, and vested interests."[16] This is certainly the case in contemporary Russian Arctic strategy.[17] Beyond Putin, a leading individual shaping Russian Arctic strategy is Nikolai Patrushev.[18] As the secretary of Russia's Security Council, he is central to all Arctic affairs and is a close and longstanding Putin ally. Patrushev is responsible for the reordering of Russia's

Table 3-1. *Russia's Arctic Policy Establishment*

Actor	Area
Presidential Administration	Policy scope
Security Council	Interagency coordination, consensus building
Ministry of Defense	Troop contingency
Ministry of Foreign Affairs	Diplomacy
Federal Security Service (FSB)	Intelligence, coast guard function
Ministry of Energy	Arctic development issues
Ministry of Natural Resources and Environment	Arctic development issues
Ministry for the Development of the Russian Far East and Arctic	Arctic development issues (economic and social)
State Commission on the Development of the Arctic	Coordination body
Gazprom	Exploration/Production of hydrocarbons
Rosneft	Exploration/Production of hydrocarbons
Ministry of Transport	NSR
Northern Sea Route Administration	NSR
Atomflot	State icebreaker fleet operations
Sovkomflot	State-owned hydrocarbon shipping firm (LNG tankers)
Rosatom	State nuclear arm (ice-breaking)
Roscosmos	State satellite and space agency

Source: Compiled by author.

maritime priorities to promote the Arctic, and to a lesser extent, the Antarctic, to greater national significance.

Another key individual in Russia's Arctic policymaking processes is Defense Minister Sergei Shoigu. He is responsible for the undercurrent of securitization within Russia's Arctic strategy. In step with Putin, Shoigu deems the Arctic to be of great strategic significance and brings the hard-line Arctic aspect to the table, as evident in the refocus and redevelopment of Russia's Arctic military capabilities. Although neither Patrushev nor Shoigu is a "free agent," both nonetheless have central roles in Arctic matters.[19] In a commercial sense, personal interests are apparent in the potential financial windfalls from Arctic resources. As the heads of the state energy apparatuses, Igor Sechin and Alexei Miller have a vested interest in seeing Russia's Arctic strategy realized.[20] This variety of individual interests helps shape Russian Arctic strategy and, against the background of shifts in Russia's relationship with the West, can at times elicit more airtime, depending on the circumstances. For example, souring relations between Russia and the West post-2014 have allowed some individual biases to emerge in Arctic decisionmaking. Despite current tensions, those at the helm of Russian foreign policy are consistently voicing calls for multilateral cooperation in the Arctic. Patrushev has declared Russia's continued commitment to "expanding the platform of international dialogue" in the Arctic, which he described as a region with the "traditions of good neighborliness and cooperation."[21]

As it pertains to institutions, Arctic policymaking in Russia is security-intelligence agency heavy. While it is normal to have these bodies engaged in Arctic strategy, this still serves to shape external views of Russian Arctic priorities. In reality, most Arctic rim states are not dissimilar in tasking their military or security agencies with Arctic policy development or implementation (and indeed, capabilities).

Overseeing the coordination of Russian Arctic policy is the State Commission on the Development of the Arctic. This body was established in 2015 by Putin to serve as "a single point of accountability for the implementation of Arctic Policy."[22] Then deputy prime minister Dmitry Rogozin, and former director of Russia's space agency Roscosmos, was selected to head up the commission. Under Rogozin the commission was a fickle beast with over seventy stakeholders and relatively little to show in output. Stakeholders spanned Russia's oil and gas industry, defense and government agencies, regional Arctic leaders, education, and nongovernmental organization (NGO) representatives, as well as stakeholders from the presidential administration. In 2018, Yuri Trutnev (also currently acting Deputy Prime Minister) replaced Rogozin and began to make changes. The commission now is, in principle, more agile and able to deliver on Russia's Arctic agenda.

The establishment of the Russian Arctic commission was evidence that Russian Arctic policy is clearly "shaped by the leading figures of

Russian President Vladimir Putin's inner circle, based on the interplay of their personal and business interests in the Arctic."[23] This assessment is not wrong. The *siloviki* and oligarchs are certainly prominent in the Arctic policy space. Nikolai Patrushev (Putin's long-term associate, a former director of the FSB, and secretary of the Security Council), Igor Sechin (head of Rosneft), Alexei Miller (head of Gazprom), and Gennady Timchenko (cofounder of the investment group that owns Novatek) are all closely tied to the policymaking processes of Russian Arctic strategy.[24] Kristian Atland once emphasized the interplay between personal and business interests in Putin's Russia, noting that "whereas Russia's Arctic policy in the past was governed by national security interests, it is now increasingly governed by national economic interests and the interests of companies closely associated with the Russian state."[25] Of course, this might bolster the cooperative agenda of Russian Arctic strategy under Putin, not least due to the personal investment stakes of Putin's "mates" in the Russian Arctic energy sphere.

RUSSIAN ARCTIC POLICY (2020–)

In 2020 a web of new projects emerged relating directly to Russian strategic thinking in the Arctic. This section assesses policy planning as of 2023. The 2013 Arctic strategy was due for review and, in March 2020, Putin signed into law the new Arctic strategy, "The Foundations of State Policy of the Russian Federation in the Arctic in the Period to 2035."[26] Alongside this, Russia's Security Council, the national interagency body for coordinating and overseeing Russian strategic planning, announced the preparation of the project for the "Strategy of Development of the Arctic Zone of the Russian Federation and the Provision of National Security for the Period to 2035" (or Strategy of Development). This project is to be the mechanism for the realization of Russia's Arctic strategy and points to a range of priorities for Russia, from national security and threats to the ecosystem and the maintenance of Russia's "scientific-technological leadership" in the region.[27] If these two documents are considered to be a "unified plan," their implementation will be based on a third document, a newly prepared edition of a state program, the "Socio-Economic Development of the Arctic Zone of the Russian Federation."[28]

Together, these 2020 documents constitute Russia's contemporary plan for the Arctic, updating and reaffirming Moscow's long-term priorities to ensure national security and protect national interests in the Russian Arctic zone. While the 2020 strategies represent traditional national interests and reflect a high degree of continuity with previous iterations, there are also some interesting changes.

As table 3-1 shows, the Arctic strategic planning burden falls across several ministries, departments, and individuals. If the Security Council oversees the wider process (one that includes defense), planning is coordinated, at least in theory, by the State Commission for Arctic Development. As noted, changes in leadership and within the body commission itself may be behind what appear to be delays in the production of some plans. Perhaps aligning priorities has taken more time than anticipated or the central body for coordinating agendas is still ineffective. Nonetheless, the commission continues to evolve. In early 2019, the government incorporated Arctic issues into the work of the Ministry for the Development of the Far East, with Alexander Kozlov as minister. In 2020, there was a major reshuffle that caused ripples across the Arctic and energy sectors. Kozlov became the new Minister for Natural Resources, replaced by Alexei Chekunkov at the Far East and Arctic post.

Putin's vision for the NSR to carry 80 million tons by 2024 is well known. Although it is widely considered an unrealistic objective, Moscow has nonetheless placed the economic potential, and the role of the NSR in delivering it, at the heart of strategic planning to 2035. Rosatom, Russia's nuclear power firm owned and operated by the state, oversees the NSR development and infrastructure now that the NSR no longer sits within the Ministry of Transport responsibility.[29] The NSR focus is further illustrated by the industrialization overseen by deputy prime minister (and presidential envoy to the Far East and Arctic) Trutnev, whose agenda includes a series of reforms and laws incentivizing Arctic and Far East resource project investments. The new interest-free and zero-tax incentives for new energy, petrochemicals, and plastics sector projects in the Russian Arctic and Far East seek to stimulate projects that can add tonnage to the NSR.

Moscow's 2020 suite of Arctic planning and strategy documents reflects a high degree of continuity. National interests remain focused upon ensuring sovereignty and territorial integrity, first and foremost. Moscow's interest in preserving the Arctic as a zone of peace and cooperation also remains a feature. However, the new framing of "stable [and] mutually beneficial" partnerships is an interesting development for Russian strategy. It suggests a slight shift from a naively cooperative agenda to one in which partnerships and cooperative ventures are equally weighted—a potential warning to Beijing or other partners in the Russian Arctic zone that Moscow writes the rules.

There is still a pointed military-security agenda. Framed as "defensive" militarization, the strategy states that Russia's military modernization program in the Russian Arctic serves to ensure Moscow can deter foreign military aggression in the region. The new strategy intends to increase the combat capabilities of Russia's armed forces in the Arctic zone, as well as to improve integrated Command, Control, Communications, Computers, Intelligence, Surveillance, and Reconnaissance (C4ISR) systems. A continued commitment to the modernization of Arctic military infrastructure and facilities is included. The 2020 strategic planning reflects various other national interests. Using the Russian Arctic zone as a "strategic resource base" for social and economic development reoccurs in the documentation, as does the priority of maintaining the Arctic as a "zone of peace and cooperation." The "preservation of the Arctic ecological system" and the promotion of the NSR as a global transportation route rounds out the Kremlin's national interests.

Efforts to ensure "sovereignty and territorial integrity" for Russia in the Arctic replace the primacy of resource development, which led Russian interests in previous Arctic policies. While Russia's indigenous Arctic population has been a component of previous iterations, the new planning documents raise the priority of the prosperity of the Russian Arctic population. The new strategy includes guarantees of high living standards to flow from the ability of the state to successfully develop the Russian Arctic as a future strategic resource base. The focus on the development and prosperity of the indigenous population reflects broader policy developments for the Russian Far East and Arctic zone. Calls for some 200,000 new jobs to be created by 2025 from Arctic energy projects are echoed in other Kremlin policies underway—in particular, the Strategy of Development.[30]

New in 2020 to Russian Arctic strategy is an assessment of security concerns, which is articulated by the "Assessment of national security in the Arctic" section of the State Policy. This provides useful insight into what the Kremlin perceives as threats in the Arctic. When it comes to the main national security threats, Russia views its declining population, the inadequate development of social, transport, and communication networks of the Arctic zone, and low rates of geological resource exploration as the three top concerns.[31]

Further components of Moscow's threat perceptions include a lack of state support for business, missed deadlines for NSR infrastructure development, and the slow manufacture rate of vehicles and aircraft for Arctic conditions. The main threats to national security in the Arctic include the lack of Russian technology for the development of the Arctic zone, as well as Moscow's inability to respond to environmental challenges.

It is important to note that Russia's threat perceptions in the State Policy consists entirely of domestic concerns. That is not to say Moscow sees no international "threat" to its Arctic ambitions; Russia has simply framed these concerns as "challenges" to overcome. The State Policy outlines attempts by foreign states to revise "basic provisions of international treaties" in the Arctic, as well as foreign states' efforts to create regulations without considering the legal treaties, as key challenges to Russian Arctic national security interests.[32] Here, it would appear that Moscow is pointing to US efforts to designate the NSR as an international waterway, affording the international community unopposed access. In the Arctic, basic geography means Russia holds the largest territorial claim. Therefore, agreed-upon international law regimes (such as UNCLOS) are in Moscow's favor to uphold.

A second challenge to Russian national security in the Arctic outlined by the State Policy is the unfinished international legal delimitation of marine spaces in the region. This refers to the overlapping claims of Russia, Canada, and Denmark to the seabed of the North Pole. While negotiations between the three states are ongoing, this extended continental shelf claim is not one that Moscow is likely to renounce. The State Policy notes the "obstruction of the implementation by the Russian Federation of lawful economic" activities by foreign states and organizations are a further challenge to Russia's national security. Another challenge for Moscow is the building up by foreign states of their "military presence in the Arctic," increasing the potential for conflict in the region.[33] Overall, the State Policy takes aim at external efforts to "discredit" Russian Arctic economic activity.[34] While other recent Arctic strategies, primarily those of the US Department of Defense, call out Russian Arctic activity, Moscow's strategy falls short of naming names. It underlines Moscow's perceived shortfalls in the Arctic zone and, in doing so, illustrates that the focus of the document is largely upon overcoming Russia's domestic challenges. Population decline, failures in transport, and communication infrastructure are issues, along with the slow pace of new geological and resource exploration projects that are crucial for delivering on the region's economic promises.

Since the previous iteration of Russian strategic planning in the Arctic, Russia's relations with the Euro-Atlantic community have sharply deteriorated. Yet the Arctic remains a zone of cooperation for the Russia-West relationship, seemingly protected from the wider tensions. The same cannot be said, necessarily, for the relationship between Russia and the North Atlantic Treaty Organization (NATO) when it comes to the Arctic. Although there are disagreements that would need to be overcome within the alliance (for example, Norway welcomes an Arctic role for NATO while Canada does not), there appears to be an effort by the alliance countries to develop a cohesive, united Arctic position should NATO table an Arctic strategy. However, Moscow would almost certainly oppose any NATO Arctic strategy as a means of expanding the reach of the institution.

Indeed, overall, the timing of Russia's 2020 strategy was interesting, not only because of the wider strategic overhaul taking place at a time of considerable flux in international affairs. Russia launched this overhaul in the lead-up to Moscow assuming the reigns of the Arctic Council presidency in 2021. While the State Policy singles out foreign military buildup in the Arctic as a national security threat, the Arctic Council is not mandated to discuss or deal with military-security concerns. Therefore, Moscow's focus on processes of militarization and securitization as Arctic challenges might flag its intent to attempt to broaden the mandate of the Arctic Council institution during Russia's 2021–2023 council presidency. Time will tell. With no viable institution currently able to serve as a forum for such issues, and given the fact most Arctic stakeholders view militarization as a security threat regarding their own national Arctic interests, reviewing the Arctic Council's mandate might find consensus support.

Under Putin, strategic planning for the Arctic tends to remain pragmatic and predictable. While Moscow's agenda for the Russian Arctic zone remains constant and unsurprising (not to mention well within international laws and norms), forces beyond Russia are cultivating geopolitical pressures within the Arctic. For example, with each iteration that comes from Washington, US Arctic strategy is increasingly suspect of Russia's rightful Arctic footprint. Great power competition narratives are figuring in Arctic rim state policies at an increasingly alarming rate. These forces in turn are placing pressure on Moscow to respond in kind, as evident in the 2020 Arctic strategy. Moscow's response to increased international attention and activity in the Arctic, as well as to pointed Arctic policies from the West, is captured in the challenge of "discrediting Russian Arctic activities." This challenge is raised in the Russian strategy as a central challenge to Moscow's Arctic agenda into the future, warranting serious attention. Russia places a premium on its Arctic great power identity, and the region is quite important to the realization of further national security strategies. The Arctic zone not only houses precious mineral wealth for the Russian Federation—playing a significant role for the state's economic bottom line—but also affords the nation sea access both east to the Pacific Ocean and west to the North Atlantic. This has national security and foreign policy implications. The Arctic zone plays a part across many Kremlin strategies and doctrines, from energy strategy and foreign policy planning to national security and maritime strategies. Some of the key documents are worth reviewing to get a sense of just how broad (and deep) Russia's Arctic stake is.

THE ARCTIC IN OTHER KREMLIN POLICIES AND PLANS TODAY

The "Concept of the Foreign Policy of the Russian Federation," approved by Putin in 2013, points to the significance of the Arctic zone to Putin's Russia.[35] The document uses the term *Arctic* fourteen times, mostly in relation to "strengthening multi-formal international cooperation" as well as "cooperation with non-Arctic actors as long as they respect the independence, sovereign rights and jurisdiction of Arctic states."[36] Likewise, the prominence of the general energy theme in the document confirms that energy had become central to Moscow's security outlook due to energy's "ability to produce high revenues and its use as an instrument of power."[37]

Russia's 2016 iteration of the foreign policy concept referred to the Arctic on nine occasions and affirmed the region as a priority zone for Moscow. Its cooperative agenda was further emphasized in terms of a policy "aimed at preserving peace, stability and constructive international cooperation" in the region.[38] However, the 2016 iteration deviated from the "mutually beneficial cooperation" platform. While the 2013 foreign policy concept cited Moscow was open to "mutually beneficial cooperation" with non-Arctic states—as long as those states respected the sovereign rights of the Arctic rim powers—this statement was removed from the 2016 update. Further, while the 2013 foreign policy concept spoke of the NSR as a national transit route "open to international shipping," the 2016 revision dropped any international shipping connotations. Where the 2013 foreign policy concept placed priority on engaging with fellow Arctic states, the 2016 version framed engagement and management of the Arctic as a "special responsibility" of Arctic states. The 2016 concept also takes a harder line approach to ensuring Russian Arctic security: "Russia will be firm in countering any attempts to introduce elements of political or military confrontation in the Arctic, and, in general, politicize international cooperation in the region."[39] Likewise, the "Military Doctrine of the Russian Federation," approved by Putin in 2014, discussed the Arctic. Here, the doctrine lists the main task of Russian troops (in peacetime) as being to "protect the national interests of the Russian Federation in the Arctic region."[40]

Russia's 2015 maritime strategy succinctly captures Moscow's blueprint for how it plans to harness "sea power." After all, as Alfred Thayer Mahan taught us, "whoever rules the waves rules the world."[41] Specifically, the Arctic is a "regional priority" theater, and Moscow's strategic interests are articulated quite simply:

> Policy in the Arctic regional area is determined by the priority to ensure the free access of the Russian fleet to the Atlantic and the Pacific oceans, by the abundance of natural resources in the exclusive economic zone and the continental shelf of the Russian Federation, by the growing importance of the Northern Sea Route for sustainable development and security of the Russian Federation, and the decisive role of the Northern Fleet in the defense of the country from the sea and ocean.[42]

Russia's maritime priorities in the Arctic include limiting external threats posed to Russian maritime interests, ensuring strategic stability in the Arctic zone, and strengthening the economic basis for Russia by facilitating access to offshore Russian Arctic resource deposits. Development of the NSR along with adequate navigation and search and rescue capabilities in the Russian Arctic zone are additional priorities.

This maritime strategy was updated in 2019 by Prime Minister Medvedev, with the unveiling of the "Strategy for the Development of Russia's Maritime Activities up to 2030." As Richard Connolly argues, the update does not serve to shift the original aims of the 2015 strategy, but rather it seeks to ensure Russia's objectives can be achieved by 2030.[43] The 2019 strategy outlines various Arctic-related challenges to the ambitions of Russian maritime activities. Those challenges include the need for new icebreakers, extraction technology for offshore Arctic resources, and related implications of international sanctions on Russian firms.

In 2015, "The Russian Federation's National Security Strategy" (National Security Strategy) had little focus on the Arctic. Despite a total of 116 paragraphs the word *Arctic* is only mentioned on three occasions.[44] The first reference is to processes of international cooperation within "a new polycentric model of world order." Here, the strategy highlights Russia's leadership "in exploiting the resources of the world's oceans and the Arctic." The second reference is in the context of "the development of equal and mutually beneficial international cooperation in the Arctic."[45] And the third reference is to "countering threats to economic security." For Russia, this involves "widening the use of the instruments of state-private partnership to perform strategic tasks in the development of the economy . . . particularly in the Arctic."[46] The earlier iteration, the 2009 "National Security Strategy of the Russian Federation to 2020," had also only mentioned the Arctic on three occasions. However, the tone was entirely different. First, the Arctic was mentioned in regard to the "long term" focus of international politics on "ownership of energy resources of the Arctic." Second, it was discussed in terms of "resolution of border security problems," and third, in terms of "ensuring national security in the medium term."[47]

The 2015 National Security Strategy document uses the term threat twenty-four times. For Olga Oliker, the strategy overall reflects an "ambitious Russia that sees constraints on its ambitions as threats to be overcome."[48] The lack of a specific Arctic discussion may reflect Putin's confidence that the West would never seriously challenge Russia's Arctic stake. But the scant reference to the Arctic in the 2015 document is nonetheless interesting, given the national security status Putin has afforded the Arctic since 2000. Possibly this was a deliberate move by Putin to distance the Russian Arctic narrative from geopolitics and soothe the growing unease in the West about Russia's more assertive posture in Arctic matters. It is more likely that Russia merely views the Russian Arctic zone as uncontested, and indeed the strong legal case by way of geography makes Russia the largest Arctic stakeholder. However, per Russian law, the National Security Strategy must be updated every six years, which means 2021 ushered in a new iteration.

In the 2021 National Security Strategy, Moscow acknowledged the international system has thrown up a "new architecture" that is "accompanied by an increase in geopolitical instability."[49] The new strategy unveiled Russia's plans to standardize its strategic engagement in the international system based on "mutually beneficial" cooperation. The new security strategy also signals that Moscow firmly sees itself as an independent stakeholder (and actor) focused on shoring up its national interests. While still committed to the existing international order—indeed, Russia remains a stalwart supporter of the UN Security Council and of principles of noninterference—Moscow's engagement within the system will be shaped by its newly articulated strategic independence.

Russia's 2021 National Security Strategy seeks to "improve predictability in relations between states" but moves away from previous iterations that outlined how it would strengthen trust and with whom Russia would work. Dropping clear goalposts and interests in its relationships with Europe and the US from the strategic document signaled the rebirth of an independent Russia. The problem is that—as the coronavirus pandemic underscored—states cannot go it alone in the global system. Going it alone becomes a stark challenge when considering Russia's strategic interests in the Arctic—a zone in which international cooperation and collaboration are considered crucial.

In contrast to the 2015 strategy, which framed climate change in terms of "consequences," the 2021 version reframes climate change as a security threat requiring "prevention" and "adaptation." There is also a clear departure from the 2015 iteration's treatment of the Arctic, with sentiments shifting from "mutually beneficial international cooperation" to "ensuring the interests of the Russian Federation" in the region. Evidently, in the space of merely six years, Moscow grew more confident in its inalienable majority stake in the Arctic zone. It is likely this confidence, further underscored by the updated National Security Strategy, will see Russia double-down on Arctic region leadership efforts.

The 2021 framing of Russia's Arctic stake is particularly interesting. This version speaks of "ensuring" Russia's interests related to "the development" of the Arctic. Previous iterations viewed the Russian Arctic as a frontier to be managed, a sovereignty challenge on the horizon. Today, the economic potential and Moscow's efforts to securitize the resource base of the Russian Arctic zone are paramount. The revised National Security Strategy clearly took some comfort in Russia's current position vis-à-vis the West, despite rather stagnated bilateral relations. Having adequately tested Western resolve to fight for Ukraine, it would seem Moscow is exploiting the public relations opportunity it now has to sell Russia's perceived victory in external security affairs to its domestic audience. Here, the narrative put forward by the security strategy appears to be one in which Russia's frontiers have been bolstered, and this in turn has afforded the Kremlin latitude to look after its citizens.

When it comes to national strategic priorities, Russia now cites the "quality of life" and "wellbeing of Russian nationals" as the top national interest. Indeed, Moscow's success in delivering on Arctic region development goals will rely upon Russia's ability to improve living standards in the High North. Attracting the dedicated workforce required for energy projects and the development of the Russian Arctic will remain a priority, and ultimately a prerequisite for realizing ambitious economic goals in the Arctic (including that lofty 80 million tons via the NSR). The revival of the Russian nation-state and a focus on its historical identity further indicate an interesting departure from previous security strategies. In reorientating human security to the prime position among Russia's strategic priorities, Moscow is also throwing down the gauntlet of a new culture war.

The 2021 National Security Strategy has cemented Moscow's intention to "go it alone" (unless it sees mutual benefit in collaborating). This has clear implications for the future of the Arctic, as this approach raises a concerning point. The spheres of Russia's 2021 national interests—including the Arctic—are zones in which international collaboration is expected, if not required. Russia promotes international law and underscores throughout the security document the primacy of the UN system in place, so an interesting test will no doubt become whether Moscow plays by the rules in the Arctic. A clear takeaway from the document is there will be no normalization or reset, let alone integration between Russia and the West in the coming years.

It is evident from a comparison of some key policy and strategy documents that there is no clear-cut answer when it comes to pondering what the future of Russia-West engagement in the Arctic looks like. Despite Russia's chest-thumping via some strategic documents, it has remained more or less in its "lane" when it comes to venturing beyond the Russian Arctic zone into the broader Arctic region.

State policies, strategies, and Kremlin rhetoric aside, Russian Arctic strategy is, at its core, driven by processes of securitization. While often framed merely in military-security terms, securitization is also a political-security process. Indeed, Russian Arctic interests are political—not least in relation to Russian history and the significance of the region to Russia's economy. Russia has an evident interest in securitizing its economic stake in the Russian Arctic, primarily in terms of the region's energy resources and the NSR. The region both is a central component of Russia's projected future budgetary position and factors into the wider great power identity project for Putin. As evidenced in the key policy documents examined above, Russia is actively working to secure not only its vast border from increasing activity, but also its claim as the Arctic's largest stakeholder. The Arctic race, as it were, has already been won in that it is likely Russia will continue to prioritize the Russian Arctic zone. As a Russian government official highlights:

> The Arctic isn't going away for Russia, the Arctic is largely Russian by default. You would have heard that polar bears are Russian. The more demand increases, the sooner we will have people approaching Russia for partnership, and this could be a powerful position for us, but we have shown—and of course, this requires careful reading of our policy documents that are made readily available to all—that we seek partnerships based on cooperation with our neighbours in the Arctic. I think this is wishful thinking in the short to medium term however, but just think about a passenger ship running into trouble on the NSR for a moment. It becomes Russia's duty to search and rescue and this

would be expected by our neighbours, and yet in order to carry out such missions, there would need to be readily deployable teams stationed nearby. We are building such teams and growing our capacity and yet Russia is criticised for these actions? Symptomatic maybe, but the West cannot have it all.[50]

Of course, the very process of securitization in Russia's Arctic zone necessarily invites discussion of Russia's militarization of the Arctic. Often confused, the two concepts are nonetheless distinct, and the confusion can result in a misreading of Russian Arctic activity if viewed purely through a militarization lens. Further, the increase in activity in the Arctic will necessitate an active coast guard operation, which most Arctic rim neighbors have already implemented. In developing Arctic coast guard capabilities, Russia is merely applying the same measures as its neighbors. Militarization has been apparent in the updating of aging Soviet hardware in the Arctic and the reopening of Soviet bases on the Arctic coast, spurred by Russia's newly formed Arctic Joint Strategic Command. This should not be a surprise, for it is a desperately overdue modernization project, given the hardware has been neglected since the fall of the Soviet Union.

This modernization agenda for Russia necessarily includes Russia's Northern Fleet. Since 2012, under Putin the pace of military modernization has increased. Beyond the reopening of Arctic bases, there has been an increase in Russian military exercises and war games. However, these activities are outlined in the Arctic security strategies. Further, most of the refurbished military outposts in the Arctic are "dual use" facilities also servicing regional search and rescue operations. But Russia's securitization efforts in the Arctic have clearly intensified, going far beyond standard coast guard strengthening capabilities. Russia's Arctic threat perceptions are more intense than in the Cold War period, as seen in the deployment of Arctic brigades. Yet, despite apparent Russian militarization, Moscow's Arctic posture remains a shadow of its Cold War footprint.

In many ways, Russian Arctic strategy (including its securitization aspect) predates Russia's current assertive foreign policy. For Stephen

Blank, Russia's militarization of the Arctic coast "highlights a certain paradox" in Moscow's Arctic strategy.[51] The bases are closely connected to the development of Russia's economic interests in the Arctic, serving to safeguard the region. However, it appears Russia is becoming increasingly alarmed about potential threats. As Blank points out, this is interesting since, to date, no Arctic Five state has "even remotely expressed the intention (let alone the desire) or demonstrated the capacity to threaten" Russia's Arctic position and interests.[52] The notion that militarization efforts are to warn off China's mounting Arctic interest is also somewhat moot, given Russia's partnership with China on Arctic energy and infrastructure investments.

Despite the contracted economic constraints, Putin has ensured military investment continues. Since 2014, the planned redevelopment of airstrips and Northern Fleet docking facilities has continued. On Russia's securitization approach to the Arctic, a Russian government official commented:

> Russian security officials, for example the FSB and some individual interests, will keep the current statist approach and continue to securitise the existing state of affairs in the Arctic. I don't see a departure from this thinking. It is important to understand that our Arctic posts have dual operational civil, industry, and defence purposes. We militarise out of necessity to match increasing human activity on our shores, as our neighbours are also doing.[53]

In any case, this Arctic retooling is long overdue for Russia.[54] Had events on the Crimean Peninsula not occurred in 2014, it is likely the modernization of Russian infrastructure in the Arctic would have been viewed in the securitization context as an expected development in the changing region. Instead, events beyond the Arctic have swayed Russia's Arctic policies more toward an intensified strategy of militarization. Note that of those Russian military bases shown, the majority date from Soviet times.

Granted, an increased Russian military footprint in the Russian Arctic zone makes it a little harder to argue that Moscow is cooperative in the region. However, with its discussion of Russian Arctic interests and the ensuing policies implemented, this book builds a persuasive argument that Russian interests are best secured by a low-tension global Arctic. Economic pressures have slowed the development of major offshore Arctic projects, and sanctions have limited Russian access to foreign capital and Western partnerships. These are adverse outcomes that Putin can only surmount by reverting to a cooperative approach, especially in the Arctic. For Russia, cash flow, investment, and technology from foreign firms are vital to getting new projects off the ground. And the global attraction Russia's Arctic energy ventures thus far have garnered seems to be doing the trick. Saudi Arabia as well as Chinese and Indian heavy hitters are just a few of the buyers lining up to secure supplies and investments in Russian Arctic energy. But secure supply for these states will necessitate a Russian Arctic free of conflict and, more broadly, an Arctic Ocean—and its passages—void of contest or congestion.

Russia's Arctic securitization agenda is not dissimilar from the agendas of other Arctic rim powers. Moreover, there is precedent of cooperation between Russia and its Arctic neighbors. There is evidence of continued commitment by Arctic powers to uphold the existing cooperation with Russia in the Arctic. Meanwhile, international attention and analysis of Russian Arctic strategy appears to remain narrowly committed to the traditional neorealist approach of viewing Russian foreign policy. This fails to account for Russia's cooperative behavior and overall modus operandi in the Arctic. For a neorealist, Russian foreign policy and aggressions under Putin—namely the contemporary Russia-Ukraine war—follow a distinct pattern of Russian foreign policy. However, Russia's Arctic strategy represents a distinct deviation from neorealist expectations.

Under Putin, Russia has increased its material capabilities thanks to financial windfalls of sky-high oil prices in the early 2000s, which filled Kremlin coffers. With that influx of cash, Russia paid off international debts and undertook a strategic modernization agenda, pushing for Russian technological development to bring the state into the twenty-first century. It is easy to forget the state is relatively young: the latest incarnation of Russia is still in its 30s. But it has not all been smooth sailing, and not all strategic objectives have been realized. Russia is still vulnerable in the energy and Arctic spheres.

Despite overlapping claims going back to the 1920s, to date there has been no military conflict between the Arctic rim states over Arctic territory. Experts recognize this is due to the fact that overlapping claims have been bilaterally resolved over the decades, and today there is not much to squabble over, as the region is more or less delineated. Frenzy is whipped up in hot-take media reports that seek to denote the Arctic as a region of tense competition over territory. In reality, there is clear precedent for cooperation between Russia and the West in the Arctic. The Russian flag-planting incident is consistently trotted out as "evidence" of Russia's expansionist agenda in the Arctic. Even then, this stunt occurred prior to the Ilulissat Declaration, in which Russia and other Arctic rim powers agreed to cooperatively determine any overlapping territorial claims.[55]

Russia's Arctic strategy under Putin remains somewhat of a siloed sphere within Russian foreign policy. The Russian Arctic is a zone that Russia has cordoned off from its aggressive and assertive foreign policy elsewhere. This does not necessarily mean the region will never host Russian aggression; I am merely arguing that aggression is not the default mode (nor the interest) for Moscow in the Russian Arctic zone. While Russia has enhanced military capacity to respond to breaches of its Arctic sovereignty and has clearly stated its commitment to use this capability to defend its national interests in the region, it is not conducive to Russia's strategic interests (exporting Arctic energy) to plunge the region into conflict. It is an undeniable fact that the Russian Arctic zone is the future resource base for the Russian economy, and conflict is bad for business.

Overall, despite assessments that Russian Arctic strategy mirrors Russian aggressive policies beyond the region, I would argue it is unlikely that military conflict will eventuate in the Arctic between Russia and the West. This chapter serves to outline the themes of Russia's Arctic strategy by unpacking various governance documents and policy positions of Moscow. By now, readers are better placed to rigorously question preexisting assumptions of Russian Arctic strategy under

Putin. This strategy is driven mostly by routine factors that do not necessarily reflect an expansionist agenda. Unlike Russia's foreign policy approach elsewhere, such as in its near abroad, Putin's approach in the Arctic has consistently been broadly cooperative. Given Putin's foreign policy style, there is potential for Russia to throw its weight around in the Arctic. In any case, a more assertive Arctic strategy would be driven by a hypernationalist, largely domestic agenda, but the notion of a Russian-controlled "global Arctic"—an Arctic wholly dominated by Russia beyond its Arctic zone—is an exaggeration of Russia's capabilities and, as this book argues, Moscow's intentions.

The following chapter moves to contextualize Russian Arctic strategy under Putin in terms of the broader Arctic geopolitical environment. In doing so, the book applies this normative understanding of what is driving Putin's Russia in the Arctic to the strategic developments underway in the Arctic region. Seeking to disprove the looming conflict narrative, the following chapter steps through the various Arctic stakeholders and their strategic interests to illustrate the Arctic is indeed unlikely to host a new Cold War.

4

CONQUERING THE ARCTIC

"POSSESSION IS NINE-TENTHS OF THE LAW."

—LEGAL TRUISM

In an ideal world, pundits would immerse themselves in a study of Arctic geopolitics only after they already possessed adequate knowledge of Russian Arctic strategy. The fact that Russia is the Arctic's largest stakeholder, in theory, ought to pave the way for any study of Arctic security to start from the agreed point: Russia is a legitimate power in the Arctic region. Instead, people often approach the issue of Arctic geopolitics from an ideologically clouded view of Russia's Arctic intent. Not surprisingly, Russia is typically cast as the villain in Arctic narratives.

This chapter examines the Arctic's resource endowment, its governance, and the competing claims of Arctic rim powers. It considers the emerging regional challenges spurred by easier Arctic access brought about by climate change and sets out the key opportunities related to the opening up of the Arctic. The chapter also provides background on Arctic geopolitics by examining the competing interests and ambitions of the Arctic Five powers and the emerging interests of some key non-Arctic powers.

This chapter deals with the rise of China's involvement in the region, particularly Beijing's strong interest in the emergence of the Northern Sea Route (NSR). It also examines the standing political stalemates of the Arctic region as well as the accommodations that have been reached in response to maritime disputes. While narratives of "conquering the Arctic" are alluring, this chapter argues the sphere is actually a zone of mutual interests and challenges faced by Arctic stakeholders.

The Arctic is a complex, "moving-target" issue in which contemporary strategic challenges are framed by journalistic historical parallels. As already outlined, the Cold War is repackaged as an Arctic new cold war and the great game in Central Asia is rehashed as the Arctic's great game.[1] The Arctic is viewed nostalgically by many as the home of polar bears, the North Pole, and crisp white snow. In reality, it is predominantly dark, bleak, isolated, and unforgiving. In recent decades, the Arctic has been a zone of military interest, used by Soviet strategic forces as a base for their nuclear submarines and as testing grounds for intercontinental ballistic missiles.

The Arctic appeared to lose its strategic significance with the end of the Cold War. However, since 2000—incidentally, when Vladimir Putin came to power—this has changed due in large part to the "combination of accelerating climate change and a rapid increase in energy prices."[2] International oil prices are an external force that fuels geopolitical competition globally. Putin's acceding to the presidency coincided with a fortuitous new cycle in the global oil markets. Figure 4-1 illustrates the rise and fall of oil prices since 2000.

Energy is a key driver of Arctic conflict narratives. Framed as a last dash to the North Pole to control the region's energy wealth, these notions might sell newspapers and garner internet traffic, but they are largely overblown—not least because there is no "looming" battle for delineated resources. In fact, global oil prices are nowhere near the territory they need to be to support commercial considerations for exploiting Arctic oil.

Figure 4-1. Oil Prices 2000–2023 (US$, Brent Crude)

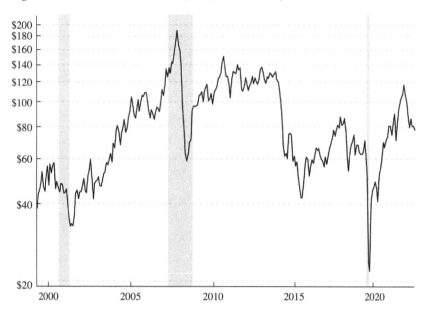

Source: Author's research. Primary data sourced and compiled online at macro trends.net.

THE ARCTIC PRIZES

What is at stake in the effort to conquer the Arctic? It holds two main "prizes" that attract keen interest from powers both within and outside the region. These Arctic opportunities are hydrocarbons and shipping—both of which are increasingly accessible as a direct result of global warming.[3] Both also represent some key challenges for Arctic rim powers, in logistics and in the international interest these opportunities attract. While this book narrows the focus of resource wealth to hydrocarbons (oil and natural gas), the Arctic region is also home to ample deposits of precious minerals.

The Arctic is home to the world's largest unexplored hydrocarbon reserves. The Arctic encompasses about 6 percent of the globe's surface, an area of more than 21 million square kilometers. The Arctic's continental shelves may constitute the largest prospective area for undiscovered oil on Earth.[4] The 2008 US Geological Survey (USGS) is

often cited as the central study on Arctic resources. It estimates t
tic accounts for 13 percent of undiscovered global oil and 30 pei
the world's undiscovered natural gas. That said, these are unexplored
deposits, and it is necessary to remember those figures are only estimates. Moreover, the study excluded any reserves of unconventional energy such as gas hydrates. Since the 2008 survey such estimates have
been overtaken due to several large discoveries throughout the Arctic.

The 2008 US Geological Survey utilized a Circum-Arctic Resource
Appraisal (CARA) model, which is based only on probabilities.[5] The
CARA methodology involved dividing the Arctic region into assessment units (AUs). Each AU is a mappable area of rock with common
geological traits found in provinces all over the Arctic. These AUs were
then assessed for their hydrocarbon potential. However, given "the
sparse seismic and drilling data in much of the Arctic, the usual tools
and techniques used in USGS resource assessments, such as discovery
process modelling, prospect delineation, and deposit simulation, were
not generally applicable."[6] This meant the CARA study team was left
to work with a probability methodology. The team concluded that the
Arctic holds approximately 90 billion barrels of oil and some 1,669 trillion cubic feet of natural gas,[7] with 84 percent of these resources located in the offshore Arctic. So essentially, the Arctic's hydrocarbon
prize is a highly informed guess.[8] Figure 4-2 illustrates the CARA findings and location of potential Arctic hydrocarbons. The important
takeaway: most hydrocarbons are adjacent to the Russian coast, well and
truly within Russia's exclusive economic zone (EEZ).

The finding that most hydrocarbons in the Arctic are located offshore raises concerns around the commercial viability of these resources. As a leading energy security academic stated:

> I don't hold my breath when it comes to Arctic hydrocarbons, sure
> there has to be some amount of resources up there but I honestly doubt
> it will be the treasure trove it is peddled to be. In any case, it's a near
> impossible feat to operate in the [Arctic] offshore environment—no
> matter how flash the technology gets, I do wonder how much risk the
> corporates will actually take on.[9]

Figure 4-2. US Geological Survey of Arctic Hydrocarbons

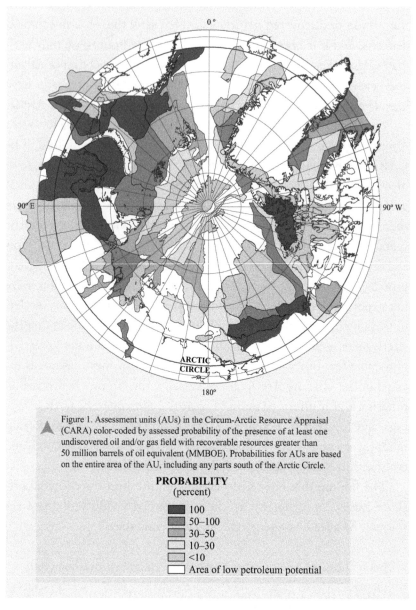

Figure 1. Assessment units (AUs) in the Circum-Arctic Resource Appraisal (CARA) color-coded by assessed probability of the presence of at least one undiscovered oil and/or gas field with recoverable resources greater than 50 million barrels of oil equivalent (MMBOE). Probabilities for AUs are based on the entire area of the AU, including any parts south of the Arctic Circle.

PROBABILITY
(percent)

- 100
- 50–100
- 30–50
- 10–30
- <10
- Area of low petroleum potential

Source: US Geological Survey, 2008. "Circum-Arctic Resource Appraisal: Estimates of Undiscovered Oil and Gas North of the Arctic Circle," http://pubs.usgs.gov/fs /2008/3049/fs2008-3049.pdf.

Nonetheless, the ever-growing global energy demand positions Arctic hydrocarbons as a strong option, and perhaps a necessity, for the longer-term future. This sentiment is echoed by a Russian academic:

> Arctic resources are Russia's lifeline. In fact, they (Arctic resources) are the Earth's lifeline; oil will remain the leading fuel choice for the next 100 years at least—I doubt the world will leave this [Arctic] resource potential in the ground. It can't. We won't.[10]

The Arctic's second prize is its transportation channels. Climate change is increasing access to Arctic shipping routes. As a direct result of climate change, the Arctic sea ice is thinning. For now the Arctic summer (June–September) sea ice in much of the Arctic Ocean's littoral seas is passable without icebreakers. The reduced need for ice-breaking support has alerted the world's shipping firms to the Arctic's potential. Through the Arctic Ocean, the Atlantic and Pacific Oceans are connected. As previously discussed, the Russian leg of the Northeast Passage (NEP) is the NSR. This is not a new addition to the Arctic's shipping routes; it has been utilized for many decades, albeit largely by Russian merchant ships between Russian ports. Traffic in the NSR appeared to peak in 1987, long before Putin's Arctic push.[11] But the NSR is still of great interest to the world's largest exporter—China.

In 2013 the first Chinese merchant ship transited the NSR and was the first container vessel to do so.[12] Travel time between Asia and Europe via the NSR is about twenty-three days on average, compared to the Suez Canal's average of thirty-seven days. Russia holds all the trump cards in relation to the NSR. As illustrated in figure 4-3, the NSR wraps along the Russian coastline for most of its route. This is important to Russia for two reasons. First, much of the NSR falls within Russia's EEZ and therefore Russia has deemed it necessary to charge transit tariffs. The tariffs have been accompanied by Russia's introduction of tight rules and domestic laws for foreign firms seeking to utilize the route. Second, Russia insists vessels can only navigate the NSR when accompanied by Russian nuclear icebreakers.[13] The NSR's potential is thus subject to strict Russian directives.

Figure 4-3. Northern Sea Route versus Suez Canal

Source: RT, 2015. "Russian PM Orders Plan to Increase Northern Sea Route Capacity by 20 Times," rt.com/business/265756-northern-sea-route-medvedev/.

The NSR cuts global shipping transit times drastically. Shorter lead times have an obvious knock-on effect, exerting downward pressure on costs. In total, the NSR is nearly 40 percent shorter than the traditional Suez Canal route.[14] But NSR efficiency goes beyond transit time. The Northern Sea Route is also a safer alternative to routes affected by high seas piracy and to ports or passages affected by political unrest. Navigation numbers had been growing steadily since 2010; however, between 2014 and 2015, transit cargo declined by 86 percent.[15] Today, most of the tonnage is liquified natural gas (LNG) and other supplies headed for Asia from the Russian Arctic. Whether the NSR will prove to re-shape global commodity shipping is still to be seen.

There are several interested stakeholders hoping to gain access to, and control of, the Arctic's resource and shipping potential. It is therefore relatively easy to draw parallels between the Arctic's trajectory and the notion of a new great game. The next section of this chapter examines contemporary Arctic stakeholders, including Arctic Five powers, China as an external power with a strong Arctic agenda, and international organizations with strong Arctic interests—the North Atlantic Treaty Organization (NATO) and the European Union (EU).

THE ARCTIC FIVE

By way of Alaska, the US is an Arctic Five power. Broadly speaking, the US approaches the Arctic from a strategic point of view because it was historically a theater of the Cold War with Russia and still serves as the shortest route for Russian missiles to reach Washington. Under the Barack Obama presidency, the US implemented a pointed environmental agenda in the Arctic. Obama also adopted, in 2013, the first US National Strategy for the Arctic Region. While it had environmental challenges and conservation of resource wealth at its core, the strategy also returned the Arctic to national US discourse. Signaling this revival of US Arctic interest under Obama was the fact that, in 2011, then secretary Hillary Clinton was the first ever US secretary of state to attend an Arctic Council meeting.

In 2015, the US assumed the rotating presidency of the Arctic Council. The Arctic Council chair serves for two years, and the position rotates between the eight Arctic state council members. The Arctic Council is further discussed later in this chapter. The US chair's theme was "One Arctic: Shared Opportunities, Challenges and Responsibilities."[16] Ostensibly, cooperation drove the agenda during the US chair. The US largely focused on bilateral Arctic issues during the Obama presidency, with key concerns including the Northwest Passage (NWP) and the Bering Strait. While there was clear elevation in US Arctic interests, movement beyond the environmental stewardship of the Arctic was limited in the Obama years.[17] The previous administration, under President George W. Bush, established a National Security Presidential Directive for the Arctic in the final days of Bush's presidency. As an Arctic politics observer states:

> Bush left a strategic doctrine for the Arctic upon exit. It urged ratification of the United Nations Convention on the Law of the Sea (UNCLOS) and outlined a leadership role for the states in the Arctic. That momentum ended with Obama; Obama is interested in the environment—the last place he was about to get involved in was the Arctic. That's pristine, that's off limits. I think that was the mentality, then perhaps it simply fell to the wayside given the domestic economic situation (jobs and debt) that has plagued his time in the White House. Either way, under Obama the Arctic has been an afterthought.[18]

In the Obama era, the strategic capabilities and capacity earmarked for development by the 2009 Bush directive dropped into the background, and as a result, the US still finds itself at an Arctic capability disadvantage. Throughout the Obama presidency, the US focus on the Arctic remained "modest" and undoubtedly served to further "undermine and limit" the US in the Arctic.[19] Toward the culmination of the US chair of the Arctic Council, in 2017, Donald Trump ascended to the presidency. For better or worse, US Arctic policy underwent a strategic awakening. However, the Trump presidency had a slow start in the Arctic strategy space, with the diplomatic post of special envoy to the Arctic remaining vacant for much of Trump's presidency. (The contours of US Arctic policy under the Joe Biden presidency are discussed later in this book.)

For Washington, UNCLOS is a perpetual challenge. Unfortunately, it also happens to be the legal governing framework agreed upon by the Arctic Five powers to navigate maritime matters within the Arctic. (This body and the wider governance components of the Arctic are examined at a later stage in this chapter.) The US is the only Arctic Five power yet to ratify UNCLOS and therefore cannot submit any formal extended continental shelf claim for consideration within the Arctic.

However, figure 4-4 illustrates the potential US extended continental shelf claim that could be submitted if the US ratified UNCLOS.

The default US domestic policy constraint restricting UNCLOS ratification (for fear of "ceding sovereignty") has further cultivated the notion that the US is a reluctant Arctic power.[20] This sentiment was captured by a leading think tank representative commenting on US-Arctic affairs:

> We [Americans] are latecomers to the Arctic; we are gearing up to take the reins of the Arctic Council next year and the truth is we are still deciding what our Arctic policy looks like. Heck, the only Americans who have the Arctic on their radar are the Alaskans. For the rest the Arctic is a vague region far out of sight and very much out of mind. Without ratifying UNCLOS the US isn't even in the game, we are parked on the bench.[21]

The notion of the US missing out on the Arctic great game is supported by a US think tank specialist on Russian affairs, who remarked, "I simply stated the US doesn't really have an Arctic strategy; this was met with laughter, but my comment really wasn't far from the truth."[22]

When Trump acceded to the US presidency, he worked effectively to dismantle most of Obama's environmental and Arctic protection initiatives. However, Washington continued to collaboratively engage with Arctic Council partners including Russia. This has perhaps remained the sole point of continuation of US Arctic policy throughout the past few administrations.

On the other hand, the other North American Arctic power has maintained an active Arctic agenda. Canada's Arctic identity is unshakable. Under Stephen Harper's leadership (2006–2015), Canada provided a strong voice in the Arctic, with a clear defense agenda. Under the Justin Trudeau prime ministership, Canada has somewhat drawn down on the military-security angle and emerged as another environmental steward. The Canadian Arctic encompasses close to 40 percent of the nation's total landmass, and two-thirds of Canada's marine coastline, but is populated by only 85,000 individuals.[23]

Figure 4-4. Potential US Extended Continental Shelf Claim

USA (submission projected by IBRU)

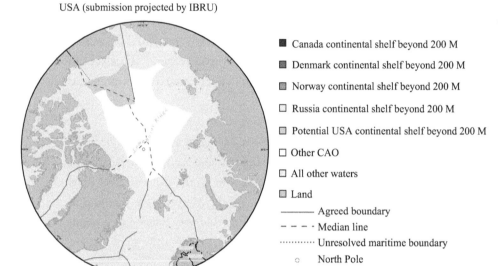

- ■ Canada continental shelf beyond 200 M
- ▨ Denmark continental shelf beyond 200 M
- ▧ Norway continental shelf beyond 200 M
- ☐ Russia continental shelf beyond 200 M
- ▨ Potential USA continental shelf beyond 200 M
- ☐ Other CAO
- ☐ All other waters
- ▨ Land
- ——— Agreed boundary
- – – – Median line
- ·········· Unresolved maritime boundary
- ○ North Pole

Source: durham.ac.uk/media/durham-university/research-/research-centres/ibru
-centre-for-borders-research/maps-and-databases/arctic-maps-2021/updated-maps
-and-notes/Map-4-IBRU-Arctic-map-07-04-21-(Focus-Maps-in-the-CAO).pdf.

Canada ratified UNCLOS in 2003 and, in line with the UNCLOS mandate, had ten years to submit a formal Arctic bid. In 2013, Canada requested an extension to gather necessary scientific support for its claim.[24] In 2014, Ottawa submitted a partial Arctic claim in the form of a preliminary submission to the Commission on the Limits of the Continental Shelf (CLCS).[25] This claim was tacked onto a formal Atlantic Ocean claim because Canada still required time for its Arctic bid but had to submit a continental shelf claim under the ten-year UN-CLOS ruling. Canada was granted an extension within the Atlantic Ocean submission to provide necessary scientific information to the CLCS in support of Canada's Arctic claim. The preliminary submission did, however, outline the direction of that Arctic claim in terms of the continental shelf. It states:

> The continental margin of Canada in the Arctic Ocean is part of a morphologically continuous continental margin around the Canada Basin

and along the Amundsen Basin. It comprises a number of seafloor elevations (Lomonosov Ridge and Alpha Ridge) and forms the submerged prolongation of the land mass of Canada. Throughout, the areas of continental shelf extend beyond 200 nautical miles from the territorial sea baselines of Canada and, on the Alpha and Lomonosov Ridges, beyond the 350 nautical mile constraint.[26]

In the 2014 partial submission, Canada flagged its intent to extend its continental shelf beyond its 200 nautical mile EEZ to include the disputed Lomonosov Ridge as Canadian Arctic. Canada's 2014 preliminary submission extended to include the North Pole. This was of interest to Arctic watchers, given the understanding that in the months leading up to the submission, the Canadian claim did not include the North Pole area. This section of the Arctic Ocean is deemed too difficult to operate in—so much so that commercial activities will likely not eventuate at the North Pole. This reality undermines the economic element to Canada's push for the North Pole, highlighting the lengths the Harper administration went to in essentially rewriting Canada's Arctic bid.[27]

For Canada, the inclusion of the North Pole was not about economics (though much of its Arctic interest is based on economic gain); rather, it was driven by domestic politics. Harper did not want to be seen as having "surrendered" the North Pole to the Russians, even if the science does not entirely support Canada's claim to the North Pole.[28] This sentiment is supported by a Russian academic who stated the following:

> Russia might have planted a flag which upset some Arctic partners, but Canada has voiced its own hostile Arctic ambitions increasingly under the Harper administration. How should Canada's Arctic neighbours respond to its "use it or lose it" comments? Canada appears to be drawing a line and yet Russia is the one scorned in popular media.[29]

In 2019, under Prime Minister Trudeau, Canada filed a partial submission to the CLCS regarding its Arctic claims under CLCS Article 76.[30] It was evident Canada had solid scientific evidence that the Arctic continental shelf (running under the North Pole) was indeed an extension of

Canada's landmass. However, Russia, Denmark, and the US have over-lapping claims of the shelf being an extension of their continental land-masses. But given the US failure to ratify UNCLOS, only Canada, Russia, and Denmark are essentially "in the running" to stake a legal claim for an extended continental shelf. In 2019, Canada issued a long-awaited "Arctic and Northern Policy Framework."[31] The document underscores Canada's Arctic priorities through 2030, to be split between maintaining sovereignty in the region and responding to environmental challenges. Canada's extended continental shelf claim as of 2021 is shown in fig-ure 4-5. This 2021 partial claim has since been revised with Ottawa sub-mitting an addendum in December 2022. Canada's Arctic shelf claim now reaches well into Russia's.

Heading to the European Arctic, Denmark is another Arctic Five (A5) power by virtue of Greenland, which is an autonomous nation within the jurisdiction of the Kingdom of Denmark. Here, national-ism and resource development drive Arctic strategy. For many security analysts the Danish extended continental shelf claim is a move to "shore up its popularity in independence-seeking Greenland, where the claim is very, very popular."[32] Predictably, Russia takes a negative view of Denmark's claim. As a Russian official comments:

> Denmark has increased spending for its navy and relocated much of it to the Arctic. Yet Denmark is not punished for seemingly militaris-ing the region. They simply state they have no coast guard and therefore this responsibility falls to their navy. This is accepted. Russia states the same reason for its increased naval presence—coast guard development—and we are therefore militarising. There is a clear dou-ble standard. It is a pure necessity for all A5 powers to increase mili-tary capabilities in the case of disaster relief.[33]

Denmark had until 2014 to submit a claim to the CLCS after ratifying UNCLOS in 2004. In December 2014, Copenhagen submitted a for-mal extended continental shelf claim amassing some 895,000 square kilometers of the Arctic beyond Greenland and the North Pole, a claim some twenty times the size of Denmark.[34] The submission was a joint

Figure 4-5. Canada's Extended Continental Shelf Claim

Canada (awaiting CLCS review)

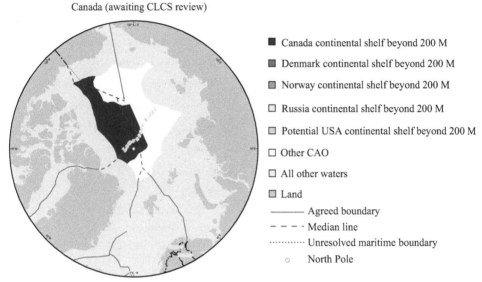

- ■ Canada continental shelf beyond 200 M
- ■ Denmark continental shelf beyond 200 M
- ▨ Norway continental shelf beyond 200 M
- ☐ Russia continental shelf beyond 200 M
- ☐ Potential USA continental shelf beyond 200 M
- ☐ Other CAO
- ☐ All other waters
- ▨ Land
- ───── Agreed boundary
- – – – – Median line
- ············· Unresolved maritime boundary
- ○ North Pole

Source: durham.ac.uk/media/durham-university/research-/research-centres/ibru
-centre-for-borders-research/maps-and-databases/arctic-maps-2021/updated-maps
-and-notes/Map-4-IBRU-Arctic-map-07-04-21-(Focus-Maps-in-the-CAO).pdf.

undertaking between the governments of Denmark and Greenland. Denmark's Arctic strategy focuses largely on securing avenues for self-sustaining growth and development in the region, protecting against climate and environment challenges, and seeking avenues for close co-operation with international Arctic partners. Denmark's extended continental shelf claim is shown in figure 4-6.

Norway responded to Denmark's claim in December 2014 by stating Norway planned to make any final delimitations on overlapping continental shelf claims "through a bilateral agreement."[35] Canada responded with no objection to Denmark's claim but stated Canada had "taken note of the potential overlap in . . . the continental shelves of Canada and the Kingdom of Denmark."[36] In 2015, the US responded with no objection.[37] Finally, Russia responded by drawing attention to "overlap of the continental shelf of the Russian Federation and that of the Kingdom of Denmark in the area referred to in the Danish

Figure 4-6. Denmark's Extended Continental Shelf Claim

Denmark (awaiting CLCS review)

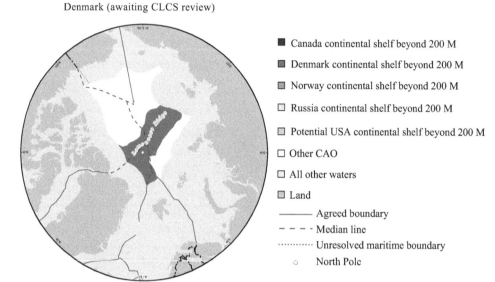

- Canada continental shelf beyond 200 M
- Denmark continental shelf beyond 200 M
- Norway continental shelf beyond 200 M
- Russia continental shelf beyond 200 M
- Potential USA continental shelf beyond 200 M
- Other CAO
- All other waters
- Land
- ——— Agreed boundary
- – – – Median line
- ·········· Unresolved maritime boundary
- ○ North Pole

Source: durham.ac.uk/media/durham-university/research-/research-centres/ibru
-centre-for-borders-research/maps-and-databases/arctic-maps-2021/updated-maps
-and-notes/Map-4-IBRU-Arctic-map-07-04-21-(Focus-Maps-in-the-CAO).pdf.

submission."[38] However, in "accordance with the agreement reached between the Russian Federation and the Kingdom of Denmark" as well as with the Canadians, Russia did not object.[39]

The other European member of the Arctic Five is Norway, whose reliance on energy exports makes its High North stake rather entrenched, as does its geography. Historically, Norway was party to one of the leading Arctic territorial disputes—that with Russia over the Barents Sea, which is analysed in chapter 5. Norway ratified UNCLOS in 1996 and had until 2006 to submit a formal continental shelf claim. In November 2006, Oslo submitted claims across three areas in the Northeast Atlantic and the Arctic:[40] the Loophole (Barents Sea), the Western Nansen Basin (Arctic Ocean), and the Banana Hole (Norwegian Sea).

In 2009, the CLCS recommended that, in regard to the Loophole, Norway "fully satisfies the requirement of a submission for continental shelf beyond 200NM from the territorial sea baselines of Norway."[41] The commission urged "a bilateral delimitation between Norway and the Russian Federation . . . to delineate the extent of each coastal state's continental shelf in the Loop Hole."[42] On the Western Nansen Basin, the commission ruled in favor of Norway's findings and recommended "the delineation of the outer limits of the continental shelf in the Western Nansen Basin area be conducted."[43] Finally, the commission agreed with the claim with respect to the Banana Hole and recommended the outer limits be determined in conjunction with the Kingdom of Denmark. The CLCS recommendation regarding Norway's Central Arctic Ocean continental shelf extension is shown in figure 4-7.

Of course, Norway benefits from a cooperative Arctic environment. After all, Norway is a NATO state that shares a border with Russia and, as such, seeks avenues to ensure open lines of communication in the region. As a Norwegian government official stated:

> Bilateral ties between Arctic nations are still strong, and I don't see that changing largely. Russia has strong and rightful interests in the Arctic and is not an expansionist actor in the Arctic.[44]

Indeed, the Putin era ushered in a breakthrough in Norwegian-Russian relations. Both rediscovered mutual interests, and the Barents Sea decision allowed for deeper trade relations. Norwegian business flourished in Russia, but some nongovernmental organizations (NGOs) did not. On one hand, Moscow saw the chance to demonstrate to an international audience a cooperative foreign policy agenda in the Arctic. On the other hand, because Russia is constrained by its lack of the required technology and finances to explore and develop the offshore Barents Sea, closer engagement with Oslo gave Moscow an avenue to take advantage of Norway's superior abilities.

Rounding out the Arctic Five stakeholders is, of course, Russia. Moscow's extended continental shelf claim was explored in chapter 2. Overall, Russia's Arctic strategy swayed in a more assertive direction in 2007 when it planted the Russian flag on the Arctic seabed. While

Figure 4-7. Norway's Recommended Extended Continental Shelf Claim

Norway (recommended by CLCS)

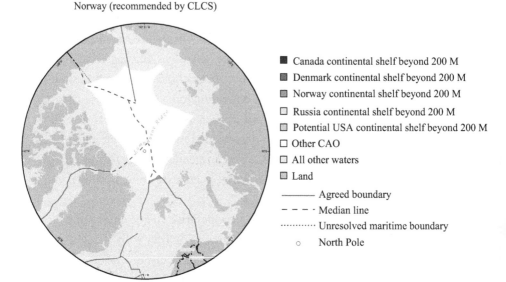

- ■ Canada continental shelf beyond 200 M
- ▨ Denmark continental shelf beyond 200 M
- ▨ Norway continental shelf beyond 200 M
- ☐ Russia continental shelf beyond 200 M
- ▨ Potential USA continental shelf beyond 200 M
- ☐ Other CAO
- ☐ All other waters
- ▨ Land
- ——— Agreed boundary
- – – – Median line
- ·········· Unresolved maritime boundary
- ○ North Pole

Source: durham.ac.uk/media/durham-university/research-/research-centres/ibru
-centre-for-borders-research/maps-and-databases/arctic-maps-2021/updated-maps
-and-notes/Map-4-IBRU-Arctic-map-07-04-21-(Focus-Maps-in-the-CAO).pdf.

the stunt was designed to symbolize Russia's Arctic quest for its domestic audience, it has since become a popular reference to the notion of Putin's conquest of the Arctic. This impedes any realistic debate on the intentions, goals, and strategies of Moscow in the Arctic, making it difficult to argue that Russia is a legitimate majority power in the Arctic and its efforts to securitize economic interests are rather benign.

THE OTHER STAKEHOLDERS

Beyond the Arctic Five powers there are a range of interested parties seeking a stake in the Arctic. This section briefly delves into the Arctic agendas of China, NATO, and the EU.[45]

China is a self-appointed "near Arctic" state (which is not near the Arctic). In 2018, Beijing doubled down on its Arctic interest by releasing a formal Arctic policy.[46] In 2013, China was granted observer status and for many this symbolized "an unspoken acceptance of Beijing's Arctic expansion."[47] Besides representing an avenue for the diversification of China's energy supplies, the Arctic is of interest to China, given the region's shipping potential. China's demand for access to NSR shipping is likely to increase, with a successful test sailing in 2013 by the vessel *Yong Sheng* encouraging other Chinese firms.[48] Official estimates signal that China still has significant plans for the NSR, with estimates of between 5 and 15 percent of China's international trade set to transit the NSR in the future.[49]

Anne-Marie Brady outlines China's strategic Arctic interests in two broad categories.[50] First, there are a range of resource-related interests spanning hydrocarbons, fishing, and tourism and transport routes. Second, China has a science and technology interest in the region: access is essential for national security information around climate change mitigation and for dual-use purposes related to space and satellite programs, both affording improved weather forecasting abilities and surveillance capacity.

Efforts to increase engagement in the Arctic are most evident in China's relationship with Iceland. It was the first European state to sign a free-trade agreement with Beijing, and Iceland was the country with which China struck its first intergovernmental framework in the Arctic, in 2012. Various Chinese state energy interests have been floated in geothermal resources in Iceland, but to date the projects have been abandoned. In 2018, the China-Iceland Arctic Science Observatory opened, providing Beijing with further footing into the Arctic. Strategically, Iceland is a logistics hub that could act as a key shipping port between Europe and Asia along the NSR.[51] It seems clear that the Chinese Arctic strategy is to internationalize the Arctic in a way that benefits China. As a leading Chinese economist notes:

> China's Arctic interest is not unlike its African interest—it's all about diversity. Diversity of resources for future growth. The slight difference is the potential of the Northern Sea Route for China; the opportunity to ship goods rapidly between Asia and Europe is a key component of maintaining Chinese global reach.[52]

China will no doubt exploit the Russians' predicament with the US and Europe. Russia requires both finance and a consumer base for various Arctic resource ventures, and China will be front and center when Russia comes knocking.[53]

Currently, China is working to increase its overall presence in the Arctic to strengthen its "right to speak" on Arctic matters at an international level.[54] China is an attractive Arctic partner for Russia, given China's willingness to invest in emerging Arctic projects and infrastructure. So long as Russia desperately needs foreign capital for its Arctic endeavors, China will be seen primarily as a valued commercial partner despite posing a potential threat. This sentiment is supported by a Russian academic who notes that "China is rejected as an A5 power, as an Arctic actor. But it is accepted as an investment partner and monetary injections are welcomed warmly."[55]

In the Arctic, China sees the potential for long-term planning around its own energy security and trade security, so for the immediate future, this bilateral relationship is a win-win scenario for both partners. A stable and peaceful Arctic is in China's best interest particularly for the use of the NSR, given its potential economic opportunity.[56]

An Arctic stakeholder much closer, physically, to the region is the European Union (EU). The Arctic is of key strategic relevance for the EU, beyond wider concern for the global environment. Three EU member states—Denmark, Sweden, and Finland—have territory located above the Arctic Circle. Further, Iceland and Norway have close relations with the EU via the European Economic Area agenda. Canada and the US are strategic partners of the EU, and Russia technically still holds a partnership and cooperation agreement with the EU.[57] All of the aforementioned nations are members of the Arctic Council. However, the EU is not, although it squarely states its strategic interest though various policy documents for the Arctic. Politics remains a hurdle for Brussels (EU headquarters) when it comes to the Arctic.

Seemingly, there are three key objectives for the EU in the Arctic, as set out in a 2016 joint communication: to preserve the Arctic's fragile ecology, to promote sustainable resource development, and to support international cooperation.[58] This 2016 policy position was superseded by the 2022 EU Arctic Strategy, which essentially codified the long-held EU position. Significantly, the current EU approach accepts the existing international legal order—notably UNCLOS—and the Arctic Council as the lead regional body. As it stands, the EU is a pending observer and must apply to attend meetings of the Arctic Council, although, the EU's applications to attend and listen have not (yet) been knocked back.

EU objectives in the Arctic remain: mitigating of climate change, support of sustainable development, and the fostering of international cooperation in the Arctic. In the immediate future, the EU will surely bolster its campaign for an observer-status seat at the Arctic Council. In 2017, the international framework "Polar Code" entered into force. The Polar Code is a mandatory framework for ships operating in the Arctic and Antarctic regions.[59] Given that the EU controls some 40 percent of global tonnage and that the development of the NSR may one day shift trade routes, the EU has a vital interest in the application of the Polar Code in the Arctic.[60]

Another institution with its eye on the Arctic sphere is the North Atlantic Treaty Organization (NATO). While NATO has no formal Arctic strategy yet, there is much debate over the role NATO should— or even could—play in the Arctic. Four of the Arctic Five states are NATO members, yet there is disagreement over the requirement for NATO to play a role in the region. For instance, Norway welcomes an active role for NATO in the Arctic, while Canada is more wary.[61] Of course, for Russia, as the sole non-NATO Arctic Five power, formal NATO engagement in the Arctic is a nonnegotiable issue.[62] The position of NATO in the Arctic is best summarized by a Norwegian government official who stated:

> Of course, there is a role for NATO in the Arctic—four of the five Arctic polar nations are NATO nations. Northern Norway is just as important to NATO as the south. NATO's role must come simply by default. This doesn't mean NATO needs a military presence or post; simply NATO must have an understanding of northern affairs and

follow developments in the Arctic. Prior to Ukraine and Crimea, this was the case, and it will continue to be the case. Perhaps closer lines of communication will develop, however.[63]

For Alexander Shaparov, NATO's interest in the region has less to do with potential military confrontation and more to do with geopolitical rivalry, which takes the form "of economic, technological and political competition."[64] Although there is still no consensus within NATO on its Arctic role, it is not a new theater for the alliance. Indeed, the High North (as the Arctic is often politically constructed and termed by Brussels) featured prominently during the Cold War. With the collapse of the Soviet Union, NATO shifted its threat perception away from the High North. For the past decade, calls for the alliance to develop a High North presence have resulted in increased military training exercises with High North Arctic partners and yet, overall, a noncommittal approach. The most recent NATO Strategic Concept (2022) made no mention of the Arctic, and reference to the High North was made in terms of Russian strategic threats looming from the region. No Arctic or High North policy was tabled per se.

In March 2016, NATO led the "Cold Response" exercise in Norway. Cold Response is an annual military exercise led by Norway since 2006. The 2016 NATO-led iteration involved 15,000 soldiers from thirteen NATO allies and partners, including all Arctic rim powers except Russia. The aim of the exercise was to develop military capabilities in the Arctic's challenging conditions. Russia sent an inspection team to monitor Cold Response and continues to do so for most regional military exercises. Another key military exercise led by NATO in recent years was Trident Juncture, held in 2018 and one of the largest NATO exercises since the Cold War. Trident Juncture was an exercise based on a NATO Article 5 (collective defense) scenario playing out in the High North; held in Norway, the exercise involved some 50,000 participants. Dynamic Mongoose (yes, actual name) was an exercise led by NATO in 2020, again focused on the High North. Dynamic Mongoose (marvelous, right?) ran off the coast of Iceland and featured anti-submarine warfare (ASW) training exercises.

ARCTIC CHALLENGES

There are challenges inherent in the opening up of the Arctic, not least stemming from the geopolitical tensions whipped up by the vast array of state and institutional interest in the region. This section reviews some of the key challenges, including issues of governance and environment, as well as military and technological concerns emerging in the Arctic. Figure 4-8 captures the overlapping extended Arctic continental shelf claims, as explored earlier in this chapter.

Responsibility for mediating these claims falls to the UN Convention on the Law of the Sea (UNCLOS). Since it was signed in 1982, the convention has been ratified by some 150 states, including four of the Arctic Five powers (as noted, the US has not ratified). Signatories have ten years from the ratification of UNCLOS to submit a claim for continental shelf extension. Multiple claims may be submitted from that point thereafter. The Commission on the Limits of the Continental Shelf (CLCS) is empowered to pass judgment regarding the validity of scientific data submitted to support shelf expansion bids; however, it is ultimately at the discretion of claimants to negotiate disputes amongst themselves. Arctic rim powers (the Arctic Five) declare an area extending 200 nautical miles as their EEZs. But further sovereign rights to resources on and beneath the seabed can be assigned to an area encompassing up to a further 150 nautical miles beyond this 200-nautical-mile point, based on an extended continental shelf claim.[65] This extended continental shelf saga is a key issue in the Arctic today. Of course, any extended continental shelf bid does not give claimants control over the water column. Much of the Arctic Ocean area that hosts overlapping extended continental shelf claims will remain international waters or high seas. Figure 4-9 illustrates the particulars of maritime zones under UNCLOS.

The Arctic's key governance institution is the Arctic Council. Established in 1996, the council is an intergovernmental forum and consensus body that focuses on the Arctic's protection and sustainable development. Military or security issues are not mandated for discussion.[66] The Arctic Council consists of eight Arctic states: Canada,

Figure 4-8. Maritime Zones and Claims in the Arctic (2021)

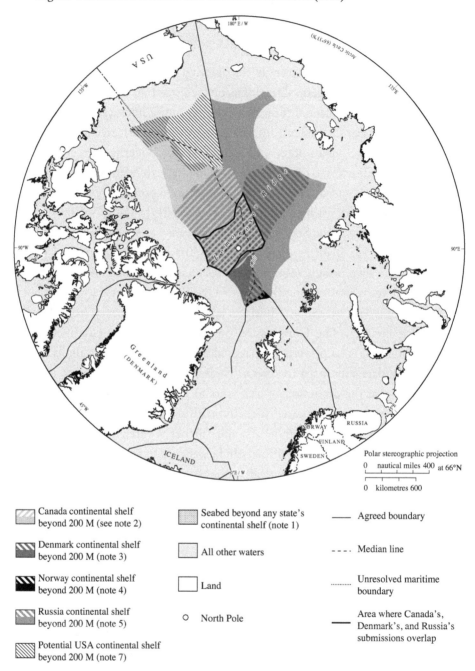

Canada continental shelf beyond 200 M (see note 2)

Denmark continental shelf beyond 200 M (note 3)

Norway continental shelf beyond 200 M (note 4)

Russia continental shelf beyond 200 M (note 5)

Potential USA continental shelf beyond 200 M (note 7)

Seabed beyond any state's continental shelf (note 1)

All other waters

Land

○ **North Pole**

—— Agreed boundary

- - - Median line

.... Unresolved maritime boundary

—— Area where Canada's, Denmark's, and Russia's submissions overlap

Source: durham.ac.uk/media/durham-university/research-/research-centres/ibru
-centre-for-borders-research/maps-and-databases/arctic-maps-2021/updated-maps
-and-notes/Map-1-IBRU-Arctic-map-07-04-21-(revised-Russia-claimed).pdf.

Figure 4-9. Maritime Zones under UNCLOS

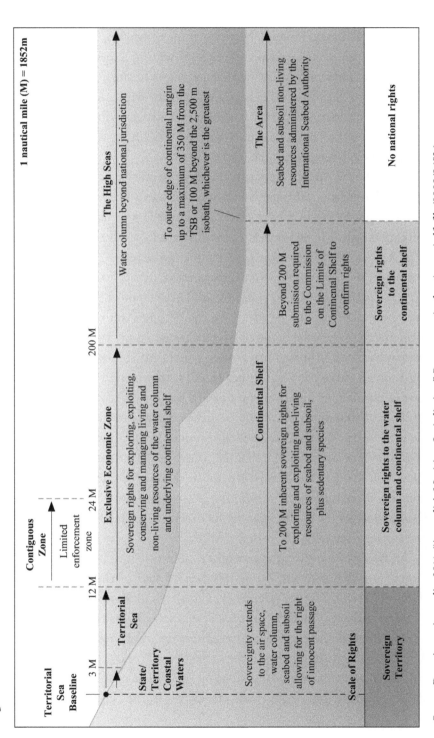

Source: Geoscience Australia, 2011. "Australia's Maritime Jurisdiction," 7, ga.gov.au/__data/assets/pdf_file/0009/86526 /Australias-Maritime-Jurisdiction.pdf.

Denmark, Finland, Iceland, Norway, Russia, Sweden, and the US. There are also several organizations representing Arctic indigenous peoples that have permanent participant status in the council. Arctic Council states decide whether to grant applicant states observer status. The following states currently hold observer status: Switzerland, Germany, the Netherlands, Poland, Spain, the UK, Italy, France, Japan, South Korea, Singapore, India, and China.[67]

In 2008, the Arctic Five members of the Arctic Council signed the Ilulissat Declaration, through which members set a firm course for cooperation, agreeing to resolve territorial disputes without resorting to military means.[68] In addition, the Arctic Five renewed their support for UNCLOS to remain the sole legal regime in the region. According to Denmark, the "landmark political declaration" sent a "strong political signal that the five coastal states (would) act responsibly concerning future development in the Arctic Ocean."[69] The Arctic Council has formalized cooperation between Arctic nations. In the past, this cooperation had been insulated from other global affairs. However, following Russia's annexation of Crimea in 2014, the Arctic Five members have largely cut defense cooperation with Russia and kept to a reduced level of collaboration on military-security dialogue outside the Arctic Council forum. The Arctic Council remained the facilitator of Russia-West dialogue up until March 2022, when the West paused engagement. While the Arctic Council's mandate does not stretch to military-security discussions or considerations, in many ways the Ilulissat Declaration serves as the impetus for Arctic Five states to negotiate and consider security affairs in the Arctic.

As alluded to earlier, the central geopolitical "race" to the North Pole is one that can only be undertaken by four of the Arctic Five states. Three of the four (Denmark, Canada, and Russia) are already well and truly mid-race via the official governance channels. The US has yet to meet the race's entry requirements (ratifying UNCLOS). The US continues to approach the underwater Arctic ridge as an oceanic ridge and thus not as an extension of any one state's continental shelf—rejecting any single claim. All claims to the ridge may be regarded as tenable by the CLCS; however, in this scenario, the CLCS would merely call on the competing claimants to settle the dispute bilaterally (or trilaterally).[70]

The three Arctic Five nations scrapping over the seabed of the North Pole have moved to focus their claims on questions of "geologic origin," with sovereignty over the ridge being based on estimates from rock deposits. Given that the rock deposits were from the same ridge, all three nations have come to the same conclusion: the ridge is a continuation of each of their particular continental shelves, and they are all connected. Trudeau's Canada is presenting itself as an advocate of international cooperation and maintains an oddly "relaxed" attitude to the Arctic. Denmark is not able to defend its claim militarily against Russia's superior forces, and it is unlikely Russia will recognize other claims. For Russia, the ridge—the Lomonosov Ridge—is synonymous with national pride, reflected in the fact that it is named after a celebrated eighteenth-century Russian polymath.

Climate change is raising Arctic temperatures at up to four times the global average. This means most territorial seas in the Arctic region already see ice-free summers. Further, a National Oceanic and Atmospheric Administration (NOAA) study has found the following:

> Rapid Arctic sea ice loss is probably the most visible indicator of global climate change; it leads to shifts in ecosystems and economic access, and potentially impacts weather throughout the northern hemisphere. . . . Increased physical understanding of rapid Arctic climate shifts and improved models are needed that give a more detailed picture and timing of what to expect so we can better prepare and adapt to such changes. Early loss of Arctic sea ice gives immediacy to the issue of climate change.[71]

A further concern for the Arctic is the waste from increased activity in the region, as well as the potential for eco-disasters. Compared to oil spills on land, those at sea are harder to contain. With higher traffic and areas of more intense resource production, tanker spills in the Arctic are a risk. Further, transportation utilizing the NSR might increase, emitting waste as a by-product of transit. Likewise, increased Arctic tourism brings with it the potential for environmental degradation.

However, with advances in technology, there is cause for optimism for the future of the Arctic as a bustling commercial hub. Advances in satellite surveillance might yet provide early warning of potential Arctic devastation.[72] Oil spills at the deep-water level are often not recognized until the oil slick appears on the surface or miles away, carried by ocean currents. Satellites provide images that penetrate deeper beneath the ocean surface and are sometimes able to detect deep spills days before they surface.

The emergence of social responsibility campaigns at international energy firms, as well as the general public's concern for the Arctic ecosystem, has resulted in a cautious operating environment for many firms. This is evident in energy firm approaches to date toward Arctic offshore exploration. Firms are going slow, investing billions in state-of-the-art technology, and pulling out of projects if there is any cause for concern. Additionally, concern for the commercial costs associated with operating in the Arctic environment are voiced by a representative of a global oil major who stated the following:

> Shell left its Arctic (Chukchi Sea) venture because it couldn't meet operational requirements. It's really that simple; although their PR machine would have you believe anything from Obama blocking license renewal, to the oil price having been too low. Shell pulled out because it rushed to the Arctic and in the rush, got caught up with inefficient deep-sea production materials. We are back to the drawing board. We have oil rigs that can't be anchored correctly—Shell lost one of their rigs and it drifted to the Alaskan shore. Like the rest of us, they now won't touch the wells until the technology is foolproof. The industry is almost there; demand will get us over the line sooner or later.[73]

That interview was conducted in 2015, and in 2020 it was announced Shell had indeed solidified plans to return to the US offshore Arctic.

Of course, it is likely that further offshore oil ventures in the Arctic will be complicated by the increasing number of financial bodies and capital lenders refusing to finance such projects.

Even still, ExxonMobil's 1989 *Valdez* and BP's 2008 Gulf of Mexico spills are ever-present in big oil thinking. These firms are risk-averse, and no one wants to be the first to spill in the Arctic. Estimates from the US Department of the Interior put the risk of Arctic spills at 75 percent, yet the department still sold licenses for offshore Arctic exploration. That said, globally there has been a decrease in oil spills despite increases in oil trade. However, the physical challenges of the Arctic environment as it relates to the great game energy narrative is problematic for efforts to exploit Arctic resources.

The Arctic's permafrost is a drilling hazard, given the accumulations of natural gas hydrates that exist within and directly beneath it. Offshore Arctic technology for drilling platforms is being updated constantly to better withstand strong storms, currents, and icebergs.[74] But the technology is still years away from being cost-effective or presenting Arctic offshore oil and gas as commercially viable for mass production. Despite grand plans for offshore Arctic hydrocarbon projects, Russia has failed to invest in the development of new technology for its Arctic endeavors. As a Russian academic states:

> Technological capability in the Arctic is a key component of Arctic development. Currently, only Russia has the icebreaker fleet capable of navigating the offshore Arctic all year round. China comes close, yet its current fleet can break 1.4 m of ice and its new fleet will be able to break 1.8 m. These ships will only be useful in summer months.[75]

The cost of the sophisticated technology needed to build Arctic projects is roughly $3 billion to $5 billion per rig. Further, the geographical constraints of Arctic production, the long supply lines, limited infrastructure, and higher salaries for the workforce are all roadblocks to rapid Arctic project development. While shallow Arctic waters have yielded resources without much hassle, depths exceeding

100 meters are another problem. The bulk of Russia's oil resources are estimated to be in the deep offshore Arctic Ocean, and it is here that extraction becomes tricky.[76] Yet, over the past ten years, the necessary technology has advanced considerably, enabled as the resource prize was deemed big enough. The 2008 US Geological Survey results gave some energy majors the confidence to attempt to overcome the major technology hurdles to "safely and economically produce large hydrocarbon accumulations in harsh environmental conditions."[77]

In the case of France's TotalEnergies (formerly Total SA), however, the company argued that the risk of Arctic spills is simply too high. The firm was the first to speak out against Arctic hydrocarbon development.[78] Arctic offshore oil is still a long-term reality, ever constrained by shifts in the global energy market. As an energy consultancy representative explained:

> Arctic oil and gas is squarely a long-term project and simply won't be feasible unless either a) oil is above $130 a barrel, or b) demand side-steps non-traditional energy routes like renewables. I don't think either are all that likely in the long term (35+ years). Of course, oil majors are strategic thinkers and no doubt we will remain fixed on the potential of the Arctic offshore.[79]

Putin has gradually developed an interest in the Arctic environment. This interest may be politically charged, as it certainly coincided with Moscow's lead-up to the presidency of the Arctic Council for 2021–2023. That said, Russia is learning through exposure to climate change perils—most recently the 2020 Norilsk oil spill. It can be argued that a tangible "cost" attributed to Russian Arctic plans and investments has forced Moscow to securitize climate change. But for now, at least, Putin continues to use the Kremlin media machine to portray himself as deeply committed to the welfare of polar bears.[80] As per Putin's previous wildlife photo shoots with tigers and whales, this is also employed to perpetuate Putin's "strongman" persona— now with a "climate warrior" element.

Militarization is a central challenge to the Arctic, but it is not a new one. In the post–Cold War period, the Arctic underwent a major decline in levels of militarization. With the collapse of the Soviet Union, Russia no longer directed funds to Far North projects, and the region became somewhat forgotten. Since 2012, there have been steady efforts by Arctic rim powers to restore and, in some cases, enhance Arctic military capabilities. It is therefore important to note that the current military buildup has the potential to surpass even Cold War levels but is not there yet.

Generally, the Arctic is viewed as the home of a new arms race and as a theater for a new cold war between Russia and the West.[81] The Arctic rim powers have actively bolstered their military presence in the region, further fueling such sentiments. In 2007, Canada launched an annual "sovereignty operation" called Operation Nanook. This exercise in the Canadian Arctic involves the deployment of 600 to 1,250 navy, army, and air force personnel to "assert Canada's sovereignty over its northernmost regions" and enhance their ability to operate in Arctic conditions.[82] Since 2007, Operation Nanook has also involved various international military partners.[83] However, many operation objectives have focused on responses to petrochemical leaks and general maritime emergency scenarios. Operation Nunalivut and Operation Nunakput were two other annual sovereignty operations conducted by Canada in the High North between 2007 and 2018. These exercises have also included various international military partners, but all are now run under the aegis of Operation Nanook.[84]

These militarization efforts are unsurprising and expected, given geopolitical pressures. Such pressures span Arctic Five economic interests and the securitization of domestic state borders as global activity increases in the region. The domestic politics of each the respective Arctic rim powers is often the leading driver of military policy in the Arctic. As Michael Byers argues in relation to the "rush" for the North Pole:

We're talking about the centre of a large, inhospitable ocean that is in total darkness for three months each year, thousands of miles from any port. . . . The water in the North Pole is 12,000 feet deep and will always be covered by sea ice in the winter. It's not a place where anyone is going to be drilling for oil and gas. So it's not about economic stakes, it's about domestic politics.[85]

Certainly, the requirement for functioning search and rescue capabilities in the region is also driving states to acquire new equipment or move existing hardware north. Disputes that could be labeled "conflicts" are cordoned off as largely bilateral issues. Further, outright military conflict in the Arctic is unlikely. This reality is supported by a Russian government official:

We have to look to capability and deployability before war can be waged in the Arctic. Military capabilities cannot change the fact that the environment is unpassable between Nov–Jan each year, the region is dark 24 hours a day and ice storms limit deployability. It is difficult to fight over a region that simply will not host the battle.[86]

Arguing that there is a correlation between increasing military activity in the Arctic and looming Arctic conflict is problematic. First, all Arctic rim nations have a history of military exercises in the region. Given that US submarine deployments to the Arctic continued after the collapse of the Soviet Union and that the annual Cold Response exercise predates the return of Russian long-range bomber patrol flights, it is evident that the Arctic was never demilitarized in the first place.[87] The installation, in Russia's case reinstallation, of military infrastructure should not be narrowly viewed as increasing Arctic tensions.

In 2015, despite Russia-West tensions, Norway and Russia conducted a joint exercise code-named Barents-2015. The two-day exercise provided training for search and rescue events in the Arctic Ocean, and was conducted despite Norway's 2014 suspension of military cooperation with Russia in the wake of Ukraine.[88] (In line with suspension of joint military activities, the annual Norwegian-Russian Arctic exercise called Pomor was suspended in 2015.[89]) Barents-2015 signaled the maintenance of some bilateral cooperation and communication between

Norway and Russia. Ultimately, the Arctic is progressing from "Cold War theatre to mosaic of cooperation"[90]—although continued regional peace is, of course, contingent on Putin's Russia cooperating.

Perhaps more pressing than the processes of militarization are the innate environmental and physical challenges posed by the Arctic. While the region is often referred to as pristine, white, and wonderful, the Arctic is better characterized by its remoteness, harshness, extreme temperatures, and long periods of darkness in winter.[91] This physical environment is undergoing profound, irreversible change as the world continues to fall short of climate targets and fails to collectively band together to mitigate global warming.

While the Arctic is viewed as a "final frontier" in some states, opportunities stemming from domestic political gains and resource potential drive Arctic Five strategies in the region. The only constant in the Arctic geopolitical narrative is the fact that the region is rapidly changing. That said, the tensions and mistrust rife in this current period of strained Russia-West relations have yet to entirely spill over into the Arctic. Sure, some aspects of Russia-West Arctic relations are affected, like the freezing of bilateral or multilateral forums and military exercises. Further, the pace of commercial projects has slowed in the offshore Russian Arctic as a result of sanctions—but arguably, more so because of stagnated global oil prices since 2014.

Arctic Five militarization efforts, inevitable in an opening Arctic, are taken as evidence of an Arctic conflict on the horizon. Yet, cooperation and regional peace within the Arctic continue to prevail. Viewing the Arctic wholly through the lens of conflict or cooperation is problematic, for it is too simplistic. The Arctic is so complex that, at any one time, it can represent elements of both conflict and cooperation. External forces might elicit more of one or the other from time to time. But generally, all Arctic Five states are geared toward cooperation in the Arctic, simply because they perceive the region to house a range of challenges conducive to bilateral and multilateral partnership. Climate change, scientific explorations, communication networks, and shipping, as well as search and rescue capabilities, are all areas in which the Arctic Five recognize the value of cooperation. Against the backdrop of Putin's resurgent Russia elsewhere, Russian Arctic strategy has remained rather collaborative and cooperative. This chapter has detailed the existing dynamics in both territorial claims and the prizes at stake in the Arctic. The coming chapters will build upon this to illustrate *why* Russian Arctic strategy is geared toward cooperation, underscoring the fact that Moscow's interests are not served by conflict or tension in the Arctic. Rather, the opposite is true.

5

COOPERATING WITH THE KREMLIN(?)

"CZAR ALEXANDER III SAID RUSSIA HAS ONLY TWO
ALLIES, ITS ARMY AND NAVY. FOR VLADIMIR PUTIN,
THEY MAY WELL BE GAS AND OIL."

—E. CHOW

This chapter uses two case studies to provide further evidence of Moscow's requirement for an air of cooperation in the Arctic. The first case study provides an overview of Russia's conduct in its state-to-state relations. Here, the case study assesses the maritime dispute between Russia and Norway in the Arctic's Barents Sea, showing how Russia exerted considerable effort to end the dispute, which had simmered since 1974.

The second case study focuses on the Kremlin's commercial engagements in the Russian Arctic. Many offshore Russian Arctic projects remain "frozen" or are still in early exploration stages. However, onshore Russian Arctic ventures on the Yamal Peninsula are either established or well under development. This case study delves into contemporary commercial relations between the Russian state and foreign energy stakeholders. International commercial cooperation is the bedrock of Moscow's desire to realize the resource potential of its Arctic zone. Russia's Arctic energy aspirations are assigned national security priority and, quite simply, delivering on these projects necessitates cooperation. Russia knows this.

CASE STUDY ONE: THE BARENTS SEA

The Barents Sea dispute had long been a difficult issue for both Norway and Russia. Historically, the maritime dispute was framed by the Cold War geopolitical context of Norway being an Arctic NATO power. This case study delves into the background of the Barents Sea dispute, examines the bilateral resolution of the issue, and assesses the contemporary state of affairs between Norway and Russia in the Barents Sea.

Situated in the High North, above the Arctic Circle and forming part of the Arctic Ocean, the Barents Sea is named after Dutch explorer Willem Barents. The sea is located off the Norwegian and Russian shorelines, extending out to Svalbard (Norway), Franz Josef Land (Russia), and Novaya Zemlya (Russia). The Barents Sea covers an area of roughly 1,405,000 square kilometers.[1]

Not only was this disputed area economically valuable, given its vast hydrocarbon reserves, but it was also strategically important for both states. For Norway, the Barents Sea is a key fisheries resource, significant for Norway's domestic market as well as its export market to the European Union (EU). For Russia, the Barents Sea provides the year-round port (located in Severomorsk) for the Northern Fleet. Today, the Barents Sea is strategically important as an entrance to the Northern Sea Route (NSR).

The Soviet Union and the Kingdom of Norway began official negotiations over the disputed Barents Sea region in 1974. The area in question measured 175,000 square kilometers. The dispute was complicated by the fact that the two parties had very different methods of delineating their Barents Sea territory. The Soviet Union (and then Russia) was firmly applying a "sectoral line" process for territorial delineation in the Barents Sea, whereas Norway based its approach on the "median line" principle. The sectoral line process refers to drawing a line from the North Pole down toward each of the Arctic Five (A5) landmasses, essentially sectioning off the Arctic according to Arctic coastlines and their line of longitude intersection with the North Pole. The median line principle uses an equidistance method in which maritime boundaries are arrived at by dividing waters at the midpoint between the bordering countries.

For Russia, the dispute had its roots in the 1926 Soviet decree "On the Proclamation of Lands and Islands Located in the Arctic Ocean as Territory of the USSR." This decree "reiterated the legal tradition in Tsarist Russia that was characterized by the notion of the sectoral line, the line of longitude that starts from the terminus of the land boundary and intersects with the North Pole."[2] This method was rejected by Norway. With neither party willing to alter its approach, the dispute entered a deadlock. It remained that way for four decades.

There was, however, a precedent for cooperation prior to the formal negotiations that began in 1974. In 1957, the USSR and Norway agreed for the first time on a maritime boundary in the Arctic. The maritime delineation was at the base of the Barents Sea in the Varangerfjord.[3] An illustration of the 1957 agreement is provided in figure 5-1. This agreement contributed to the overall maintenance of good-neighborly relations between Norway and the Soviet Union.[4]

Building upon the Varangerfjord momentum, Norway requested negotiations over the wider Barents Sea region in 1957. The Soviet Union ignored these requests, and it was not until 1970 that Norway and the Soviet Union informally discussed the outstanding delimitation issue, with formal negotiations not taking place until 1974. At the time, the formal negotiations were driven primarily by fisheries disagreements in which both states argued the other was actively fishing in its sovereign territory.

Throughout the dispute, Norway applied the median line principle in which it argued the Barents Sea boundary should be determined via the equidistant point of the nearest two state coastlines. As noted earlier, the Soviet Union relied on its 1926 decree that based its argument on a sectoral line drawn from the coast straight to the North Pole. With neither party prepared to move from its position, the region fell into a "gray zone" where the parties simply agreed to disagree.[5] In 1980 the

Figure 5-1. 1957 Barents Sea Maritime Agreement

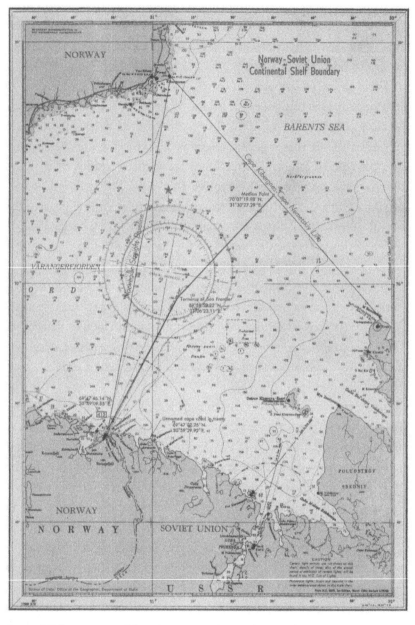

Source: US Department of State International Boundary Study, 1970.
"Varangerfjord," www. state.gov/wp-content/uploads/2019/10/LIS-17.pdf.

two nations signed a moratorium to that effect, which banned hydro-carbon exploration in the disputed area. Norway and Russia continued to work together in areas of fisheries management and of joint search and rescue exercises.

With prospective economic windfalls for both parties, the Barents Sea issue returned to the Russia-Norway agenda in 2007. In 2007, the 1957 Varangerfjord agreement was revisited and the two nations ex-tended the agreed-upon median line some distance farther off the coastline. Further, in 2007 Vladimir Putin invited Norwegian partner-ship in a joint venture with Gazprom to develop the Shtokman natural gas field in the Russian zone of the Barents Sea. The Shtokman field is potentially one of the world's largest gas fields. Discovered in 1988, it was only slated for development from 2005, but this never eventuated, and it has been shelved.

Since 2005, Gazprom has signed a range of agreements for the field, spanning partnerships with ConocoPhillips, ExxonMobil, Statoil, To-talEnergies, Royal Dutch Shell, Chevron, and Norsk Hydro. But in a series of backflips, Gazprom rejected all other foreign bids and agree-ments to develop the consortium Shtokman Development AG in 2007 with TotalEnergies and Statoil. At the time, this indicated Russia's read-iness to engage cooperatively and signaled the potential mutual eco-nomic benefits to be gained by delineating the Barents Sea.[6]

In Murmansk on September 15, 2010, Russian president Dmitry Medvedev and Norway's prime minister Jens Stoltenberg announced an agreement on the forty-year Barents Sea dispute. This was a surprise "to the public and experts alike in both Norway and Russia, as there had been no leaks in advance," with both governments remaining ex-tremely discreet throughout the negotiations.[7] Ratification documents were exchanged in Oslo on June 7, 2011. The treaty is illustrated in figure 5-2. whereby the disputed 175,000 square kilometers was simply split into two nearly equal parts. Figure 5-2 also shows the original boundary proposed by Russia (as it had also been by the Soviet Union) and the boundary proposed by Norway throughout the dispute.

The delineation was complicated by two very different interpreta-tions of the legal framework of the UN Convention on the Law of the

Figure 5-2. 2010 Treaty Agreement

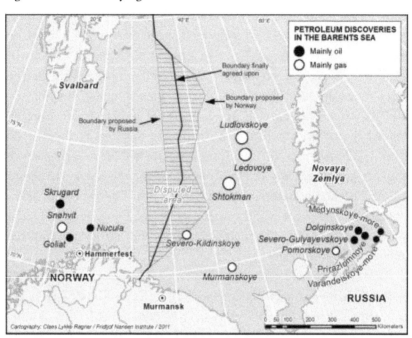

Source: Moe, A., Fjærtoft, D., and Øverland, I., 2011. "Space and Timing: Why Was the Barents Sea Delimitation Dispute Resolved in 2010?" *Polar Geography*, 34:3.

Sea (UNCLOS). Specifically, Norway and Russia had different readings of a key provision in Article 15 of "Part II: Territorial Sea and Contiguous Zone," which states:

> Where the coasts of two States are opposite or adjacent to each other, neither of the two States is entitled, failing agreement between them to the contrary, to extend its territorial sea beyond the median line every point of which is equidistant from the nearest points on the baselines from which the breadth of the territorial seas of each of the two States is measured. The above provision does not apply, however, where it is necessary by reason of historic title or other special circumstances to delimit the territorial seas of the two States in a way which is at variance therewith.[8]

Russia argued that such "special circumstances" did exist and rejected the median line principle, citing the 1926 Soviet decree as precedent of Russia's historic title and its naturally larger coastline. For Norway, the clear application of the median line principle was the only way to delineate the maritime boundary. Yet, the resulting 2010 agreement saw Russia yield entirely and adopt the median line approach.

Significantly, both parties conceded a substantial amount of claimed maritime space in this agreement. Such a concession is of interest because it contrasts with Russia's foreign policy elsewhere even at that time. The Barents Sea resolution was viewed as a valuable model for how best to delineate overlapping Arctic maritime claims. For Medvedev, the resolution reflected a "practical illustration of the principle that all disputes in the Arctic [could] be tackled by the Arctic nations by way of talks and on the basis of international law."[9] The nations' joint statement on the Barents Sea resolution rested heavily on the primacy of UNCLOS as the selected regime for the Arctic as well as the importance of the 2008 Ilulissat Declaration for settling any overlapping claims in the region.

The agreement touted bilateral cooperation as key to keeping the region peaceful, urging claimants with outstanding disputes to follow suit and resolve them swiftly. Certainly, the timing of the Barents Sea resolution is of interest, in terms of what was driving the dispute and why the two nations opted to resolve it after almost forty years.

It is likely the two nations sought a resolution, above all, so that their respective resource industries could start formally exploring the resource-rich basin. Economic drivers were probably the key rationale for the resolution. In Russia's case, however, it was also attractive to demonstrate a cooperative approach to the Arctic in the lead-up to its revised extended continental shelf bid for the North Pole seabed. After all, much of the bid discussed Russia's adherence to international law and its interest in the peaceful development of the Arctic. The Barents Sea provided at least some precedent. A Norwegian government official provides some insight into how the two nations came to the sudden agreement:

The Soviets were not in a position to compromise over the Barents Sea, and I don't think that would have changed given the Cold War setting. Timing is everything in politics. Russia likes international law in the Arctic—oddly enough, the cornerstone of Russia's Arctic strategy is adherence to international law—and the pressures of potential resource development in the region meant Russia now wanted an agreement.[10]

The Barents Sea dispute between Russia and Norway shifted over time from a dispute over fisheries to one driven by mutual gains in the hydrocarbons realm. Certainly, the resolution required a large concession by Russia, for it ceded waters deemed Russian under the 1926 Soviet decree that dictated the use of the sectoral line in all maritime issues. The Norwegians praised the resolution and soon after began exploratory expeditions in their half of the previously disputed region of the Barents Sea.

In Russia, the resolution was met with some criticism linked to the notion that Medvedev was the softer in the "tandemocracy" with Putin when it came to Russian leadership.[11] In the case of the Barents Sea, there was domestic backlash in Russia over Medvedev seemingly ceding sovereignty to Norway.[12] The Medvedev presidency coincided with Russia's push for recognition as a constructive international player, to some extent influenced by Medvedev's own more liberal inclinations. But as Roman Kolodkin (head of the Russian delegation to the delineation talks) pointed out, concessions were made on both sides of the dispute. Kolodkin highlighted that not only had Russia accepted the median line principle over its historically preferred sectoral line principle, but also Norway accepted that the median line would have to be slightly altered to account for Russia's larger coastline.[13]

Overall, the agreement "angered vocal Russian nationalists who strongly criticized the Russian leadership for the deal," with the treaty ratification bill passing in the Duma with 311 votes in favor, 57 opposed, and 82 not voting.[14] Given the criticism of the agreement, the Russian Foreign Ministry issued a formal statement denying it had ceded a vast amount of resource-rich territory to Norway, stating that it "knew what resources were there and had received equally lucrative deposits as part of the deal."[15] These efforts did little to lift the domestic blame directed toward Medvedev over the concession, with the Russian press scapegoating Medvedev even years later. For instance, in 2013 the Russian newspaper *Ekho Russkogo Severa* ran a front page headlined "Aleksandr II sold Alaska, Dmitry Medvedev gave Norway the part of the Barents Sea with huge reserves of hydrocarbons."[16] Like earlier attacks on Medvedev, this probably reflected Putin's favor among domestic media, both before and, more particularly, after his return to the presidency in 2012.

Of course, Putin was in favor of an agreement with Norway in the Barents Sea. For Putin, the Barents Sea agreement was useful for Russia's cooperative Arctic narrative. It was evidently also good for Putin to have the more nationalist resentment for the agreement deflected to then president Medvedev. In 2010, as prime minister, Putin addressed the international forum "The Arctic: Territory of Dialogue," noting the 'Arctic was at the juncture of serious geopolitical and economic interests."[17] Putin stated:

> I have no doubts at all that the existing issues in the Arctic, including those related to the continental shelf, can be resolved in a spirit of partnership through negotiations and on the basis of existing international law. . . . As an example, I want to mention the recently signed Russian-Norwegian treaty on the delimitation of the maritime area and cooperation in the Barents Sea. The negotiations were exhausting. They went on for decades and sometimes reached deadlocks. However, we finally found a way out, the treaty was concluded; I believe that it is a very good example of the possibility of finding a compromise acceptable for all parties. In the given case, both parties really wanted to produce a result and were making steps to meet each other halfway. The Arctic is a special region that requires responsible balanced solutions. And mutual trust, of course.[18]

A changing economic landscape affected the Norway-Russia Shtokman development venture in 2012. Norwegian state-owned Statoil walked away from the consortium, claiming the shale gas revolution was decimating Shtokman's potential market base. This is interesting, given the vast number of Norwegian ventures that popped up in the western Norwegian section of the Barents Sea soon after. Gazprom shelved Shtokman in 2014, citing low gas prices. In June 2015, the remaining consortium partner, France's TotalEnergies, pulled out of the project. TotalEnergies expressed interest in cooperating further should the project enter an active phase, but this is unlikely to occur now that new, cheaper, onshore Russian Arctic gas ventures have taken off. As recently as April 2020, Gazprom signaled a new round of preinvestment studies in the field, but no one knows what, if anything, will come of this iteration of the project's lifespan.

The year 2014 ushered in a new low in Russia-West relations, with Moscow annexing Crimea and unleashing relenting aggression toward Ukraine. Not being an EU member, Norway imposed independent sanctions on Russia in October 2014 following its Ukrainian aggression. Best described as "restrictive measures," these sanctions have no time limit, unlike the EU and US variants.[19] Norway's sanctions include freezing of assets and travel restrictions for some individuals, a ban on imports from Crimea, an import/export ban on arms and defense-related products, and bans on financial investment. Later, in February 2015, Norway's defense minister, Ine Erkisen Soreide, noted that when it came to Norway-Russia ties, "There is no going back to some sort of normality or back to normal business, because that normality does not exist."[20]

Significantly for the Barents Sea issue, Norwegian restrictive measures also covered the export of products to be used for deep-water oil exploration and production in the Arctic. However, the "small print" of such measures included a caveat around the Russian petroleum sector, saying that authorization from Norway's Ministry of Foreign Affairs is available where necessary. This represents a concession to Russia in that Norway's Ministry of Foreign Affairs can, at its discretion, still approve contracts in the energy sphere with Russia.[21] This stated "room for discretion" was utilized in early 2016 when bilateral discussions began for joint Barents Sea exploration.

Technically, Norwegian sanctions ban the export of products to Russia for deep-water, shale or Arctic exploration. The measures do not ban the import of Russia's technology, nor do they restrict Russian capital or joint venture partnership in such projects. In May 2016, the Norwegian government awarded prospecting licenses to thirteen oil firms in the Norwegian territory of the previously disputed Barents Sea zone. Despite low oil prices, future planning is well underway in the Norwegian resource sector. The previously disputed region has been off-limits to eager firms for almost forty years but is thought to hold the richest deposits of hydrocarbons in the Barents Sea. The firms who picked up the licenses include Norway's Statoil, Sweden's Lundin Petroleum, and the US's Chevron and ConocoPhillips. Norway also awarded licenses to Russia's Lukoil and to DEA, a German-based firm owned by Russian oligarch Mikhail Fridman. Russia's Lukoil secured a 20 percent stake in two separate blocks located on the Norway-Russia maritime border. The award, the first joint venture with Russia since the 2014 sanctions, came shortly after Norwegian prime minister Erna Solberg stated she sought cooperation with Russia in the High North because "we have a long history of cooperating with Russia, even in times of political differences."[22]

Yet, this business relationship with Russia in the Barents Sea is inconsistent with Norway's vocal dismay over Russian aggression in Ukraine. It is also at odds with Norway's position as a NATO member. And it is curious, given Norway's increase in defense spending and focus on the High North, along with the reopening of its previously closed, northern Cold War military bases. Evidently, the economic windfall in the Barents Sea trumps strategic concerns elsewhere. Deeper analysis of Norway's Barents Sea stake suggests that there is simply too much to lose for Norway if it were to deny Russia partnership in this Arctic region. The Barents Sea license sale was also the first time since 1994 that Norway had offered foreign access to its Barents Sea region. The sale of these licenses is an attempt by Norway to maintain its resource output after Norwegian crude production peaked back in 2000. Norway is Western Europe's biggest oil producer, and in a bid to maintain its primacy, it was necessary to open the Barents Sea to make up for falling production from aging fields. The Barents Sea region is estimated to hold almost 50 percent of Norway's unexplored 18 billion barrels of oil and gas.[23]

In many ways, the 2010 Barents Sea agreement was about Russia tying up loose ends in regard to its outstanding legal disputes in the Arctic region. It is likely that, although Medvedev was the face of the agreement, Putin played a key role in the background. Not only did the agreement provide precedent for Russia adhering to the norms of international law, but it also signaled Russian interest in engaging with neighbors over Arctic disputes. The Barents Sea agreement was important for Russia's broader aim of maintaining UNCLOS as the key avenue for legal governance within the Arctic.

The fact remains that Russia conceded claimed maritime space to a (militarily) weaker Norway. This represents a clear divergence from Russia's overall foreign policy under Putin since 2000. The Barents Sea resolution ultimately indicates that Putin views the Arctic as a siloed special region of Russian foreign policy. The historical reasons for confrontation in the Barents Sea, namely the Cold War strategic environment, had abated, and cooperation based primarily on mutual interest had emerged. Since the 2010 agreement, this cooperation has been tested—namely, on the grounds of Norway hosting US and NATO hardware, developments in Ukraine since 2014, as well as a recurring tension over Svalbard—and yet pragmatic cooperation between Norway and Russia in the Arctic has occured.

CASE STUDY TWO: FOREIGN ENERGY FIRMS
IN THE RUSSIAN ARCTIC

In 2008, Putin passed new legislation for Arctic offshore licensing. Offshore licenses could only be granted to companies where the Russian state held a majority share and the firm had at least five years' experience working in the Russian Arctic. This rendered Rosneft one of only two companies that met such criteria (Gazprom was the other). In this way, Putin found an avenue to ensure all future Russian Arctic offshore exploration and production would fall under the jurisdiction of the Kremlin. Foreign firms were only able to gain access to the offshore resource bounty via joint ventures with the Kremlin's two preferred firms. Rosneft long attempted to secure joint venture partnerships with Western firms for its key offshore Arctic projects in the Kara Sea and the Barents Sea. Rosneft required these partnerships because the firm lacks the advanced technological know-how to operate in such a challenging environment. Further, the Kremlin lacks the funds to finance the ventures independently. Russia's cooperative Arctic agenda and the reasons for it emerge clearly in reviewing Rosneft's corporate endeavors to partner with foreign firms in the offshore Russian Arctic.

In 2010, Rosneft formally launched its key offshore Arctic projects in the Kara and Barents Seas. The firm also secured additional licenses in the offshore Russian Arctic, this time further afield in the Laptev and East Siberian Seas. Rosneft now owns about 75 percent of all drilling rights and licenses available in the offshore Russian Arctic.

In January 2011, Rosneft announced a strategic partnership with BP to explore and develop the Prinovozemelsky field. The two firms established a consortium for the joint venture, with Rosneft holding a 66.67 percent share and BP holding the remaining 33.33 percent share.[24] In line with Kremlin objectives, BP was to finance the exploration stages of the venture and provide all necessary technology to do so. The partnership involved a $16 billion asset and share swap. Touted as a "global strategic alliance," it was the first of its kind to create an equity partnership between a state-owned firm and an international oil company.[25] Beyond the share swap, the agreement included the establishment of an Arctic technology research center to develop offshore technology and safety capabilities.[26]

In March 2011, the deal was blocked by BP's Russian subsidiary, TNK-BP. It was a consortium of Alfa Access Renova (AAR), which comprised Russian oligarchs, and BP, each with a 50 percent stake. Oligarch Mikhail Fridman (mentioned in the previous case study as a successful licensee in Norway's Barents Sea sale) led the challenge to the Rosneft-BP Arctic partnership. Under the TNK-BP deal, BP was required to offer any commercial opportunities to TNK (AAR) first.

Fearing exclusion from future Arctic ventures, AAR sought legal recourse through an arbitration tribunal. The tribunal ruled in favor of AAR and prevented the $16 billion deal from going ahead.[27] In an attempt to salvage it, BP agreed to let TNK hold a stake in the deal, which was welcomed by TNK. However, Rosneft opposed the inclusion of TNK, primarily because of the stake it would hand to AAR. The Kremlin evidently did not want AAR to have a stake in the venture; in other words, the Kremlin did not want a private Russian interest in state business.

The BP-Rosneft deal could not be saved, for the Kremlin was not willing to negotiate further on the inclusion of TNK in the deal. Eventually, BP sold its Russian joint venture with TNK to Rosneft for a 19.75 percent stake in Rosneft. BP was keen to walk away from the embarrassment, coming so soon after its 2010 Gulf of Mexico spill. Reactions to the spectacular commercial failure were varied. When Putin was asked why Russia opted to negotiate with the firm tainted so publicly by the Gulf of Mexico disaster, he cited the Russian proverb, "the man who's been beaten is worth two who haven't."[28] In the US, Washington publicly voiced concern for the attempted partnership, with the House Committee on Natural Resources noting, "BP once stood for British Petroleum, it now stands for Bolshoi Petroleum."[29] Possibly as punishment for derailing the BP deal, Rosneft absorbed TNK-BP in 2013. Rosneft struck a deal to purchase AAR's remaining stake in TNK-BP for $55 billion, utilizing funds from the Chinese prepayment of $60 billion for Rosneft's $270 billion deal to double oil supplies to China.[30]

In August 2011, just months after the Rosneft-BP deal fell apart, Russia announced a partnership between ExxonMobil and Rosneft for Arctic exploration. Despite Washington's concern over commercial energy ventures with Putin's Russia, it is widely known that ExxonMobil's then CEO (and briefly, subsequent US secretary of state) Rex Tillerson has for some time had a close personal relationship with Putin.[31] The deal was valued at $3.2 billion and focused on the exploration and development of the Prinovozemelsky field in the Kara Sea, as well as the Laptev and East Siberian Seas.

For ExxonMobil, the partnership was significant because the Russian Arctic is "the most promising and least explored offshore area globally."[32] For Rosneft, this strategic alliance was even more momentous, given the fact that ExxonMobil surrendered a stake in its projects in Texas and the Gulf of Mexico to Russia. Remaining from the Rosneft-BP partnership, an Arctic research center was also a key part of the Rosneft-ExxonMobil deal. ExxonMobil and Rosneft assess the reserves in the Kara Sea's Prinovozemelsky field to be more than those of Saudi Arabia.

Drilling in the Kara Sea was slated to start in 2015, but this never eventuated. The 2014 sanctions for Russia's actions in Ukraine brought Rosneft-ExxonMobil Arctic exploration to a halt, blocking ExxonMobil from working with Rosneft in the Russian Arctic. In December 2014, the two firms canceled contracts for exploratory service vessels (operated by Norway's Siem Offshore Inc.) when it became apparent the sanctions were to be extended. ExxonMobil's annual report noted that "in compliance with the sanctions and all general and specific licensees, prohibited activities involving offshore Russia in the Arctic regions have been wound down."[33] Some flexibility in the sanctions was evident in ExxonMobil's ability to press Washington successfully for a two-week extension to safely wrap up exploration before sanctions took hold. Rushing a halt to its Arctic activity was never an option for risk-averse ExxonMobil, ever keen to avoid another disaster like *Valdez*.

By 2018, ExxonMobil had formally exited its joint ventures with Rosneft in the Kara Sea offshore Russian Arctic. In August 2020, Rosneft returned to the Kara Sea venture, albeit alone. Soon after, Rosneft announced it had struck black gold, arguing that the Kara Sea region is comparable to the Gulf of Mexico.[34] But it is important to note that ExxonMobil sought to remain wedded to Russian energy. For instance, ExxonMobil remained a 30 percent stakeholder of Russia's Sakhalin-1 project only until it was unilaterally seized by Putin in late 2022.

Like the Kremlin, Rosneft is highly vested in the development of the offshore Arctic. The region is crucial for the firm because of the vast potential (and discovered) resource base it represents for the company's future bottom line. There are no large onshore project licenses left for Rosneft to buy, leaving the firm's future tied largely to the offshore Arctic region. Additionally, offshore Arctic projects are important to Rosneft to further develop its technical expertise and major project management skillset, and to remain competitive within the industry.

The continuation of Western sanctions and futher souring of ties since February 2022 has severely delayed Rosneft's Arctic ambitions due to complications with foreign partnership. For now, Rosneft is busy assuring the West that the firm is willing to proceed with offshore Arctic exploration without US firms like ExxonMobil. When discussing the fallout of Western sanctions on Arctic progress, CEO of Rosneft (and close ally of Putin) Igor Sechin announced, "We will do it on our own, we'll continue drilling here next year and the years after that."[35] Back in October 2014, Putin approved the creation of RBC, a new energy services firm owned and operated by the state.[36] The firm's mission is to reproduce services provided by oil industry giants Halliburton and Schlumberger. Such services include, but are not limited to, geological data management, drilling technology, rig construction and completion, project management, subsea testing, and spill prevention and cleanup. While Russia's ambition may be to proceed independently in the offshore Arctic, its actual capabilities will limit Russia's success. Without the advanced technology or finance required to start rapidly developing the offshore Arctic, Russia is reliant upon joint venture partnerships for offshore Arctic projects. Rosneft has not explained how it will make up for the tens of billions of dollars it lost when ExxonMobil, Italy's Eni, and Norway's Statoil walked away from various Arctic Russian joint ventures.

Sanctions are not solely to blame for the delay in Rosneft's offshore Arctic exploration plans. The situation is compounded heavily by the 2014 oil price dive. With prices still struggling to lift much above $70 per barrel in early 2023, it is evident the global energy market is still in a difficult position. It is not commercially viable to bring offshore Arctic oil online while the oil price is so low. Of course, oil price estimates are notoriously unreliable because they are dictated by variables beyond anyone's control and often defy solid prediction. The only certainty in the oil price game is that, in the longer term, the price will inevitably rise, due in part to the basic global supply-demand realities. On the other hand, how long this will take and how long prices will stay high are constant unknowns for the industry.

Rosneft has demonstrated its "untouchable" standing in the Russian energy industry as a result of the firm's Kremlin ties. Given that oil revenues are a key contributor to the Kremlin's budget, it is evident that there is a state interest, as well as a corporate interest, in Rosneft weathering low oil prices. Not only did the Kremlin provide ample tax breaks for Rosneft in the form of a lowered tax rate on mineral extraction, but also with the ruble weakening along with the oil price, the result was the ruble price per barrel of oil fell less steeply than it did in dollars.

Rosneft will continue to seek foreign partnership and cooperation for its offshore Arctic ventures. Non-Western firms appear to be of increasing interest, due largely to Western sanctions. However, Western firms are finding ingenious ways to remain relevant in the Russian Arctic market. In fact, US and European energy firms are still able to bid publicly on Russian Arctic proposals by exploiting a loophole that says the sanctions do not apply to an energy firm's foreign subsidiaries. If the US and European firms are part of a consortium with a foreign firm, they are not technically doing business directly with Russia. The same goes for bans on importing Russian Arctic energy—indirect European imports via third parties are actively occurring.

Both the low oil price and sanctions have slowed Russia's offshore Arctic development in the short to medium term. In the long term, foreign energy firms are eager to have a stake in Russia's offshore Arctic projects. Whether Russia is bluffing about its ability to explore the offshore Russian Arctic alone remains to be seen, but certainly it will endeavor to do so. With Chinese and Indian interest in the Russian offshore Arctic growing, and firms like ExxonMobil playing the long game from the sidelines, it is evident that the offshore Russian Arctic is still very much open for business.

The story is similar when it comes to Rosneft's onshore Arctic energy game, where Rosneft's flagship project is Vostok Oil. Located in the Taymyr Peninsula of the Russian High North, the project is evidence of unprecedented Russian Arctic industrialization. Home to an estimated 5 billion tons of oil, Vostok is expected to produce roughly 100 million tons of oil per year by 2030. Easy access to the NSR via ports in the region will ensure ease of delivery from Vostok to Russia's Asian and European customers. Vostok Oil will also build and operate its own fleet of oil tankers and ice-class vessels. In 2020, Singapore's Trafigura became the first major partner in Vostok, acquiring a 10 percent stake. This was sold in July 2022 to NordAxis—a Hong Kong registered trading firm. It is likely Indian and Chinese firms will soon join the Vostok Oil team as shareholders too. Vostok Oil is set to develop the oil and gas province of Taymyr, and along with that, it plans to build some fifteen towns in the province to support the labor-intensive industry. Two airports are slated for development, and the Vostok Oil endeavor is expected to create 130,000 jobs. Well, at least those are the Kremlin planning stats for Rosneft's Vostok venture.

Further collaboration between Russian energy firms and international partners is on display in other onshore Russian Arctic megaprojects. Liquified natural gas (LNG) ventures Yamal LNG and Arctic LNG-2, from Russian private firm Novatek, are also attracting vast global interest. Figure 5-3 illustrates key onshore Arctic ventures.

Despite not being state owned, Novatek is nonetheless closely tied (read: toes the line) to the Kremlin. Owned by Putin-ally oligarch Leonid Mikhelson, Novatek might be privately owned and operated, but its orbit is Kremlin sanctioned. It is worth noting France's TotalEnergies also owns a 19.4 percent stake in Novatek, a stake which it has not divested—merely "written off" since late 2022 to signal European solidarity with Ukraine. In the onshore Russian Arctic, Novatek leads the way in cultivating and managing cooperative joint energy ventures with foreign firms. Online in 2017, Yamal LNG was running at full capacity (three LNG trains) by 2019, producing 16.5 million tons of LNG per year. A fourth LNG train was added in 2019 to lift Yamal LNG's capacity to 17.4 million tons per year. (Here, a "train" refers to an LNG plant's liquefication and purification facility, or the machines that convert natural gas to LNG.) Novatek's stake in Yamal is 50.1 percent, France's TotalEnergies and China's CNCP both hold 20 percent shares and the balance of 9.9 percent is held by Beijing's Silk Road

Fund. The Silk Road Fund is the Chinese government's investment fund that finances projects across the Eurasian sphere under Beijing's "One Belt, One Road" initiative. Further evidence of Moscow's international engagement on the strategically crucial Yamal project is the fact that the purpose-built LNG vessels—the Arc7 series—were constructed by South Korea's Daewoo Shipbuilding and Marine Engineering. South Korea built fifteen Arc7 LNG vessels between 2017 and 2019. Most Yamal LNG exports are tied to long-term (twenty- to thirty-year) contracts.

Arctic LNG-2 is another Novatek project steeped in cooperation with international firms. This project is based some 70 kilometers across Ob Bay from Yamal LNG. Despite technically being a floating plant (where liquification of gas will occur on slightly offshore moored platforms), which implies technical challenges, Arctic LNG-2 is meant to be online by the end of 2023, although sanctions appear to be slowing Russia's progress. Arctic LNG-2 is slated to have an annual production capacity of 19.8 million tons of LNG. Novatek holds a 60 percent share in the project. China's CNPC and CNOOC firms each hold 10 percent, and 10 percent is held by a consortium made up of Japanese firms Mitsui and Jogmec. The final 10 percent is held by France's TotalEnergies. The firm 'exited' the grassroots venture in 2022, simply writing off the loss. A number of European firms were engaged to design and support engineering aspects of the Arctic LNG-2 venture, including Germany's Siemens, Norway's Olav Olsen, and Italy's Saipen. Following Russia's sustained aggression toward Ukraine, many of these firms have since withdrawn support. Some forty-two Arc7 LNG carriers are required for the Arctic LNG-2 project. While early indications saw foreign shipyards in South Korea continuing to build these vessels, western sanctions have since stymied these plans.

Novatek has more plans underway for the Gydan and Yamal Peninsula zones of the Russian Arctic. By 2030, the firm hopes to break ground on at least four more mega-LNG ventures, including Arctic LNG-1, 2, and 3 as well as Ob-LNG. It is uncertain whether these LNG ventures will secure competitive contracts in Asia (and Europe) and have earmarked enough capacity in an Arc7 fleet to actually deliver

Figure 5-3. Key Novatek Arctic Projects

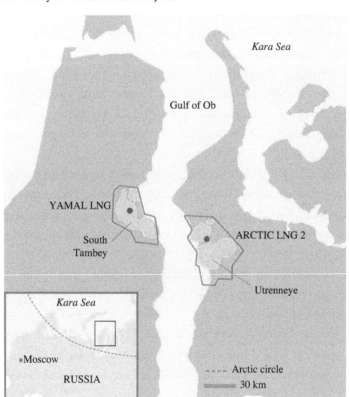

Source: novatek.ru.

on (assumed) demand, it is also unknown which foreign firms will secure investment stakes in these megaprojects.

These two case studies provide evidence of Russian efforts to seek
cooperative arrangements in the Russian Arctic, whether in state-state
agreements or in international joint ventures and partnerships with energy firms. As for the Barents Sea agreement, Russia did not necessarily have to strike a deal with Norway, because a decade later, there has
been very little development. Delineating the disputed zone, and thus
ceding territory to Norway, was evidently part of an actively conces-
sionary policy on Russia's part.

Likewise, the commercial dealings of Rosneft in the offshore Russian Arctic also indicate a strong interest in cooperating with non-Russian firms, albeit with less than ideal results. Onshore, however, it appears to be a very different tale, with Russian energy ventures experiencing no shortage of international interest and partnerships. The 2014 sanctions and low oil price have complicated the commercial operational environment for all, but this has not stopped all foreign energy firms from lining up partnerships with Moscow in the Russian Arctic. Russian Arctic offshore oil reserves may one day—perhaps in another thirty years—be required in accordance with assumed supply-demand rules of the global energy system. Global energy firms plan for the long-term and are likely well aware of the potential need to develop Arctic ventures decades before they become profitable.

Novatek's LNG ventures in the Russian Arctic already illustrate the breadth of international cooperation Russia seeks to ensure that its energy projects deliver results. Cooperation features quite strongly in Russia's Arctic commercial and political dealings. It is a key component of the Kremlin's long-term fiscal business case.

Of course, the popular neorealist "resource race" theories fail to account for such cooperation. Yet, these notions of Russian exceptionalism and neoimperialist objectives cannot explain why Russia agreed to split previously claimed territory with Norway. Putin's Russia actively seeks such cooperative joint ventures in the Arctic energy realm. Sure, Russian failure, until now, to invest in necessary offshore Arctic technology and sovereign capabilities has made foreign energy partnerships necessary. But this aside, cooperation with foreign energy firms is Russia's new normal in the Arctic resource sphere.

Certainly, Russia's array of joint ventures with foreign firms is manipulated by Putin for domestic political gain. By demonstrating continued foreign interest in accessing Russia's Arctic resource bounty, Putin can exploit the sentiment of Eastern and rising state eagerness for doing business with Russia. While commercial engagement and project partnership are largely on Russian terms and work in Russia's favor, they are cooperative nonetheless.

6

A "NEW" COLD WAR?

*"WE USED TO SAY THAT IN THE HIGH NORTH WE HAVE LOW
TENSIONS AND WHAT WE'VE SEEN IN THE LAST YEARS IS
INCREASED CHALLENGES."*

—J. STOLTENBERG

If Russia's Arctic interest is built from a legitimate territorial footprint and Russian geoeconomic strategy in the region necessitates cooperation, then why do murmurs of Arctic conflict persist? Where do the connotations of an Arctic security "meltdown" and whispers of a "new" cold war originate? Are tensions really increasing? These are complex questions to answer. But they are not new. The notion of Arctic conflict is steeped in international history, since the region has served as a strategic frontier for centuries.

The Arctic region, particularly the European Arctic, was a critical maritime arena during both World Wars. Further, it has always represented a crucial sea line of communication (a primary maritime route) between North America and Europe. The Cold War era saw the region featured in popular culture as the direct frontier through which the Soviets might invade American homes. Indeed, the Arctic has remained home to Russia's strategic nuclear arsenal. So, there is nothing "new" in the notion of the Arctic hosting great conflict.

Yet the idea of a new cold war or looming conflict in the Arctic persists. Indeed, postulating future frontiers of great power conflict and clashes keeps the strategist's world turning—and think tank funds flowing. Insistent calls of a new cold war in the Arctic are fueled in much the same way most global security narratives are—by the media. The contemporary, universal hollowing out of credible media reportage and a lax public interest in weeding fact from fiction have exacerbated the challenge of countering perceptions of Arctic war. This challenge is made more difficult by both the proliferation of the 24-hour news cycle and the rise of social media platforms wading into political affairs—often serving as a one-stop shop for individuals to access news content.

In the Arctic war narrative, Russia is (spoiler alert) cast as the villain. What this book has tried to do is illustrate why this approach might not be helpful. I have outlined the drivers of Russian Arctic strategy to argue two things. First, Russia's Arctic interest and position are legitimate. Whether by way of geography, international legal norms, or history, one cannot deny Russia's majority stake in the Arctic. Second, it is difficult to ignore evidence. Despite worsening strategic ties between Russia and the West, primarily over Ukraine, war has not returned to the Arctic zone.

For at least twenty years, the Arctic has been a zone of predictability and entrenched circumpolar communication. Table 6-1 offers a snapshot of the extent of Russia-West cooperation in the Arctic as of early 2023. It highlights the reality of widespread, persistent cooperation between the Arctic Five powers within the region. The domestic US debate over whether to ratify the UN Convention on the Law of the Sea (UNCLOS) long predates the Vladimir Putin presidency and is not a response to Russian Arctic ambitions, so the US failure to ratify is not considered a signal of an uncooperative Arctic agenda. In terms of the region's forum for military dialogue, the Arctic Security Forces Roundtable (ASFR), Russia has suspended its participation since events surrounding Ukraine in 2014 but has still maintained membership.[1]

Table 6-1. *Precedent of Arctic Five Cooperation within the Arctic*

	Russia	US	Norway	Denmark	Canada
Avenue					
Arctic Council	✓	✓●	✓●	✓●	✓●
Agreement on Cooperation on Aeronautical and Maritime Search and Rescue	✓	✓	✓	✓	✓
Agreement on Enhancing International Arctic Scientific Cooperation	✓	✓	✓	✓	✓
Marine Oil Pollution Preparedness and Response Agreement	✓	✓	✓	✓	✓
Arctic Security Forces Roundtable	✓●	✓	✓	✓	✓
Agreement on the Conservation of Polar Bears	✓	✓	✓	✓	✓
UNCLOS	✓	✓●●	✓	✓	✓
Polar Code	✓	✓	✓	✓	✓
Agreement to Prevent Unregulated High Seas Fisheries in the Central Arctic Ocean	✓	✓	✓	✓	✓
International Maritime Organization	✓	✓	✓	✓	✓
International Arctic Science Committee	✓	✓	✓	✓	✓

Key	
✓	Signatory
●	Suspended
●●	Not Ratified

Source: Compiled by author.

Despite Moscow's suspended participation in the ASFR, state-to-state defense dialogue and ministerial communication (at least publicly) did continue until the March 2022 decision by Western states to pause Arctic Council activity. And despite this pause, backchannels of unofficial communication have endured between Russia and its Arctic neighbors. This further dilutes the notion that Russia and the West are headed for war in the Arctic.

Russian Arctic strategy consists of relatively unsurprising drivers. The securitization of Russia's vast open and increasingly active Arctic border, as well as protection of its economic assets, is central to Russian strategy. It is this securitization process that continues to attract international media attention and to serve as a roadblock for levelheaded discourse on Arctic security and Russia's role within it.

Even though Russia-US relations are at their lowest point since the end of the Cold War, there is still an avenue for communication and dialogue within the Arctic context. Russia set a cooperative precedent through its adherence to international law in the region, demonstrated by Russia's engagement with the Commission on the Limits of the Continental Shelf (CLCS); various search and rescue activities with Arctic Five neighbors; and joint military activities with Norway.[2] Russia has maintained its commitment to fostering a cooperative Arctic environment, as indicated through its July 2015 signing of the Arctic Ocean fisheries ban moratorium.[3] The agreement to ban commercial fishing in the central Arctic Ocean entered into force in June 2021, signed by the Arctic Five and Arctic Council observers such as China, South Korea, and Japan, as well as the external actors like the European Union (EU).

The fisheries ban had been under negotiation since early 2014, but Russia's actions in Ukraine soon brought discussions to a halt. However, this did not stymie multilateral action for long. The signing of the agreement by Russia in 2015 and the ban's taking effect in 2021 signal that parties found avenues for Arctic dialogue with Russia to continue. The 2014 creation of the Arctic Coast Guard Forum is a further indication of dialogue and cooperation between Russia and the West on military-security issues within the Arctic, despite tensions further afield.

For Russia, the Arctic also represents a conduit for international prestige and international relevance. Russia's Arctic strategy is informed, like its overall foreign and strategic policy, by the desire to consolidate what the Russian political class believes is its rightful great

power status. But here, Russia's great power quest does not lead necessarily to military confrontation. Russian Arctic strategy is not driven
by a military-expansionist agenda. However, Russian aggression elsewhere has colored the common reading of Russia in the Arctic. The
process of securitizing Russia's Far North territory should not of itself
be deemed aggressive.

Despite calls of an expansionist Russia, Moscow has still opted to
await the CLCS ruling on the matter of its extended continental shelf
claim. With three nations providing evidence of their continental shelves
extending along the underwater Lomonosov Ridge, the claimants will
likely be asked to resolve the overlapping claims among themselves.
Denmark's claim extends far beyond the North Pole and into Russian
Arctic territory. Both Russia and Denmark are planning ahead, knowing
full well that the CLCS could take more than a decade to consider the
evidence. In a formal response to the UN regarding the extended continental shelf claim from Denmark, Russia noted that the two nations had
cooperated at all stages of each other's continental claim process. This
statement by Russia ended with a note that the question of who "owns"
the seabed of the North Pole will ultimately be decided via bilateral or
multilateral "negotiation and on the basis of international law."[4]

The Arctic has been sheltered from external "ups and downs" between Russia and the West primarily because the Arctic Five powers
have successfully branded the Arctic as a global zone of peace and cooperation[5]—at least in practice, although some appear to have "missed
the memo." Indeed, under the Joe Biden presidency, shared climate
change challenges and an interest in promoting Arctic stability (read:
keep China out) have served as a blueprint for US engagement with
Russia within the Arctic. With overwhelming areas of shared interest
in the Arctic, the region has remained safeguarded from tensions
prevailing outside the High North. In 2015, the US took up its two-
year Arctic Council chair, and despite the 2014 Ukraine events, the key
objective was to maintain a window for cooperation with Russia—
which it did at the time.

From a purely commercial standpoint, Russian onshore energy
ventures in the Arctic are "thriving" despite being sidelined, given the

complicated international political context. Igor Veselov, head of the Russian Emergencies Ministry's representation in the EU, confirmed that "despite the difficult international situation, we have good relations with the United States and with other neighbours regarding Arctic cooperation."[6] This sentiment is echoed by Admiral Robert Papp, the US State Department's former special representative for the Arctic, who said, "Our cooperation is very strong. The Secretary of State [John Kerry] and [Russian Foreign] Minister Lavrov often hold talks. We hope that Minister Lavrov will attend our events in the future. I don't know any problem in the world that can be solved by stopping communication."[7]

There are growing calls for a revised mandate for the Arctic Council or the creation of a new body to deal with military-security challenges in the Arctic. Something along these lines was expected to be proposed by Moscow on the sidelines of its 2021–2023 Arctic Council chair. Indeed, any potential body or conduit for Arctic security dialogue will be a nonstarter if Russia is not at the development table.

Realistically, the key challenge of the Arctic has nothing to do with a resource clash or staving off the "new cold war" between Russia and the US. The likely challenge is a collective question of how to exploit Arctic resources safely and sustainably. Arctic Five state Norway released a 2020 Arctic white paper that clearly featured these two priorities. References to a "green Arctic economy," sustainable development of energy deposits, and the emerging potential of hydrogen to fuel Arctic shipping are all garnering increased airtime in the Arctic context. These Arctic opportunities bond the Arctic Five states together, and shared challenges related to delivering on the economic potential of the Arctic further incentivise the states' cooperation. While most of Arctic is clearly delineated, environmental challenges do not recognize sovereign borders. Indeed, Arctic Five powers are aware of this reality, and behind closed doors it would appear collaborative and cooperative discussions are necessary.

Climate change is opening up the Arctic, and global energy insecurity is propelling interest; these notions are fanned by hot takes on the internet. But constructive governance of the region remains a priority for the Arctic Five powers. Those at the table recognize good governance is an impossible feat if cooperation between the Arctic Five ceases entirely. This is not constructive for the Arctic geopolitical narrative. Preexisting notions of Russia, or expectations of Russian strategic playbooks beyond the Arctic, do not apply neatly to the High North. Attempts to cut and paste Moscow's assertive foreign policy in the Middle East or Eastern Europe to the Arctic zone will simply result in strategic fog.

Efforts to isolate Russia from a region it considers to be not only the cornerstone of its economic future, but also strategically significant to its international standing, will likely backfire. Such policies might back the Kremlin into a corner it will most definitely feel compelled to fight its way out of. While Russia's economy is increasingly burdened by Western sanctions, Moscow has recently made crucial headway with its Northern Sea Route (NSR) transport corridor, which could have far-reaching economic and geopolitical consequences. For much of the past decade, analysts have said the NSR is merely a pipe dream. It does not help that Putin has mandated lofty visions of the NSR delivering 80 million tons per year to customers. Congestion in the existing maritime corridors will only continue to rise, threatening supply security for much of the energy market. In its role of Arctic Council chair for 2021–2023, Russia continued to promote the NSR as a hallmark of Russia's cooperative Arctic agenda. Despite the NSR tariff potential and windfalls for the Kremlin, the bigger prize for Russia is that a competitive NSR will theoretically gift Moscow with control over a vast amount of global trade. Whether any of this eventuates is another question all together.

PUTIN, TRUMP, AND BIDEN WALK INTO A BAR . . .

The Arctic is a natural geopolitical theater for Russia-US tensions. History, geography, and contemporary political discourse further sharpen the Arctic frontier for both Washington and Moscow. While the zone might host competition, there is little basis for this competition to spill over into Arctic conflict. Nonetheless, under US president

Donald Trump, a pointed US-Arctic "America first" interest emerged. In line with efforts to roll back Barack Obama's environmental record (like exiting the Paris Climate Accord), Trump worked to reverse Obama's protectionist legacy in the US Arctic. From a publicized interest in "buying" Greenland and a memo to plug the polar icebreaker "gap," to selling off licenses to drill in the Alaskan Arctic Refuge, Trump recast US domestic interest in the Arctic.

The 2016 election was to be the reset of the reset for US-Russia relations. But for all the talk of relationship resets and warm ties between Putin and Trump, the Trump era ended with very little to show for this "bromance." The Arctic represented a viable avenue for strides forward in the bilateral relationship. Russia-US maritime borders had long been delineated, and engagement and cooperation were alive and well, both within the Arctic Council context and among policymakers in each country. Quite simply, Obama's legacy delivered a road map for Russia-US cooperation in the Arctic context that required little more than following it. Under Trump, not only did ties fail to intensify in the Arctic, but also the administration appeared to chuck out the road map altogether.

A watershed moment for the Arctic Five states (and the world) in terms of US abdication of its Arctic-stewardship role under Obama was probably the 2019 Arctic Council Ministerial Meeting in Rovaniemi, Finland. In a speech by then US secretary of state Mike Pompeo, littered with factual inaccuracies and a brash delivery, even Canada found itself in Pompeo's crosshairs. Referring to what he called an ongoing feud, Pompeo noted Canada's "illegitimate" claim over the Northwest Passage (NWP) was at odds with Washington's view that it is an international waterway. He then spoke in condescending terms of the Arctic Council, stating it has "had the luxury of focusing almost exclusively on scientific collaboration, cultural matters, and on environmental research." Confused attendees wondered if Pompeo was aware this was in fact the actual mandate of the Arctic Council.

Following the 2019 Rovaniemi meeting, the divergence between US and Russian Arctic positions became more pronounced. Trump's administration viewed the region as an "arena for power and for competition" yet displayed no real leadership in stewarding the region through the challenges. Indeed, the 11th Arctic Council Ministerial Meeting went down in history as the first time the meeting had produced no ministerial declaration. Abroad, Trump's US was cast as the Arctic Council spoiler. Things were not any better at home in Arctic affairs. Throughout the Trump presidency, US Coast Guard polar cutter capabilities continued to fall into disrepair. While Russia was ordering icebreakers and planning procurement into the 2030s, the US in 2023 still only operates two icebreakers.

The Trump presidency also oversaw the reduction of Arctic budgets. The National Science Foundation (NSF) and Environmental Protection Agency (EPA) attracted huge cuts—particularly the US Office for Polar Programs and the Directorate for Geosciences. Likewise, the National Oceanic and Atmospheric Administration (NOAA) lost all funding for its Sea Grant and Coastal Zone Management programs.

Early on, Trump moved to hand key portfolios to climate skeptics and representatives of Big Oil. Scott Pruitt was handed the leadership of the EPA, an agency he had sued over a dozen times for environmental legislation overreach when he was Oklahoma's attorney general. Pruitt left the EPA post only to be replaced by coal industry alumnus Andrew Wheeler. Trump then appointed ExxonMobil's Rex Tillerson secretary of state, essentially making energy firms a representative to the Arctic Council forum. In line with the high attrition rate of the Trump administration, Tillerson was replaced with Mike Pompeo, who has strong ties to Koch Energy and is a staunch climate skeptic.

Under Trump, the Arctic lost the small amount of momentum it had gained under Obama in the US strategic outlook. The region did not get even a single mention in the 2018 National Defense Strategy; similarly, Trump's 2017 National Security Strategy failed to engage with the climate change challenge and only mentioned the Arctic in passing with regard to multilateral institution building. Not even the deepwater port that was long promised and desperately needed in Nome, Alaska, was built.

Perhaps the sole achievement of Trump's abandonment of the Arctic region is that this move ensured for some time the continuation of low tension between Russia and the West. In 2016, the promise of a Trump White House was tantalizing for Moscow. Russia foresaw the relaxation (perhaps scrapping) of US sanctions on Russian Arctic energy projects. Indeed, with the former CEO of ExxonMobil sitting in the secretary of state role, Moscow probably expected the Rosneft offshore Arctic venture to come back online. However, none of these eventuated; sanctions remained and, indeed, were strengthened.

Repeated engine fires on its *Healy* vessel meant that the US entered 2021 down to one functioning ice breaker, the *Polar Star*. Pulled from her usual Antarctic missions, the vessel replaced the *Healy* for the 2021 Arctic summer season. In the final six months of Trump's presidency, a presidential memorandum was released tasking relevant bodies to come up with a plan to close Washington's icebreaker gap. The allotted time came and went without any real result or clarity around next steps to be taken for the US to rectify its lackluster polar capabilities.

With the Biden presidency, the US appeared to return to the Arctic—albeit, led by its armed forces. A litany of strategies dropped in 2021: In March, the US Army produced its first ever Arctic strategy. Focused on "regaining Arctic dominance," the strategy underscored a clear shift in mentality toward the Arctic region. The US Navy's 2021 Arctic strategy, the 2021 updated Arctic policy documents from the Department of Homeland Security and the Coast Guard, and the US Air Force's 2020 Arctic strategy all signaled a somewhat unilateral inward focus when it came to the region. Projections of stability and aspirations for regional leadership were replaced with a siege mentality. References to existing and thriving regional cooperation were supplanted by great power competition conceptualizations across most of these updated or new doctrines coming out of Washington. Some even went so far as to lump Russia in with China as neoimperialist actors in the Arctic—oddly missing the fact that Russia is already the largest Arctic stakeholder. But Biden did return environmental security to the US conception of its Arctic interest. For Washington, nowhere are the implications of climate change more apparent than in the US Arctic.

Trump was unable to forge ties with Russia in the Arctic, and he was under an air of suspicion with regard to his pro-Putin outlook. So, perhaps any close policy collaboration between Trump and Russia in the Arctic would have become a sideshow for domestic political point scoring. On the other hand, Biden has repeatedly drawn red lines for Russia and called Putin out. Therefore, any bilateral US-Russia collaboration in the Arctic space or engagement on mutual interests in the region will be viewed as legitimate. After decades of avoiding serious climate action in the Russian Arctic, the Kremlin spent most of 2020 recalibrating its outlook on the climate threat. The clearest indication of the securitization of global warming under Putin is that Russia's 2020 Arctic Development Strategy singled out climate change as a roadblock in Moscow's efforts to implement and deliver on Arctic interests. Therefore, mutual interest in mitigating climate change in the Arctic could serve as a basis for closer Russia-US engagement.

Further areas of commonality in the Arctic for Moscow and Washington include their respective "retooling" agendas. Washington must work to rebuild its ice-breaking capabilities, and there already are plans to house most of the US Pacific air power in the Arctic state of Alaska. Russia continues to industrialize its Arctic zone, and in turning it into Moscow's resource base for the next century, further efforts to secure these investments with dual-use military installations are likely. While these Arctic developments are an opportunity to engage on lessons learned and best practices, it is probable these areas will also intensify competition between Moscow and Washington. Indeed, the Bering Strait may emerge in the crosshairs of the US-Russia relationship. A Bering Strait that is busier and congested with liquified natural gas (LNG) tankers, or potentially, more Chinese military vessels, may shape up to be a real choke point.

For now at least, Russia's Arctic priority remains the western Russian Arctic zone, specifically the Yamal Peninsula. The majority of Russia-West tensions will therefore continue to emerge in this European Arctic region, potentially extending out to the Greenland-Iceland-

United Kingdom (GIUK) gap. However, this does not negate the strategic value of Russia's eastern Arctic flank. Russian cooperation with international partners is also a reality of the underdeveloped Russian eastern Arctic zone. Along the Laptev and Kara Seas, US firm ExxonMobil remains interested in offshore oil plans. Despite one of the biggest write-downs of its commercial history, ExxonMobil's offshore Russian Arctic investments located here are still on the books. Again, energy giants think long-term and pragmatically.

Any real opportunity for Russia-US and broader US reengagement with the Arctic will likely build upon Washington's 2022 National Strategy for the Arctic Region. Early signs, however, indicate that US policy has been unable to move away from the reactionary, great power contest-ridden views of the Arctic. However, reactionary strategy is rarely ever smart policy, nor does it prove successful in communicating the contours of long-term interests. Alliances can shift, powers can wax and wane, security threats come and go, technology advances, but geography is fixed. The US is an Arctic Five power and owes the region (and itself) a considered, cohesive long-term Arctic strategy.

While the world probably expected too much from both Obama and Trump in terms of long-term visions for the Arctic, Biden stepped into the driver's seat at the right time. Indeed, much of geopolitics is about timing. Since 2016, Russian Arctic interests have been more or less clearly articulated to the world. Moscow has set about building and delivering what it said it would in the Russian Arctic zone. With this sense of predictability and pragmatic planning, it is easier for neighboring states to engage with Moscow within the Arctic and formulate their own Arctic initiatives. The cloud of historical preconceptions of a "spoiling" Russia in the Arctic is unfounded, and there are now years of consistent Arctic collaboration to show for this.

Today, Moscow is not planting flags on the Arctic seabed or undertaking a domestic public relations program heralded by Arctic exceptionalism. Russia's domestic narrative is the unprecedented industrialization of the Russian Arctic and the primacy of a socioeconomic agenda for achieving (sometimes lofty) Arctic visions based around "sustainable resource development." Likewise, Arctic Five states Norway, Canada, and Denmark (Greenland) are reorientating their Arctic resource development agendas to be framed in terms of "sustainable development." Norway's Arctic energy ventures are booming, in part due to the EU ban on Russian gas. These states are not walking away from their resource potential. This is another unifying element for the Arctic.

Biden likely seeks an environmental legacy, and any such agenda for the region would have to be built on cooperative foundations with Russia. After all, environmental challenges know no maritime or territorial boundaries. Any effective climate agenda from the White House will necessitate Russia-US collaboration.

7

FUTURE ARCTIC HISTORIES

"IF SOMEONE WERE TO INVADE THE CANADIAN ARCTIC,
MY FIRST TASK WOULD BE TO RESCUE THEM."

—GENERAL W. NATYNCZYK

It is unlikely that military conflict will eventuate in the Arctic, not only because of a lack of serious intent to go to war in the region, but also because of a broad lack in current capability to do so. As an operational environment, the frigid Arctic Ocean—characterized by extreme weather events and long periods of complete darkness—is a theater that would be hell for individuals, for technology and hardware, for resupply missions, and for military planning. Of course, never say never. Perhaps as readers peruse this book, World War III is raging in the Arctic?

Russian Arctic strategy under Putin is driven mostly by routine factors that do not necessarily reflect an expansionist agenda. Unlike Russia's foreign policy approach elsewhere (for example, Ukraine since 2014), Putin's Russia has consistently approached the Arctic in a broadly cooperative manner. Given Putin's foreign policy style, there is still the potential for Russia to throw its weight around in the Arctic. But the intrenched international collaboration and partnerships that are allowing Russia to deliver on its strategic resource agenda in the Arctic would be unsanctioned casualties of any aggressive agenda. Any increase in the assertiveness of Russia's Arctic narrative will be driven by a hypernationalist, largely domestic agenda. The notion of a "global Russian Arctic," in which the Arctic region is wholly dominated by Russia, is an exaggeration of Russia's capabilities and its intentions.

Domestic economic pressures and pandemic-related delays have slowed the development of new major offshore Russian Arctic projects. Western sanctions have limited Russian access to Western capital and Western partnerships. And yet, much of Russia's onshore Arctic zone has continued to grow, particularly on the Yamal Peninsula. Russia has overcome external challenges and tensions placed on its Arctic industrialization agenda by reverting to a more moderate and cooperative approach overall, especially in Russia's western Arctic region. For Russia, cash flow, investment, and technology from foreign firms are vital to getting liquified natural gas (LNG) projects up and running. Securing long-term customer contracts in Asia has assisted many of the current Russian Arctic LNG ventures in gaining international commercial viability.

It is difficult to separate Russia's military-security footprint from its industrializing program in the Arctic. Of course, Russia's military interests (particularly the Northern Sea Fleet) predate the contemporary Arctic geopolitical picture. In painting the Arctic as a theater of renewed cold war tensions, many forget the realities of the actual Cold War period and what it meant for the Arctic. US and Soviet military gear substantially outnumbered Washington and Moscow's arms today in the region. The ideological "bloc" factor that once carved up the Arctic Five is no longer a tangible component of the Arctic narrative. Today, sustainable development of the Arctic appears to be the unifying Arctic identity, if not ideology. As this book has discussed, Moscow has recalibrated its security capabilities on its wide-open (and increasingly busy) Arctic flank. This has involved reopening Soviet-era bases, building new military infrastructure, and investing in capabilities to deliver on commitments to patrolling the largest search and rescue zone in the Arctic region.

Russia's securitization agenda is not dissimilar from that of other Arctic Five powers. Neighboring states have stepped up Arctic commands and institutions like the North American Aerospace Defense Command (NORAD), and the North Atlantic Treaty Organization (NATO) has recalibrated its outlook to cater to intensified activity in the region. Sweden and Finland now plan to join NATO. This will then mean Russia is the sole Arctic Eight power (states with territory above the Arctic Circle) without a NATO membership. The evolution of military planning is such that any pragmatic state continues to plan regardless of the actual contemporary, tangible security threat, because no military can be effective in last-minute terms. No forward-thinking military or body tasked with perpetual defense of homeland or national interests, simply sits on its hands, and waits for the threat to materialise. Even military-security initiatives in the Arctic necessitate collaboration. While Russia has taken up invitations to observe western-led military exercises in the region, it is the case that any exercise planned to occur in nearby zones to the Russian Arctic— are often flagged prior with Russian defense officials. Even at the depths of strained tensions between Russia and the West, behind the scenes avenues of communication are kept open and are utilized.

A traditional neorealist reading of Russian strategy fails to account for Russia's cooperative behavior and overall modus operandi in the Arctic. For the neorealist, Georgia, Ukraine, and Crimea follow a distinct pattern of Russian foreign policy. However, Russia's Arctic strategy represents a distinct deviation from the neorealist framework. After more than a decade of waiting for Russia to repeat its expansionist playbook in the Arctic, realists still fail to explain this divergence and continue to overlook the primacy of geography in the Arctic political context.

The Arctic is a unique challenge in that it has become both a major regional geopolitical theater and a crucial global environmental issue. Not only are these key strategic issues for the Arctic Five powers, but also Arctic environmental developments are of great concern to the planet as a whole. Asian coastal states will be increasingly affected by the intense weather systems that the changing Arctic environment creates. New shipping potential also poses an economic threat to Asian shipping states like Singapore. At the crux of this regional versus global conception of the Arctic is the question of whether the region is a global commons. In international law, a *global commons* refers to su-pranational resource domains. While there is a section of the Central Arctic Ocean that can be deemed international waters or high seas, once the continental shelf debate is resolved between Russia, Canada, and Denmark (and potentially the US), the resources of (and under) the seabed will no longer be considered a supranational resource domain. The debate of whether the Arctic is rightfully classified as a global commons is also complicated by the geographical features of the region, which comprises a pocket of international sea surrounded by territorial seas and long-resolved maritime delineations. This is another aspect of Arctic "exceptionalism." It is also a unifying feature of Arctic Five engagement on Arctic futures—in which the largest stakeholder, Russia, maintains a legitimate seat at the table.

The Russian Arctic energy playbook is about investing in the region as a future economic base and welcoming foreign partnership in ventures. The Arctic represents another divergence for Russian foreign energy strategy under Putin, in that Moscow does not always have the upper hand in commercial negotiations. China often has the edge in energy contract negotiations with Russia—securing a reduced price for Russian gas, given the Kremlin's current political isolation.

While the primacy of energy in Russia's Arctic strategy is evident, notions of Russia as a future energy superpower, however, will require a substantial bolstering of Russian capabilities. Without access to foreign capital and technology, Russia's offshore Arctic exploration has been delayed, and sanctions have been extended time and again. Perhaps the (re)installation of populist European governments in time will change this reality. A silver lining for Putin's Russia is that it has been forced to develop some indigenous technology capabilities. This process has yielded mixed results. Of course, the crisis of corruption throughout the energy and finance sectors in Russia may hinder any real progress. Indeed, despite sanctions, there is no shortage of foreign energy firms seeking to partner with Russia in the Arctic.

Overall, Russian visions of "superpowerdom" are still half-baked. That said, Western commentators have potentially also underestimated the capacity of Russia's Arctic LNG projects. By 2035, Russia seeks to capture 20 percent of the global LNG market, with 70 percent of this export potential originating from its Arctic ventures.[1] For now, it seems that Russia cannot operate alone in the Arctic, as its ambitions are limited by its technology and capital shortcomings. But ultimately, Russia will fill the gap between ambition and capability with capital and technology from foreign partners, likely from the East.

Under Putin, Russia has actively sought cooperation with the West in the Arctic. The question remains, how long will this continue? In 2011, Putin clearly signaled that Russia would "defend [its] own geopolitical interests firmly and consistently."[2] Commitment to cooperation and a determination to vigorously defend Russia's perceived national interest in the Arctic appear to be two sides of the same coin. In the Arctic, Putin's Russia has continued to voice a hard-line, neoimperialist rhetoric and yet deliver a softer cooperative approach to the region as compared with its behavior in the near abroad. This seems at variance with the narrative that depicts the region as an emerging flashpoint of international conflict over access to, and control of, its resources. Such an approach seems to imply that energy is more likely to be a conflict amplifier than a direct cause of conflict. Generally, Russia aims to regain international standing by using energy and has continued to use resources in a coercive way in the near abroad. However, when it comes to the Arctic, Russia seems to prefer measured cooperation.

The global community should expect to see Putin's Russia continuing to cooperate, albeit on Russian terms, in the Arctic. Externally, the changing global energy mix, spurred by the shale revolution and the rise in renewables, complicates the current balance, and will provide Russia's customers with more options in the future. Nonetheless, in the long term, Russian Arctic offshore hydrocarbons might yet be tapped.[3] This book has argued one should not expect to see any serious military confrontation in the Arctic.[4] Today, Russia has near-complete control of its Arctic border. Russia's military deployment and redevelopment of infrastructure are still modest compared to Soviet Arctic levels. Discussion of militarization of the Arctic is therefore somewhat misleading; if anything, there is a return to the normalization of Russia's military presence in the Arctic.

Arctic ice cover is melting, but this does not mean easier access to the region's resource endowment. Just how large the hydrocarbon prize is and whether the Northern Sea Route (NSR) will be a viable option for global transit are points of continuing uncertainty. Likewise, with shale and new sources of energy (including renewables) entering the global energy mix, can offshore Arctic oil compete, given the exorbitant barrel price it will demand? Further, there are outstanding overlapping extended continental shelf claims to consider. The Commission on the Limits of the Continental Shelf (CLCS) cannot rule on claims per se; all parties will have to agree on a compromise.[5] Could Russia reinforce its claims to said sovereign (resource) rights with military might and refuse to negotiate? These are just a few "known unknowns" when it comes to contemporary Arctic geopolitics.

Cooperation between Russia and the West in the Arctic was protected more or less until the February 2022 invasion of Ukraine. As the Russia-Ukraine war rages on, far from resolved conflict has not emerged in the Arctic. Indeed, further "new" lows are consistently found in the Russia-West relationship—from election interference charges to cyberattacks. When it comes to Russia-US ties, the two states are constantly discovering a "new floor" to the depths of post–Cold War tensions.

So, can the Arctic really and truly remain "siloed" from Russia-US tensions elsewhere? This book has argued it can and, there exists strong precedent. Despite overlapping claims dating back to the 1920s, to date there has been no military conflict between the Arctic Five over Arctic territory. Indeed, in 2022, NATO released an updated Strategic Concept which omitted any reference to the "Arctic" (despite NATOs evident interests). This book has sought to shift the focus on Russian Arctic strategy away from what Russia could do in the Arctic and toward the realities of what Putin's Russia will do in the Arctic. Despite Russia's assertive foreign policy elsewhere, it is likely that the Arctic will remain a foreign policy anomaly for Putin's Russia. Indeed, the Arctic will probably remain an incongruity of cooperation between Russia and the international community post-Putin.

This book has offered a strong case for Russian cooperation with the West in the Arctic. It has illustrated how Arctic cooperation results from Russia's technological and investment requirements from the foreign firms; Russia's solid legal case in the Arctic with regard to the extended continental shelf debate; and finally, the strong precedent of cooperation over Arctic matters to date. In coming years, Russia may try to repair relations with the West, where possible, including in the Arctic, and foreign energy and corporations will want to respond positively. Even if tensions persist, the new cold war paradigm will not neatly apply to the notion of conflict over Arctic resources or governance issues.

Russia reassumed the chair of the Arctic Council in 2021. For two years, Moscow will lead the region's sole governance body—whether western engagement remains "paused" or not. There is no logical reason to believe that, under Russian stewardship, the council will oversee such rapid deterioration of the region's status quo that the zone will descend into conflict. Yet, it would be prudent to consider that the Arctic Council is not capable of ensuring status quo cooperation for decades to come. Could the past twenty-plus years of Russian cooperation under Putin in the Arctic context have been merely blind luck? To consider this, I offer three future scenarios across the conflict-cooperation spectrum in the Arctic.

FUTURE ONE: ARCTIC ARMAGEDDON

In this future, the Arctic "turns red," bringing back Washington's Cold War anxieties over Russia's reach across the Arctic. But in this scenario the US must welcome a new player into the Arctic strategic theater: China. Ideologically bound together, Moscow and Beijing unite to overhaul Arctic strategic planning. "Might is right" becomes the marching orders for the Arctic region, and the zone is plunged into conflict. In this future, the Arctic is characterized by an intensified China-Russia relationship resulting in economic coupling, joint ventures, and military exercises. With Washington having long warned of great power competition sharpening in the region, China and Russia indeed delivered. This future is heavy on the doom and gloom.

FUTURE TWO: ARCTIC MELTDOWN

In this future, despite the international focus on great power competition and aggressive actions by Russia in the Arctic, it is all for nothing. There is no Arctic left to fight over. Ravished by climate change, the region turns on its stakeholders and threatens Arctic Five national security across the board. Billions (perhaps trillions) of dollars are needed to fortify northern flanks, not in terms of military hardware but in terms of mitigating infrastructure erosion and bolstering socioeconomic livelihoods against global warming. To date, states have focused largely on maintaining standing armies instead of funding climate mitigation strategies. Ironically, eroded Arctic permafrost means military structures became the first casualties of the morphing Arctic environment. Extreme weather events in the Arctic Ocean make navigation untenable, and thousands of lives are lost in maritime accidents.

FUTURE THREE: ARCTIC ENTENTE
(WITH RUSSIAN CHARACTERISTICS)

A third scenario sees the geopolitical situation remaining as it is: the Arctic status quo survives. Here, Arctic Five actors continue to put forward strategies that safeguard stability and "low tension" in the Arctic. Much of the hot air regarding Russian expansionist activities and the looming new cold war remains outside the Arctic. International cooperation is heralded in the Arctic, and governance continues to be coordinated via the Arctic Council, with the agreed international legal contours of the region remaining robust. As the largest stakeholder, Russia remains a key figure in the Arctic's future. Years of international collaboration to deliver on Moscow's strategic priorities in the Russian Arctic have meant predictability and pragmatism continue to define Moscow's Arctic strategy. Competition bubbles up from time to time, namely via the increased activity within the Arctic region by China, NATO, and the

EU. However, these activities are conducted in line with international law and serve no basis for any state to rewrite the Arctic rulebook.

These three futures are useful for testing the utility of contemporary Arctic assumptions. This book has focused on fact-checking the Arctic Armageddon assessment, the future scenario apparently very popular in most corners of the world. Of course, continuous publication of doctrine and strategy out of Washington casting Beijing and Moscow as Arctic "spoilers" with expansionist agendas serves to cloud reality. But more realistically, a Russia-China relationship that does intensify in the Arctic will remain tied to the energy potential and shipping realms. Here, Moscow will seek to maintain the controlling share of the partnership, and China will jump through Moscow's hoops to ensure access to the NSR and deliver on China's "Polar Silk Road" ambitions. Meanwhile, Russia will actively offset any potential overreliance on Chinese capital and partnership by courting India and the Arab states to dilute any potential Beijing leverage.

Arctic Armageddon aside, the pragmatic Arctic partnership between Russia and China is no alliance, nor will it ever likely be one. Moscow and Beijing have both learned that nations do not have allies but should only seek mutually beneficial relationships. That sentiment frames Sino-Russian engagement in the Russian Arctic. Of the eight members of the Arctic Council, Russia took the most convincing to grant China its observer status in 2013. Moscow approved membership, and with it, legitimacy, on the basis that Beijing explicitly acknowledged the sovereignty of Arctic rim states and reaffirmed its commitment to the legal architecture of the Arctic region, the UN Convention on the Law of the Sea (UNCLOS). China is also engaging in a mutually beneficial arrangement with Russia to access the NSR, which presents attractive savings for Chinese shipping. But Russia has not given China privileged use of the route. Russia has refused entry to Chinese vessels, and those that do pass must abide by Russian transit laws: vessels must have Russian pilots and pay tolls, and Russia must be prewarned about trips. Meanwhile, China is actively engaging with other Arctic rim powers and has commercial ventures, investment plans, and entrenched soft-power strategies in Norway, Canada, Iceland, and Greenland.

There are elements of all three Arctic futures sketched that are viable. Indeed, there are also aspects of each that are already apparent. In rising to the challenge posed by an opening Arctic, Russia will require a decent amount of cooperation to deliver on and realize its strategic national interests. Russia is already hedging its bets against an Arctic Armageddon future by diversifying partners in its Arctic resource ventures. The Arctic Meltdown narrative is less a scenario than a ticking time bomb. Under Biden and Putin, the US and Russia have only recently started to securitize climate change in the Arctic context. Securitizing a problem is a necessary first step in crafting any political response or action. It is likely that, soon enough, climate change will be a collective security issue that outpaces the economic windfalls of the Arctic. The Arctic Meltdown scenario also underscores the shortsightedness of the Arctic great power competition narrative. The "icebreaker gap" that the Trump presidency fixated on becomes a folly when there is no year-round ice to break. While a warming Arctic might yet hand states easier access to hydrocarbons offshore, there is no certainty around exploitation.

It is nonetheless interesting to track the ways in which Arctic Five energy exporters are repackaging resource exploitation in the climate-aware era. Norway is the latest Arctic Five state to jump on the "sustainable development" bandwagon with regard to Arctic hydrocarbons. Sentiments of a "green circular economy" in the Arctic are becoming hallmarks of Arctic Council chairs too. New energy technologies are also ushering in a rebrand of sorts when it comes to hydrocarbon exports by Arctic five states. For example, much of the Arctic shipping industry is looking toward hydrogen power as the future building block of a circular, sustainable green economy in the Arctic.

Aspects of the third future, Arctic Entente, also already exist. Each consecutive Arctic Five strategy document doubles down on the primacy of the Arctic rim states in dictating the region's future. Sentiments of collaboration, cooperation, and dialogue are featured as best practice in Arctic Five politics. A status quo Arctic environment is the path of least resistance and the avenue that offers ample opportunity for regional consensus and collaboration. How long can the Arctic status quo hold? Russia has not grasped opportunities throughout this period of status quo to "grab" territory beyond the Russian Arctic zone. On the question of who holds the sovereign rights to seabed resources of the North Pole, Moscow continues to defer to the CLCS process that is already underway. Furthermore, Arctic maritime disputes—notably with Norway in the Barents Sea—have long been resolved. Although Russia has yet to ratify the 1990 Bering Strait agreement—signed by its Soviet predecessor and ratified by Washington—Moscow has continued to abide by the terms of the delineation agreement. Joint coast guard patrols and search and rescue activities are ongoing in the region between Russia and the US. So, it begs the question, where beyond the Russian Arctic zone is Moscow expanding?

Russia is unlikely to plunge into conflict the region that it holds the largest stake in and to which it has tied its future economic and social security. More likely, Arctic tensions will stem from a misreading of Russian interests or a misunderstanding of basic geography and international law—or perhaps both.

LOOKING AHEAD: THE ARCTIC AS A CONDUIT
FOR RUSSIA-WEST RELATIONS

The Arctic is a complex geostrategic challenge. Perhaps breaking the region into subtheaters better clarifies the expected geopolitical trajectories. There is the European Arctic, on the front lines of Russia's Arctic-located nuclear military might on the Kola Peninsula. The European Arctic is navigating what role, if any, both NATO and the EU should have in the broader Arctic context. European states here, and particularly those in Scandinavia, have long coexisted with Russia.

Then there is the North American Arctic, referring to Canadian and US regional interests. Home to NORAD and of consequence in the evolving NATO-Arctic debate, the North American Arctic is oversimplified as Russia's competing bloc in the region. In fact, Canada and Russia continue to produce sustainable dialogue on the extended continental shelf debate and have a mutual challenge in ensuring the Northwest Passage (NWP) and NSR are acknowledged as internal waters.

The global Arctic is best narrowed to the Central Arctic Ocean. This is the media darling, apparently home to polar bears and pristine white ice. For China, the notion of a global Arctic is expansive and all encompassing; for others, it is the high seas of the Arctic Ocean.

The Russian Arctic, the focus of this book, accounts for over 50 percent of the Arctic region and is home to the future resource base of the Russian Federation. Moscow's conceptualization of national security in the Russian Arctic is deeper than military-security—it is about the future security of Russia's socioeconomic, environmental, developmental, and technological interests.

Overall, these various perceptions of the Arctic facilitate competing interpretations of legitimacy, Arctic Five strategic intent, international law applicability, and assessments of what constitutes security. That is not always a helpful thing.

Indeed, an overlooked component of Arctic geopolitics is the power and potential of interpretation. One often sees what one expects from actors or at least extrapolates preconceptions based on one's own highly politicized interpretation of foreign policy. As such, Red Arctic for some will speak to the Cold War undercurrents of the Arctic—cultivating notions of the return to Soviet-era grand plans underway in the Russian Arctic. For others, it may elicit a warning light of looming catastrophe as the region warms at twice the rate of the rest of the world. Here, Red Arctic foretells the melt of Arctic ice and the geopolitical peril that a rush to resources this might bring about. Red Arctic is also a reminder to stop and consider the sustainability of hydrocarbons in the global energy mix.

Perception is a powerful component of the Arctic geopolitical narrative. One woman's doom and gloom is another woman's opportunity. Indeed, transnational security challenges in the region must involve Arctic stakeholder collaboration. The Arctic is a bellwether for climate change and indigenous peoples' rights and traditions, as well as a "health check" on the durability of international legal agreements. In cautioning against assumptions of Russian expansion and aggressive intent in the region, this book calls for better informed judgment of the real drivers of Russian Arctic strategy under Putin.

AFTERWORD

Publishing a book during a time in which the central character—Putin's Russia—has unleashed devastation and further embroiled itself in war is challenging, to say the least. Such a task is further complicated when the key thesis of said book is that Putin's Russia is a cooperative Arctic stakeholder. However, events since the writing of this book was completed continue to serve as a litmus test for Putin's Arctic strategy. True, active collaboration and cooperation via the Arctic Council remains "frozen," paused while Moscow holds the chairmanship. Indeed, as this chairmanship cycles to Norway in 2023 it is likely that engagement with Russia by way of the Arctic Council will remain paused.

Of note, however, are several long-term implications of protracted suspension in Arctic dialogue. Special Envoy to the Arctic for China Feng Gao noted in October 2022 that Beijing simply would not support or acknowledge the Arctic Council if Russia remained sidelined. Of course, an isolated Russia in the Arctic only advances China's Arctic agenda. Should the West expect a "new" Arctic forum for governance, management, collaboration, and perhaps even military-security affairs? That all sounds rather enticing for China, aligning with Beijing's Polar Silk Road strategy and its resource needs well into the next century.

Due to the polarity that exists in international relations scholarship, the preceding pages may of course appear sympathetic to Putin's Russia in the Arctic "great game." Some readers may find raising the question of how the world—specifically, how Arctic-rim states—rebuild some sort of relationship with Russia in the Arctic as altogether premature. But sooner or later the West is going to have to come back to the cooperation agenda in the Arctic.

Indeed, global reactions to the war in Ukraine are not necessarily uniform—much of the developing world, along with Asia and Africa, continues to abstain from (or veto) United Nations Security Council resolutions denouncing Moscow. Interestingly, many of these states are the emerging energy markets and transportation clients that are eyeing the opening Arctic region—looking at least twenty years ahead to secure their strategic needs.

Red Arctic was written as an audit of Russia's Arctic strategy and composed largely before the invasion of Ukraine in February 2022. That said, the main dynamics of Putin's Arctic agenda and Russian strategy remain in play. Putin's Russia still needs foreign capital and technology to deliver on ambitious Russian Arctic planning to future proof Moscow's economic base. These needs will likely be met by new actors—Middle Eastern and Asian stakeholders are going to take advantage of Western firms' exit from projects. Of course, some states in the Western camp (read Japan) will continue to put national strategic interests first and remain invested in Russian energy projects in the Far East.

The central dynamics of Russian Arctic strategy, inclusive of the need for foreign cooperation and engagement, remain. It is merely a case of new players entering the arena, different foreign stakeholders for Moscow to collaborate with. Of course, this begs the question long term: Will punishing Russia in the Arctic, suspending public cooperation and dialogue, amount to a greater strategic problem for the West when it comes to the Arctic theater? Crucially, there is a "punishment paradox" emerging in the Arctic.

This age of Arctic exceptionalism is gone: the region is no longer a protected sphere of Russia-West engagement and dialogue. There is a litany of second-order effects that stem from the cessation of dialogue with Russia in the Arctic context. Washington should expect new Arctic players, namely China and India, in its polar backyard, with the region set to become a more crowded, and contested, strategic theater.

Make no mistake: Russia is doubling down on ushering in new Arctic stakeholders. Of course, increased investment often leads to a clear business case for enhancing military footprints by stakeholders keen to protect national (economic) interests: just look at China's footprint in Africa. Beijing repeating this strategy in the Russian Arctic is not altogether unlikely.

Further, throughout the Ukraine war and cessation of Arctic engagement, the world has witnessed clear indications of a booming Russia-India relationship. India has long signaled its intent to deepen ties with Russia in the Arctic and in mid-2022 even tabled its first Arctic strategy.

Another new Arctic player taking advantage of prolonged suspension in Arctic dialogue and cooperation is the United Arab Emirates. The UAE has even developed a specialized fleet of ice-hardened container ships to take advantage of Russia's Northern Sea Route.

Putin's Russia remains committed to cooperation and dialogue in the Arctic—only now with different counterparts. But in order to uphold the integrity of certain existing Arctic agreements, cooperation with Russia will need to be re-established. A clear example is the fisheries ban in the Central Arctic Ocean. The initial period covered by the ban extends until 2037, during which time Arctic states will need Russian support if China is to be held accountable for any violations. It is a simple reality that no other Arctic state has the same means that Russia has to counterbalance Beijing.

There are other agreements as well, whose enduring success hinges on engagement with Russia. An increase in Arctic tourism—a region with lots of natural danger and few resources to respond to emergencies—makes ensuring an adequate maritime search-and-rescue capability a priority. This is a challenge if over 50 percent of the maritime resources in the region are cut out of the dialogue. Likewise, addressing Arctic environmental and marine catastrophes and facilitating Arctic scientific cooperation requires dialogue between all Arctic states.

Russia's Arctic strategy remains geared toward cooperation, meaning foreign investment, partners, and indeed foreign clients and markets. Neighboring Arctic states ought to re-establish cooperation, however limited or restrained, in the Arctic region. This is not an argument against measures taken to punish Russia for its aggression toward Ukraine, nor to condone Russia's war on Ukraine. This is a case for protecting what is left of the Arctic's status quo and the atmosphere of low tension that has been the norm for some forty years.

Of course, maybe the opportunity has come and gone. Perhaps in time we will see that Russia has little to no interest in reengaging with the West in the Arctic. The West has essentially pulled the pin on engagement and dialogue with Russia in the Arctic and, according to the new 2022 United States Arctic Strategy, this will remain the norm for "the foreseeable future."

This means that new players, new expectations, and essentially new interpretations of international rules are no doubt set to emerge in the Arctic. *Red Arctic* has argued there is a fundamental cooperative gearing to Russian Arctic strategy under Putin. This is charted via state-state engagements in the Arctic, characterized by the resolution to the decades-old maritime dispute over the Barents Sea between Norway and Russia. The cooperative requirement of Russian Arctic strategy is also illustrated through Russia's need to attract foreign energy corporations in the Russian Arctic to deliver on projects. These central dynamics remain, despite (even) worse tensions between Russia and the West.

Indeed, it is valuable to return to the three future scenarios for the Arctic, as described in chapter 7, to consider the evolution of Arctic geopolitics and the continued fallout from Russia's war in Ukraine. It would appear elements of both Future One (Arctic Armageddon) and Future Two (Arctic Meltdown) are emerging. Today, Washington's Cold War anxieties have indeed returned to the region with Beijing featuring as the peer competitor. Only China has been offered an avenue to compete with Washington, much closer to home than the South China Sea. Indeed, should China follow through with threats to disengage with the Arctic Council under Norwegian chairmanship,

Washington should expect intensified China-Russia relations in the Arctic—certainly, in the realm of economic and joint ventures, but likely also in the sphere of joint military exercises. Given the investment at risk, however, shots being fired is unlikely given the strategic interest for China to maintain secure lines of resource supplies and transportation avenues in the Russian Arctic. Could the West have a brewing China-Russia confrontation in the Arctic on its hands?

The continued lapse in scientific and climate collaboration between the West and the Arctic's largest stakeholder appears set to deliver on the worst aspects of Future Two (Arctic Meltdown). Ecological disasters abound, with the knock-on effects not confined to the Russian Arctic Zone. Likewise, the continued suspension of scientific research and collaboration with Russia that is designed to grasp the Arctic's role in weather patterns and global systems spells doom and disaster for the entire globe. Categorizing the current state of Arctic scientific engagement as "missed opportunities" utterly fails to grasp the fact that we simply don't have any time to waste in the first place.

Of course, there may be time to salvage the Arctic theatre, and we might yet see glimmers of Future Three (Arctic Entente). But the Arctic's status quo, preserved rather effectively under the Arctic Council for decades, needs to be rediscovered. Fast. Much of the key dynamics of Russian Arctic strategy explored in this book continue to remain. Russia remains the largest stakeholder and Russia continues to seek foreign cooperation and collaboration to deliver on its strategic priorities. However, prolonged disengagement between Russia and the West in the Arctic region has already ushered in an era of new Arctic players.

Inadvertently, freezing cooperation has resulted in a new iteration of strategic Arctic competition, now with China squarely in the mix. Arctic stakeholders should be seriously pondering the likelihood of Beijing remaining content with its Arctic footprint within the bounds of agreed international law and norms in the region. Punishing Russia in the Arctic is already giving China a blank check to start rewriting the Arctic rulebook. Is the West ready to deter Chinese strategy? Capabilitywise, is Washington even able to respond?

NOTES

Preface

1. Keohane, R., 1984. *After Hegemony: Cooperation and Discord in the World Political Economy*, 1st ed. (Princeton University Press).

Chapter 1

1. See, for example, Blank, S., 2011. *Russia in the Arctic* (Pennsylvania: US Army War College Press); Lucas, E., 2009. *The New Cold War* (London: Bloomsbury Publishing); Stulberg, A., 2007. *Well-Oiled Diplomacy* (State University of New York Press); Sakwa, R., 2008. "'New Cold War' or Twenty Years' Crisis? Russia and International Politics." *International Affairs*, 84:2; Borgerson, S., 2013. "The Coming Arctic Boom," *Foreign Affairs*, 92:4; Gupta, A., 2009. "Geopolitical Implications of Arctic Meltdown," *Strategic Analysis*, 33:2.

2. Borgerson, S., 2008. "Arctic Meltdown," *Foreign Affairs*, 87:2.

3. See, for example, Klare, M., 2008. *Rising Powers, Sinking Planet: The New Geopolitics of Energy* (New York: Metropolitan Books); Howard, R., 2010. *The Arctic Gold Rush* (London: Bloomsbury Books).

4. Haas, M., 2009. "Russia's Arctic Strategy: Challenge to Western Energy Security," *Baltic Rim Economies Review*, 4.

5. Cohen, A., 2007. "Russia's Race for the Arctic," Heritage Foundation, heritage .org/research/commentary/2007/08/russias-race-for-the-arctic.

6. Blank, S., 2011.

7. Schepp, M., and Traufetter, G., 2009. "Riches at the North Pole: Russia Unveils Aggressive Arctic Plans," spiegel.de/international/world/riches-at-the-north-pole-russia -unveils-aggressive-arctic-plans-a-604338.html.

8. See, for example, Pohler, M., 2009. *Russia's Energy Assets: Security and Foreign Policy Issues* (Hauppauge, NY: Nova Science); Balzer, H., 2005. "The Putin Thesis and Russian Energy Policy." *Post-Soviet Affairs*, 3; Tulupov, D., 2013. "Time for Russia and China to Chill Out over the Arctic," russia-direct.org/analysis/time-russia-and -china-chill-out-over-arctic; Laruelle, M., 2014. "Continuing Cooperation Patterns with Russia in the Arctic," wilsoncenter.org/publication/continuing-cooperation -patterns-russia-the-arctic-region; Lackenbauer, P. W., 2016. "Canadian Arctic Security: Russia's Not Coming," newsdeeply.com/arctic/op-eds/2016/04/14/canadian-arctic -security-russias-not-coming; Conley, H., and Rohloff, C., 2013. *The New Ice Curtain* (Washington: CSIS); Zagorski, A., 2013. *The Arctic: A New Geopolitical Pivot?* (Moscow: Russia Direct/Russia Beyond the Headlines); Trenin, D., and Baev, P., 2010. *The Arctic: A View from Moscow* (Moscow: Carnegie Endowment for International Peace).

9. For a good discussion of Arctic geopolitics, see Byers, M., 2009. *Who Owns the Arctic? Understanding Sovereignty Disputes in the North* (Vancouver: Douglas & McIntyre).

10. Unconventional sources are energy sources beyond traditional hydrocarbons (oil and natural gas), such as shale gas and oil sands which involve complicated technology to extract.

11. Shaffer, B., 2009. *Energy Politics* (Philadelphia: University of Pennsylvania Press).

12. Laruelle, M., 2014. *Russia's Arctic Strategies and the Future of the Far North* (Philadelphia: Routledge).

13. Brigham, L., 2010. "Think Again: The Arctic," *Foreign Policy*, 181:71.

14. Klimenko, E., 2016. "Russia's Arctic Security Policy: Still Quiet in the High North," *SIPRI Policy Paper*, 45.

15. Konyshev, V., and Sergunin, A., 2014. "Is Russia a Revisionist Power in the Arctic?" *Defense and Security Analysis*.

16. Le Miere, C., and Mazo, J., 2014. *Arctic Opening: Insecurity and Opportunity* (London: Adelphi Series).

17. Øverland, I., 2010. "Russia's Arctic Energy Policy," *International Journal*, Autumn.

18. See Howard, R., 2010.

19. Baev, P., 2007. "Russia's Race for the Arctic and the New Geopolitics of the North Pole," Jamestown Foundation.

Chapter 2

1. Goldman, M., 2010. *Petrostate: Putin, Power and the New Russia* (Oxford University Press).

2. Goldman, M., 2008. "Moscow's New Economical Imperialism," *Current History*, 323.

3. Olcott, M., 2004. *The Energy Dimension in Russian Global Strategy: Vladimir Putin and the Geopolitics of Oil,* http://carnegieendowment.org/files/wp-2005-01_olcott _english1.pdf.

4. *Moscow Times,* 2016. "Russian Government Presents Rosneft Privatization Guidelines," themoscowtimes.com/2016/07/15/russian-government-moving-ahead-with-rosn eft-privatization-a54612.

5. Rumer, E., 2007. "Russian Foreign Policy beyond Putin," International Institute for Strategic Studies, Adelphi Paper 390.

6. Pirani, S., 2010. *Change in Putin's Russia: Power, Money and People* (London: Pluto Press).

7. For further discussion of Putin's rise to power, see Gessen, M., 2012. *The Man without a Face: The Unlikely Rise of Vladimir Putin* (New York: Riverhead Books).

8. Pirani, S., 2010.

9. Szászdi, L., 2008. *Russian Civil-Military Relations and the Origins of the Second Chechen War* (Lanham, MD: Rowman & Littlefield).

10. Ibid.

11. Ibid.

12. Perovic, J., Wenger, A., and Orttung, R., 2009. *Russian Energy Power and Foreign Relations: Implications for Conflict and Cooperation* (London: Routledge).

13. Gessen, M., 2012.

14. Bugajski, J., 2008. *Expanding Eurasia: Russia's European Ambitions,* Center for Strategic & International Studies.

15. Olcott, M., 2004.

16. Ross, C., 2004. *Russian Politics under Putin* (Manchester University Press).

17. Appel, H., 2008. "Is It Putin Or Is It Oil? Explaining Russia's Fiscal Recovery," *Post-Soviet Affairs,* 24:4.

18. Pirani, S., 2010.

19. Duncan, P., 2007. *Oligarchs' Business and Russian Foreign Policy: From El'tsin to Putin,* Center for the Study of Economic and Social Change in Europe. For further discussion, see Sakwa, R., 2014. *Putin and the Oligarch* (London: I.B Tauris & Co.).

20. Hoffman, D., 2003. *The Oligarchs: Wealth and Power in the New Russia* (New York: PublicAffairs).

21. Ibid.

22. Ibid.

23. Sakwa, R., 2014.

24. Hoffman, D., 2003.

25. Ibid.

26. Perovic, J., Wenger, A., and Orttung, R., 2009.

27. Pirani, S., 2010

28. Smith, K., 2004. *Russian Energy Politics in the Baltics, Poland, and Ukraine: A New Stealth Imperialism?* Center for Strategic and International Studies.

29. Kryshtanovskaya, O., and White, S., 2015. "Inside the Putin Court: A Research Note," *Europe-Asia Studies,* 57:7.

30. Renz, B., 2006. "Putin's Militocracy? An Alternative Interpretation of *Siloviki* in Contemporary Russian Politics," *Europe-Asia Studies* 58:6.

31. Ibid.

32. Ibid.

33. Olcott, M., 2004

34. Hanson, P., and others, 2012. *Putin Again* (London: Chatham House).

35. For a more extensive review of the Khodorkovsky case, see Sakwa, R., 2014. *Putin and the Oligarch: The Khodorkovsky-Yukos Affair* (London: I.B Tauris & Co.).

36. Ibid.

37. Colton, T., and others, 2005. "Russia in the Year 2004," *Post-Soviet Affairs*, 21:1.

38. Perovic, J., Wenger, A., and Orttung, R., 2009.

39. Pirani, S., 2010.

40. Shlapentokh, V., 2006. "Russia as a Newborn Superpower: Putin as the Lord of Oil and Gas," *Johnson's Russia List*, 18.

41. Poussenkova, N., 2010. "The Global Expansion of Russia's Energy Giants," *Journal of International Affairs*, 63:2.

42. Ibid.

43. Russia's constitution at the time permitted only two consecutive presidential terms. Note that Putin's changes to the Russian constitution in the final days of his second presidency meant that foreign policy issues were moved partially to the prime minister's portfolio.

44. Neef, C., and Schepp, M., 2011. "The Puppet President: Medvedev's Betrayal of Russian Democracy," Spiegel Online, spiegel.de/international/world/the-puppet-president-medvedev-s-betrayal-of-russian-democracy-a-789767.html.

45. Baev, P., 2013. "Russia's Arctic Ambitions and Anxieties," *Current History*, October.

46. Buchanan, E., 2014. "Consumers, Not Strategists, Are the Winners in the China-Russia Gas Deal." *East Asia Forum*, eastasiaforum.org/2014/06/19/consumers-not-strategists-are-the-winners-in-china-russia-gas-deal/.

47. Medvedev, D., 2009. "Go Russia," http://en.kremlin.ru/events/president/news/5413

48. Luhn, A., and Macalister, T., 2014. "Russia Signs 30-Year Deal Worth $400bn to Deliver Gas to China," *Guardian*, theguardian.com/world/2014/may/21/russia-30-year-400bn-gas-deal-china.

49. For the purposes of this book, I focus primarily on the sanctions related to Russia's energy market. For a wider discussion of sanctions against Russia, see Council of the EU and the European Council, 2022. "EU Restrictive Measures in Response to the Crisis in Ukraine," consilium.europa.eu/en/policies/sanctions/ukraine-crisis/.

50. Whitmore, B., 2015. "Why Putin Is Losing," rferl.org/content/why-putin-is-losing/27181633.html.

51. Jensen, D., 2013. "The Kremlin Tries to Roll Back the 'Shale Revolution,'" Institute of Modern Russia, http://imrussia.org/en/economy/524-the-kremlin-tries-to-roll-back-the-shale-revolution.

52. See Gideon, R., 2014. "Power to the People: What Will Fuel the Future?" *Foreign Affairs*, 93:3; Morse, E., 2014. "Welcome to the Revolution: Why Shale Is the Next Shale." *Foreign Affairs*, 93:3.

53. Stevens, P., 2012. *The "Shale Gas Revolution": Developments and Change* (London: Chatham House).

54. Godier, K., 2013. "Putin Defends Russia's Unconventional Gas Stance," *ROGTEC*, rogtecmagazine.com/putin-defends-russias-unconventional-gas-stance/.

55. Trenin, D., and Baev, P., 2010. *The Arctic: A View from Russia* (Washington: Carnegie Endowment for International Peace).

56. White, S., 1993. *After Gorbachev* (Cambridge University Press).

57. Ibid.

58. Perovic, J., Wenger, A., and Orttung, R., 2009.

59. Wegren, S., and Herspring, D., 2010. *After Putin's Russia* (New York: Rowman & Littlefield Publishers).

60. Dibb, P., 2006. "The Bear Is Back," *The American Interest*, 2:2.

61. *CIA Factbook*, "Russia," cia.gov/the-world-factbook/countries/russia/.

62. For further discussion of the role of oil and gas in Russia's national narrative and identity, see Rutland, P., 2015. "Petronation? Oil, Gas and National Identity in Russia," *Post-Soviet Affairs*, 31:1; Easter, G., 2008. "The Russian State in the Time of Putin," *Post-Soviet Affairs*, 24:3.

63. Shearman, P., 2001. "The Sources of Russian Conduct: Understanding Russian Foreign Policy," *Review of International Studies*, 27:2.

64. The "near abroad" refers to the newly independent republics established as a result of the 1991 dissolution of the USSR.

65. Shearman, P., 2001.

66. Rose, R., 2007. "New Russia Barometer XV: The Climax of the Putin Years" in *Studies in Public Policy* (Glasgow, UK: Centre for the Study of Public Policy).

67. Goldman, M., 2010.

68. Ibid.

69. Stanislaw. J., 2008. "Power Play—Resource Nationalism, the Global Scramble for Energy," Deloitte Center for Energy Solutions.

70. Cohen, A., 2007. *Europe's Strategic Dependence on Russian Energy* (Washington: The Heritage Foundation).

71. Klare, M., 2008. *Rising Powers, Shrinking Planet? The New Geopolitics of Energy* (New York: Metropolitan Books).

72. For further insight, see Henderson, J., and Mitrova, T., 2015. *The Political and Commercial Dynamics of Russia's Gas Export Strategy*, Oxford Institute for Energy Studies.

73. Shaffer, B., 2009. *Energy Politics* (Philadelphia: University of Pennsylvania Press).

74. From my interview with an IOC representative.

75. Pirani, S., 2010.

76. Yasman, V., 2007. "Russia: Race to the North Pole," Radio Free Europe/Radio Liberty, rferl.org/content/article/1077849.html.

77. Olenicoff, S., 1972. *Territorial Waters in the Arctic: The Soviet Position*, RAND Corporation, rand.org/content/dam/rand/pubs/reports/2009/R907.pdf.

78. Ibid.

79. Emmerson, C., 2010. *The Future History of the Arctic* (New York: Public Affairs).

80. McCannon, J., 1998. *Red Arctic: Polar Exploration and the Myth of the North in the Soviet Union, 1932–1939* (Oxford University Press).

81. Horensma, P., 1991. *The Soviet Arctic* (New York: Routledge).

82. Ibid.

83. Laruelle, M., 2013. *Russia's Arctic Strategies and the Future of the Far North* (New York: M.E. Sharpe).

84. Armstrong, T., 2011. *The Northern Sea Route: Soviet Exploration of the North East Passage* (Cambridge University Press). "Five-year plans" refer to a series of centralized economic plans for the Soviet Union.

85. Emmerson, C., 2010.

86. Laruelle, M., 2013.

87. Exner-Pirot, H., 2012. "How Gorbachev Shaped Future Arctic Policy 25 Years Ago," Alaska Dispatch Publishing, adn.com/arctic/article/how-gorbachev-shaped-future-arctic-policy-25-years-ago/2012/10/01/.

88. See similar initiatives such as his 1986 Vladivostok speech on the Asia Pacific.

89. Gorbachev, M., 1987. "Speech in Murmansk at the Ceremonial Meeting on the Occasion of the Presentation of the Order of Lenin and the Gold Star to the City of Murmansk," barentsinfo.fi/docs/Gorbachev_speech.pdf.

90. Ibid.

91. Ibid.

92. Lackenbauer, W., 2010. "Mirror Images? Canada, Russia and the Circumpolar World," *International Journal*, 65:4.

93. Ibid.

94. Gizewski, P., 1993. "Arctic Security after the Thaw: A Post–Cold War Assessment Report of the Panel on Arctic Security," *Aurora Papers*, 17:2.

95. See Margaret Thatcher's 1984 BBC quote, "I like Mr Gorbachev. We can do business together," margaretthatcher.org/document/105592.

96. Yeltsin, B., 1992. "Boris Yeltsin to Both Houses of Parliament in Canada," House of Commons Debates, 34th Parliament, 3rd Session.

97. International Arctic Science Committee, 2016. "History," https://iassa.org/about-iassa/history.

98. International Arctic Science Committee, 2016. "Objectives," http://iassa.org/about-iassa/objectives.

99. Government of Finland, 1991. "Arctic Environmental Protection Strategy," http://library.arcticportal.org/1542/1/arctic_environment.pdf.

100. Arctic Council, 1996. "Declaration on the Establishment of the Arctic Council," https://oaarchive.arctic-council.org/bitstream/handle/11374/85/EDOCS-1752-v2-ACMMCA00_Ottawa_1996_Founding_Declaration.PDF?sequence=5&isAllowed=y.

101. Exner-Pirot, H., 2012.

102. Gorbachev, M., 1987.

103. Pavlov, A., and Digges, C., 2014. "Russia, Norway Urge Raising of Dumped Soviet-Era Nuclear Subs," Bellona Foundation, http://bellona.org/news/nuclear -issues/2014-04-russia-norway-urge-raising-dumped-soviet-era-nuclear-subs.

104. Digges, C., 2012. "Russia Announces Enormous Finds of Radioactive Waste and Nuclear Reactors in Arctic Seas," Bellona Foundation, http://bellona.org/news /nuclear-issues/radioactive-waste-and-spent-nuclear-fuel/2012-08-russia-announces -enormous-finds-of-radioactive-waste-and-nuclear-reactors-in-arctic-seas.

105. Editorial Board, 2007. "Ships, Subs and Missiles," *Economist*, economist.com /node/9622181.

106. Ibid.

107. BBC News, 2007. "Russia Ahead in the Arctic 'Gold Rush,'" http://news.bbc .co.uk/2/hi/in_depth/6925853.stm.

108. See, for example, Hosa, J., 2018. "Strategy on Ice: Has Russia Already Won the Scramble for the Arctic?" European Council on Foreign Relations, https://ecfr .eu/article/commentary_strategy_on_ice_has_russia_already_won_the_scramble_for _the_arct/.

109. Parfitt, T., 2007. "Russia Plants Flag on North Pole Seabed," *Guardian*, theguardian.com/world/2007/aug/02/russia.arctic.

110. Spiegel International, 2007. "Claim-Jumping the North Pole? Russian Subs Dive to the Arctic Ocean Floor," spiegel.de/international/world/claim-jumping-the -north-pole-russian-subs-dive-to-the-arctic-ocean-floor-a-497774.html.

111. Dodds, K., and Powell, R., 2014. *Polar Geopolitics? Knowledges, Resources and Legal Regimes* (Cheltenham, UK: Edward Elgar Publishing).

112. Chivers, C., 2007. "Russians Plant Flag on the Arctic Seabed," *New York Times*, nytimes.com/2007/08/03/world/europe/03arctic.html?_r=0.

113. From my interview with a Russian academic.

114. Gorenburg, D., 2011. "Russia's Arctic Security Strategy," *Russian Analytical Digest*, 96.

115. Permanent Mission of Canada to the United Nations, 2002. "Notification Regarding the Submission Made by the Russian Federation to the Commission on the Limits of the Continental Shelf," un.org/depts/los/clcs_new/submissions_files/rus01 /CLCS_01_2001_LOS__CANtext.pdf.

116. Permanent Mission of Denmark to the United Nations, 2001. "Notification Regarding the Submission Made by the Russian Federation to the Commission on the Limits of the Continental Shelf," un.org/depts/los/clcs_new/submissions_files/rus01 /CLCS_01_2001_LOS__DNKtext.pdf.

117. Permanent Mission of Norway to the United Nations, 2002. "Notification Regarding the Submission Made by the Russian Federation to the Commission on the Limits of the Continental Shelf," un.org/depts/los/clcs_new/submissions_files/rus01 /CLCS_01_2001_LOS__NORtext.pdf.

118. Permanent Mission of the United States of America to the United Nations, 2002. "Notification Regarding the Submission Made by the Russian Federation to the Commission on the Limits of the Continental Shelf," un.org/depts/los/clcs_new /submissions_files/rus01/CLCS_01_2001_LOS__USAtext.pdf.

119. Ibid.

120. Ibid.

121. Ibid.

122. Government of the Russian Federation, 2015. "Partial Revised Submission of the Russian Federation to the Commission on the Limits of the Continental Shelf," un.org/depts/los/clcs_new/submissions_files/rus01_rev15/2015_08_03_Exec _Summary_English.pdf.

123. Ibid.

124. Ibid.

125. Ibid.

126. Ibid.

127. Permanent Mission of Denmark to the United Nations, 2015. "Notification Regarding the Revised Partial Submission Made by the Russian Federation to the CLCS," un.org/depts/los/clcs_new/submissions_files/rus01_rev15/2015_10_07_DNK_NV_UN _001_15-00785.pdf.

128. Ibid.

129. Permanent Mission of the United States of America to the United Nations, 2015. "Notification Regarding the Revised Partial Submission Made by the Russian Federation to the CLCS," un.org/depts/los/clcs_new/submissions_files/rus01_rev15 /2015_11_02_US_NV_RUS_001_en.pdf.

130. Permanent Mission of Canada to the United Nations, 2015. "Notification Regarding the Revised Partial Submission Made by the Russian Federation to the CLCS," un.org/depts/los/clcs_new/submissions_files/rus01_rev15/2015_30_11_CAN _NV_en.pdf.

131. Editorial, *New York Times*, 2015. "As the Arctic Thaws, New Temptations," nytimes.com/2015/08/07/opinion/as-the-arctic-thaws-new-temptations.html?_r=0.

132. The Conversation, 2015. "The Truth about Politics and Cartography: Mapping Claims to the Arctic Seabed," http://theconversation.com/the-truth-about-politics -and-cartography-mapping-claims-to-the-arctic-seabed-46043.

133. From my interview with a Russian government official.

134. Wilson Rowe, E., and Blakkisrud, H., 2014. "A New Kind of Arctic Power? Russia's Policy Discourses and Diplomatic Practices in the Circumpolar North," *Geopolitics*, 19:1.

Chapter 3

1. Ukaz Prezidenta no. 296, "O sukhoputnykh territoriyakh Arkticheskoi zony Rossiiskoi Federatsii," May 2, 2014, kremlin.ru/acts/bank/38377.

2. For an in-depth discussion of Soviet symbolism in Russia, see Gill, G., 2013. *Symbolism and Regime Change in Russia* (Cambridge University Press).

3. For further discussion of Putin's efforts to revitalize Stalinist culture in Russia, see Baev, P., 2013, "Russia's Arctic Ambitions and Anxieties," *Current History*, October.

4. A detailed review of these documents can be found in Mehdiyeva, N., 2018. "Russia's Arctic Papers: The Evolution of Strategic Thinking in the High North," *Russian Studies*, 4/18, November 19, ndc.nato.int/research/research.php?icode=567.

5. Government of the Russian Federation, 2008. "Principles of the State Policy of the Russian Federation in the Arctic for the Period until 2020 and Beyond," govern ment.ru/media/files/A4qP6brLNJ175I40U0K46x4SsKRHGfUO.pdf.

6. Ibid.

7. Ibid.

8. Ibid.

9. Ibid.

10. Ibid.

11. From my interview with a Russian policymaker.

12. Government of the Russian Federation, 2013. "Strategy for the Development of the Arctic Zone of the Russian Federation and Provision of National Security to 2020," static.government.ru/media/files/2RpSA3sctElhAGn4RN9dHrtzk0A3w Zm8.pdf.

13. Ibid.

14. Ibid.

15. Putin, V., 2014. "On the Implementation of Russia's State Policy in the Arctic in the Interests of National Security," at the Meeting of the Security Council on State Policy in the Arctic, http://en.kremlin.ru/events/president/news/20845.

16. Bobo, L., 2015. *Russia and the New World Disorder* (Brookings Institution Press).

17. As is the case for Russian politics more broadly, for further discussion on the latent brittleness of Putin's power base in terms of his elite management, see Gill, G., 2016. "The Basis of Putin's Power," *Russian Politics*, 1.

18. From my interview with a Russian government official.

19. Ibid.

20. Ibid.

21. Rossiya Segodnya, 2015. "Patrushev: Arctic Should Be an Area of Dialogue, Peace, and Good Neighborliness," arctic.ru/international/20150916/167048.html.

22. High North News, 2014. "Russia Considers to Establish Arctic Ministry," highnorthnews.com/russia-considers-to-establish-arctic-ministry/.

23. Klimenko, E., 2016. *Russia's Arctic Security Policy: Still Quiet in the High North?* (Stockholm International Peace Research Institute).

24. Ibid.

25. Atland, K., 2011. "Russia's Armed Forces and the Arctic: All Quiet on the Northern Front?" *Contemporary Security Policy*, 32:2.

26. Ukaz 164, "Ob Osnovakh gosudarstvennoi politiki Rossiiskoi Federatsii v Artkike na period do 2035 goda," Russian Presidential Administration, http://static .kremlin.ru/media/events/files/ru/f8ZpjhpAaQ0WB1zjywN04OgKiI1mAvaM.pdf.

27. "Nachalas podgotovka proekta Strategii razvitiya Arkticheskoi zony Rossiiskoi Federatsii i obsepechenia natsionalnoi bezopasnosti na period do 2035 goda," Security Council of the Russian Federation, scrf.gov.ru/news/allnews/2737/.

28. "Prezident Rossii utverdil Osnovy gosudarstvennoi politiki Rossiiskoi Federatsii v Arktike na period do 2035," Security Council of the Russian Federation, scrf.gov.ru/news/allnews/2750/.

29. Mehdiyeva, N. "Development Strategy of State Corporation Rosatom to 2030," *Russian Studies Series*, ndc.nato.int/research/research.php?icode=584.

30. PortNews, 2019. "Draft Strategy for the Development of Russia's Arctic through 2035 to Be Presented to Vladimir Putin by Year End," en.portnews.ru/news/288635/.

31. Ukaz 164, sections 7a, b, c.

32. Ukaz 164, section 8a.

33. Ukaz 164, section 8.

34. Ukaz 164, section 8e.

35. Government of the Russian Federation, 2013. "Concept of the Foreign Policy of the Russian Federation," https://thailand.mid.ru/en/concept-of-the-foreign-policy-of-russia.

36. Ibid.

37. De Haas, M., 2009. "Medvedev's Security Policy: A Provisional Assessment," *Russian Analytical Digest*, 62:09.

38. Government of the Russian Federation, 2016. "Foreign Policy Concept of the Russian Federation," https://mid.ru/en/foreign_policy/fundamental_documents/1538901/.

39. Ibid.

40. Government of the Russian Federation, 2014. "The Military Doctrine of the Russian Federation," rusemb.org.uk/press/2029.

41. Mahan, T. A., 1987. *The Influence of Sea Power Upon History* (New York: Dover Publications).

42. Government of the Russian Federation, 2015. "Maritime Doctrine of the Russian Federation," https://rulaws.ru/acts/Morskaya-doktrina-Rossiyskoy-Federatsii/.

43. Connolly, R., 2019. "Review of Russia's Strategy for the Development of Marine Activities to 2030," NATO Defense College, ndc.nato.int/research/research.php?icode=618.

44. Staalesen, A., 2016. "What Russia's New Security Strategy Says about Arctic," *Barents Observer*, thebarentsobserver.com/security/2016/01/what-russias-new-security-strategy-says-about-arctic.

45. Government of the Russian Federation, 2015. "The Russian Federation's National Security Strategy," https://russiamatters.org/node/21421.

46. Ibid.

47. Government of the Russian Federation, 2009. "National Security Strategy of the Russian Federation to 2020," https://thailand.mid.ru/en/national-security-strategy-of-the-russian-federation.

48. Oliker, O., 2016. "Unpacking Russia's New National Security Strategy," Center for Strategic and International Studies, csis.org/publication/unpacking-russias-new-national-security-strategy.

49. Government of the Russian Federation, 2021. "National Security Strategy of the Russian Federation," http://scrf.gov.ru/media/files/file/l4wGRPqJvETSkUTYm hepzRochb1j1jqh.pdf.

50. From my interview with a Russian policymaker.

51. Blank, S., 2015. "Russia's New Arctic Base Continues the Militarization of the High North," *Eurasia Daily Monitor*, 12:202.

52. Ibid.

53. From my interview with a Russian policymaker.

54. For a discussion on Russia's downsizing of the Northern Fleet during the 1990s, see Baev, P., 2013.

55. Norwegian Government, 2008. "The Ilulissat Declaration," Danish Ministry of Foreign Affairs, regjeringen.no/globalassets/upload/ud/080525_arctic_ocean_con ference-_outcome.pdf.

Chapter 4

1. Laruelle, M., 2013. *Russia's Arctic Strategies and the Future of the Far North* (New York: Routledge).

2. Gorenburg, D., 2011. "Russia's Arctic Strategy," *Russian Analytical Digest*, 96.

3. The Arctic's summer sea ice is thinning, yet the coverage in winter months remains. This means the Arctic is becoming easier to navigate (without icebreaker assistance, in some cases) in the summer months.

4. US Department of the Interior, 2008. "Circum-Arctic Resource Appraisal: Estimates of Undiscovered Oil and Gas North of the Arctic Circle," US Geological Survey, http://pubs.usgs.gov/fs/2008/3049/fs2008-3049.pdf.

5. From my interview with a US government official.

6. US Department of the Interior, 2008.

7. Ibid.

8. From my interview with a US government official.

9. Ibid.

10. Ibid.

11. Economist Intelligence Unit, 2014. "The Northern Sea Route: Rivalling Suez?" eiu.com/industry/article/591780243/the-northern-sea-route-rivalling-suez/2014-05-02.

12. Staalesen, A., 2013. "First Container Ship on Northern Sea Route," *Barents Observer*, http://barentsobserver.com/en/arctic/2013/08/first-container-ship-northern-sea-route-21-08.

13. Alexandrova, L., 2013. "Moscow Intends to Expand Its Arctic Zone," ITAR-TASS, http://special.itar-tass.com/en/opinions/762930.

14. Schoyen, H., 2011. "The Northern Sea Route versus the Suez Canal: Cases from Bulk Shipping," *Journal of Transport Geography*, 19:4.

15. Pettersen, T., 2016. "Declining Interest in Use of the Northern Sea Route," *Barents Observer*, https://thebarentsobserver.com/en/industry/2016/03/declining-interest-use -northern-sea-route.

16. Arctic Council, 2016. US Chairmanship, https://arctic-council.org/about/pre vious-chairmanships/

17. Interview with author, Washington.

18. Ibid.

19. The Conversation, 2015. "As the Arctic Melts, the US Needs to Pay Attention," http://theconversation.com/as-the-arctic-melts-the-us-needs-to-pay-attention-35578; Ebinger, C., 2014. *Offshore Oil and Gas Governance in the Arctic* (Brookings Institute).

20. Huebert, R., 2009. *United States Arctic Policy: The Reluctant Arctic Power*, School of Public Policy, University of Calgary.

21. From my interview with a US think tank official.

22. Ibid.

23. Arctic Council, 2016. Past Chairmanships: Canada (1996–1998), https:// arctic-council.org/about/previous-chairmanships/.

24. Associated Press, 2013. "Canada to Claim North Pole as Its Own," *Guardian*, theguardian.com/world/2013/dec/10/canada-north-pole-claim.

25. Government of Canada, 2013. "Preliminary Information Concerning the Outer Limits of the Continental Shelf of Canada in the Arctic Ocean," un.org/depts /los/clcs_new/submissions_files/preliminary/can_pi_en.pdf.

26. Ibid.

27. Chase, S., 2013. "Turf War with Russia Looms over Ottawa's Claim to Arctic Seabed." *The Globe and Mail*, theglobeandmail.com/news/politics/turf-war-with-russia -looms-over-ottawas-claim-to-arctic-seabed/article15777123/.

28. Associated Press, 2013.

29. From my interview with a Russian academic.

30. Government of Canada, 2019. "Submission to the Commission on the Limits of the Continental Shelf," un.org/Depts/los/clcs_new/submissions_files/can1_84 _2019/CDA_ARC_ES_EN_secured.pdf.

31. US Government, 2009. "National Security Presidential Directive and Home-land Security Presidential Directive," https://irp.fas.org/offdocs/nspd/nspd-66.htm.

32. Barkham, P., 2014. "Why Does Denmark Think It Can Lay Claim to the North Pole?" *Guardian*, theguardian.com/world/shortcuts/2014/dec/16/why-denmark-thinks -it-can-lay-claim-to-north-pole.

33. From my interview with a Russian academic.

34. Ibid.

35. Permanent Mission of Norway to the United Nations, 2014. Response to Con-tinental Shelf Notification, un.org/depts/los/clcs_new/submissions_files/dnk76_14/2014 _12_17_nor_nv_dnk4_001.pdf.

36. Permanent Mission of Canada to the United Nations, 2014. Response to Continental Shelf Notification, un.org/depts/los/clcs_new/submissions_files/dnk76 _14/2014_12_29_CAN_NV_DNK4_001_en_15-.pdf.

37. Ibid.

38. Permanent Mission of the Russian Federation to the United Nations, 2015. Response to Continental Shelf Notification, un.org/depts/los/clcs_new/submissions_files/dnk76_14/2015_07_21_RUS_NV_NV_001_15-00554.eng.pdf.

39. Ibid.

40. Kingdom of Norway, 2009. Submission to the Commission on the Limits of the Continental Shelf, un.org/depts/los/clcs_new/submissions_files/submission_nor.htm.

41. Ibid.

42. Ibid.

43. Ibid.

44. From my interview with a Norwegian official.

45. For in-depth studies of China in the Arctic, see Jakobson, L., 2010. "China Prepares for an Ice-Free Arctic," *SPIRO*, March; Blank, S., 2014. "Enter Asia: The Arctic Heats Up," *World Affairs Journal.*

46. State Council Information Office of the People's Republic of China, 2018. "China's Arctic Policy," http://english.www.gov.cn/archive/white_paper/2018/01/26/content_281476026660336.htm.

47. Guschin, A., 2015. "China, Iceland and the Arctic: Iceland Is Playing a Growing Role in China's Arctic Strategy," *Diplomat*, http://thediplomat.com/2015/05/china-iceland-and-the-arctic/.

48. Staalesen, A. 2013. "First Container Ship on the Northern Sea Route," *Barents Observer*, https://barentsobserver.com/en/arctic/2013/08/first-container-ship-northern-sea-route-21-08.

49. Zysk, K., 2014. "Asian Interests in the Arctic: Risks and Gains for Russia," *Asia Policy*, 18.

50. Brady, A., 2018. *China as a Great Polar Power* (Cambridge University Press).

51. Ibid.

52. From my interview with a Norwegian official.

53. From my interview with a US think tank official.

54. Brady, A., 2018

55. From my interview with a Russian government official.

56. Deng, B., 2016. "The Impact of U.S.-Russian Relations on Chinese-Russian Cooperation in the Arctic," Russia in Global Affairs, http://eng.globalaffairs.ru/number/Arctic-Geopolitics-18074.

57. European Parliament, 2008. "Communication from the Commission to the European Parliament and the Council: The European Union and the Arctic Region," http://eur-lex.europa.eu/legal-content/EN/ALL/?uri=CELEX%3A52008DC0763. Note: Although the Russia-EU strategic partnership was signed in 2011, it was challenged in 2015 following Russia's annexation of Crimea. For further discussion, see European Parliament, 2015. "Russia Is No Longer a Strategic Partner of the EU, Say MEPs," press release, europarl.europa.eu/news/en/news-room/20150604IPR62878/Russia-is-no-longer-a-strategic-partner-of-the-EU-say-MEPs.

58. European Parliament, 2008.

59. Gard, 2015. "New Mandatory Regulations for Vessels Operating in Polar Waters," gard.no/web/updates/content/20872272/new-mandatory-regulations-for-vessels-operating-in-polar-waters-.

60. Oxford Economics, 2014. "The Economic Value of the EU Shipping Industry," https://marine-digital.com/article_eu_shipping_industry.

61. Coffey, L., 2012. "NATO in the Arctic: Challenges and Opportunities," Heritage Foundation, heritage.org/research/reports/2012/06/nato-in-the-arctic-challenges-and-opportunities.

62. For further discussion, see Smith-Windsor, B., 2013. "Putting the N back into NATO: A High North Policy Framework for the Atlantic Alliance?" NATO Research Division.

63. From my interview with a Norwegian government official.

64. Shaparov, A., 2013. "NATO and a New Agenda for the Arctic," http://eurodialogue.eu/energy-security/NATO-and-a-New-Agenda-for-the-Arctic.

65. United Nations General Assembly, December 10, 1982. *United Nations Convention on the Law of the Sea*, Section 2, Article 4, un.org/depts/los/convention_agreements/texts/unclos/unclos_e.pdf.

66. Brigham, L., 2014. "The Changing Arctic: New Realities and Players at the Top of the World," *Asia Policy*, 18.

67. Arctic Council, 2016. "About," https://arctic-council.org/about/.

68. Dodds, K., 2013. "The Ilulissat Declaration (2008): The Arctic States, 'Law of the Sea' and the Arctic Ocean," *SAIS Review of International Affairs*, 33:2.

69. Kingdom of Denmark, 2011. *Strategy for the Arctic 2011–2020*. http://library.arcticportal.org/1890/1/DENMARK.pdf. Note: In June 2021, Greenland's self-rule government noted it would develop its own foreign and security strategy for the Arctic.

70. Stimson Analysis, 2013. "Evolution of Arctic Territorial Claims and Agreements: A Timeline (1903–Present)," stimson.org/content/evolution-arctic-territorial-claims-and-agreements-timeline-1903-present.

71. Ibid.

72. Offshore Technology, 2014. "The Remarkable Decline of Oil Spills in the Baltic Sea—Lessons Learnt?" offshore-technology.com/features/featurelessons-learnt-the-remarkable-decline-of-oil-spills-in-the-baltic-sea-4379564/.

73. Interview with author, Washington.

74. Bishop, A., 2010. "Petroleum Potential of the Arctic: Challenges and Solutions," *Oilfield Review*, 22:4.

75. Interview with author, Moscow.

76. Hamilton, J., 2011. "The Challenges of Deep-Water Arctic Development," *International Journal of Offshore and Polar Engineering*.

77. Ibid.

78. Chazan, G. 2012. "Total Warns against Oil Drilling in Arctic," *CNN*, https://edition.cnn.com/2012/09/25/business/total-arctic-drilling-warning/index.html.

79. From my interview with an IOC representative.

80. Baev, P., 2013. "Russia's Arctic Ambitions and Anxieties," *Current History*, October.

81. See, for example, Lucas, E., 2008. *The New Cold War* (London: Bloomsbury); Blank, S., 2014. "The Russian Arctic: Between Economic Development and Accelerating Militarization," *Eurasia Daily Monitor*, 11:199; Blank, S., 2015. "Russia's New Arctic Base Continues the Militarization of the High North," *Eurasia Daily Monitor*, 12:202; Borgerson, S., 2013. "The Coming Arctic Boom," *Foreign Affairs*, July/August.

82. Government of Canada, 2022. "Current Operations and Joint Military Exercises List," canada.ca/en/department-national-defence/services/operations/military -operations/current-operations/list.html.

83. For example, NANOOK 2015 included US troops with UK observation. NANOOK 2010 involved members of the Royal Danish Navy and the US Coast Guard.

84. Government of Canada, 2022. "Current Operations and Joint Military Exercises List."

85. Associated Press, 2013.

86. From my interview with a Russian academic.

87. Keupp, M., 2016. "Five Nations Jockey for Military Influence in Arctic," *National Defense*, nationaldefensemagazine.org/articles/2016/2/29/2016march-five-nations -jockey-for-military-influence-in-arctic.

88. Eye on the Arctic, 2015. "Russia, Norway Team Up for Joint Exercise in Barents Sea," rcinet.ca/eye-on-the-arctic/2015/03/11/norway-and-russia-join-forces-in-arctic -response-drill/.

89. Pettersen, T., 2010. "Russian-Norwegian Naval Exercise in Arctic Waters," *Barents Observer*, http://barentsobserver.com/en/sections/topics/russian-norwegian -naval-exercise-arctic-waters.

90. Greaves, W., 2016. "Thinking Critically About Security and the Arctic in the Anthropocene," Arctic Institute, thearcticinstitute.org/thinking-critically-about-security -and-the-arctic-in-the-anthropocene/.

91. Royal Dutch Shell. 2016. "Energy and Innovation," shell.com/global/future -energy/arctic/arctic-technology.html.

Chapter 5

1. Einstein, N., 2005. "Barents Sea Map," Wikipedia, https://en.wikipedia.org /wiki/Barents_Sea#/media/File:Barents_Sea_map.png.

2. Heininen, L., Sergunin, A., and Yarovoy, G., 2014. *Russian Strategies in the Arctic: Avoiding a New Cold War*, Valdai Discussion Club, uarctic.org/media/857300/arctic _eng.pdf.

3. Division for Ocean Affairs and the Law of the Sea, Office of Legal Affairs, 2022. "Agreement between the Royal Norwegian Government and the Government of the Union of Soviet Socialist Republics Concerning the Sea Frontier between Norway and the USSR in the Varangerfjord," un.org/depts/los/LEGISLATIONANDTREATIES /PDFFILES/TREATIES/NOR-RUS1957SF.PDF.

4. Ibid.

5. Arctic Forum Foundation, 2014. "Delimitation Agreement: A New Era in the Barents Sea and the Arctic?" http://eu-arctic-forum.org/allgemein/delimitation-agreement-a-new-era-in-the-barents-sea-and-the-arctic/.

6. Orttung, R., and Wenger, A., 2016. "Explaining Cooperation and Conflict in Marine Boundary Disputes Involving Energy Deposits," *Regional Studies of Russia, Eastern Europe, and Central Asia*, 5:1.

7. Moe, A., Fjærtoft, D., and Øverland, I., 2011. "Space and Timing: Why Was the Barents Sea Delimitation Dispute Resolved in 2010?" *Polar Geography*, 34:3.

8. United Nations, 1958. "Convention on the Territorial Sea and the Contiguous Zone Done at Geneva on 29 April 1958," http://legal.un.org/ilc/texts/instruments/english/conventions/8_1_1958_territorial_sea.pdf.

9. Harding, L., 2010. "Russia and Norway Resolve Arctic Border Dispute," *Guardian*, theguardian.com/world/2010/sep/15/russia-norway-arctic-border-dispute.

10. From my interview with a Norwegian government official.

11. For a discussion on the "Medvedev thaw," see Wilson, K., 2015. "Modernization or More of the Same in Russia: Was There a 'Thaw' under Medvedev?" *Problems of Post-Communism*, 62:3.

12. Putin distanced himself from the initiative, and despite the nature of the Russian tandemocracy, there is little doubt that Medvedev acted without Putin's full consent.

13. Orttung, R., and Wenger, A., 2016.

14. Ibid.

15. Ibid.

16. Business New Europe, 2013. "Medvedev's $30bn Giveaway," Johnson's Russia List, http://russialist.org/medvedevs-30bn-giveaway.

17. Government of the Russian Federation, 2010. Prime Minister Vladimir Putin addresses the international forum "The Arctic: Territory of Dialogue," http://archive.premier.gov.ru/eng/events/news/12304/print/.

18. Ibid.

19. EU sanctions were extended six months, until July 31, 2016, while Norwegian measures will stay in force simply until lifted. See European Council, 2015. "Russia: EU Prolongs Economic Sanctions by Six Months," press release, consilium.europa.eu/en/press/press-releases/2015/12/21-russia-sanctions/.

20. Krever, M., 2015. "Norway: We Are Faced with a Different Russia," CNN, http://edition.cnn.com/2015/02/25/world/amanpour-norway-ine-eriksen-soreide/.

21. Government of Norway, 2015. "Restrictive Measures against Russia," press release, regjeringen.no/en/aktuelt/Restrictive-measures-against-Russia-/id765896/.

22. Maritime Executive, 2016. "Norway Offers Barents Sea Licenses," maritime-executive.com/article/norway-offers-barents-sea-licenses.

23. Holter, M., 2016. "Norway Opens Arctic Oil Exploration in Russian Border Area," Bloomberg, bloomberg.com/news/articles/2016-05-18/norway-awards-new-oil-licenses-along-arctic-border-with-russia.

24. Ibid.

25. BP, 2011. "Rosneft and BP Form Global and Arctic Strategic Alliance," https://www.bp.com/en/global/corporate/news-and-insights/press-releases/rosneft -and-bp-form-global-and-arctic-strategic-alliance.html.

26. Ibid.

27. Webb, T., 2011. "BP's Russian Deal with Rosneft Blocked by Court," *Guardian*, theguardian.com/business/2011/mar/24/bp-russian-deal-rosneft-blocked-court.

28. Bowers, S., 2015. "BP Ditched Arctic Concerns for Strategic Deal with Russia," *Guardian*, theguardian.com/environment/2015/may/20/bp-ditched-arctic-concerns-for -strategic-deal-with-russia.

29. Ibid.

30. Pinchuk, D., 2013. "Rosneft to Double Oil Flows to China in $270 Billion Deal," Reuters, reuters.com/article/us-rosneft-china-idUSBRE95K08820130621. From my interview with a US think tank official.

31. Ibid.

32. Englund, W., 2011. "Exxon Mobil Signs Russian Oil Pact," *Washington Post*, washingtonpost.com/world/exxonmobil-signs-russian-oil-pact/2011/08/30/gIQAp IvypJ_story.html.

33. Exxon Mobil Corporation, 2014. "Form 10-K Annual Report Pursuant to Section 13 of 15(d) of the Securities Exchange Act of 1934," US Securities and Exchange Commission, sec.gov/Archives/edgar/data/34088/000003408815000013/xom10k2014 .htm.

34. Staalesen, A., 2020. "Rosneft Makes New Arctic Discovery, Compares Kara Sea with Gulf of Mexico and Middle East," *Barents Observer*, https://thebarentsobserver .com/en/industry-and-energy/2020/12/rosneft-makes-new-arctic-discovery-compares -kara-sea-gulf-mexico-and.

35. Kramer, A., 2014. "Russia Vows to Drill Alone in the Arctic," Financial Review, afr.com/news/policy/climate/russia-vows-to-drill-alone-in-arctic-20141029-11e652.

36. Kramer, A., 2014. "The 'Russification' of Oil Exploration," *New York Times*, nytimes.com/2014/10/30/business/energy-environment/russia-oil-exploration -sanctions.html?_r=0.

Chapter 6

1. Klimenko, E., 2016. *Russia's Arctic Security Policy: Still Quiet in the High North?* (Stockholm International Peace Research Institute).

2. For Arctic Council search and rescue agreements, see Arctic Council, 2015. "Agreement on Cooperation on Aeronautical and Maritime Search and Rescue in the Arctic," https://oaarchive.arctic-council.org/handle/11374/531; Pettersen, T., 2010. "Russian-Norwegian Naval Exercise in Arctic Waters," *Barents Observer*, http:// barentsobserver.com/en/sections/topics/russian-norwegian-naval-exercise-arctic -waters. Note that Russia-Norway Arctic "war games" continued throughout the 2008 Georgian war.

3. BBC News, 2015. "Arctic Deal Bans North Pole Fishing," bbc.com/news/world -europe-33549606.

4. Ministry of Foreign Affairs of the Russian Federation, 2015. Comment by the Information and Press Department on Russia's application for Arctic shelf expansion, mid.ru/foreign_policy/news/-/asset_publisher/cKNonkJE02Bw/content/id/1633205.

5. Wilson Rowe, E., and Blakkisrud, H., 2014. "A New Kind of Arctic Power? Russia's Policy Discourses and Diplomatic Practices in the Circumpolar North," *Geopolitics*, 19:1.

6. Sputnik International, 2016. "Russia Confirms Int'l Arctic Projects Thriving Despite Political Situation," http://sputniknews.com/world/20160407/1037653060/arctic-political-situation.html.

7. Rossiya Segodnya, 2016. "Russia-US Cooperation within the Arctic Council Remains Successful," http://arctic.ru/international/20160126/276745.html.

Chapter 7

1. Sukhankin, S., 2021. "Russia's LNG Strategy: Foreign Competition and the Role of the Arctic Region," *Eurasia Daily Monitor*, 18:116, https://jamestown.org/program/russias-lng-strategy-foreign-competition-and-the-role-of-the-arctic-region/.

2. Wilson Rowe, E., and Blakkisrud, H., 2014. "A New Kind of Arctic Power? Russia's Policy Discourses and Diplomatic Practices in the Circumpolar North." *Geopolitics*, 19:1.

3. From my interview with a US think tank official.

4. See the NATO report that states, "The threat of armed conflict in the Arctic is still very low": NATO Parliamentary Assembly Science and Technology Committee, 2015. *The High North: Emerging Challenges and Opportunities*, https://www.nato-pa.int/document/2015-177-stcees-15-e-bis-high-north-bak-report.

5. Baev, P., 2015. "Russia's Arctic Illusions," Brookings, brookings.edu/blogs/order-from-chaos/posts/2015/08/27-russia-arctic-geopolitics-baev.

REFERENCES

Alexandrova, L., 2013. "Moscow Intends to Expand Its Arctic Zone," ITAR-TASS, http://special.itar-tass.com/en/opinions/762930.

Appel, H., 2008. "Is It Putin or Is It Oil? Explaining Russia's Fiscal Recovery," *Post-Soviet Affairs*, 24:4.

Arctic Council, 1996. "Declaration on the Establishment of the Arctic Council," https://oaarchive.arctic-council.org/bitstream/handle/11374/85/EDOCS-1752 -v2-ACMMCA00_Ottawa_1996_Founding_Declaration.PDF?sequence=5&is Allowed=y.

Arctic Council, 2015. "Agreement on Cooperation on Aeronautical and Maritime Search and Rescue in the Arctic," https://oaarchive.arctic-council.org/handle /11374/531.

Arctic Council, 2016. "About," https://arctic-council.org/about/.

Arctic Council, 2016. Past Chairmanships, https://arctic-council.org/about/previous -chairmanships/.

Arctic Forum Foundation, 2014. "Delimitation Agreement: A New Era in the Barents Sea and the Arctic?" http://eu-arctic-forum.org/allgemein/delimitation-agreement -a-new-era-in-the-barents-sea-and-the-arctic/.

Armstrong, T., 2011. *The Northern Sea Route: Soviet Exploration of the North East Passage* (Cambridge University Press).

Associated Press, 2013. "Canada to Claim North Pole as Its Own," *Guardian*, theguardian .com/world/2013/dec/10/canada-north-pole-claim.

Atland, K., 2011. "Russia's Armed Forces and the Arctic: All Quiet on the Northern Front?" *Contemporary Security Policy*, 32:2.

Baev, P., 2007. "Russia's Race for the Arctic and the New Geopolitics of the North Pole," Jamestown Foundation.

Baev, P., 2013. "Russia's Arctic Ambitions and Anxieties," *Current History*, October.

Baev, P., 2015. "Russia's Arctic Illusions," Brookings Institution, brookings.edu/blogs /order-from-chaos/posts/2015/08/27-russia-arctic-geopolitics-baev.

Balzer, H., 2005. "The Putin Thesis and Russian Energy Policy." *Post-Soviet Affairs*, 3.

Barkham, P., 2014. "Why Does Denmark Think It Can Lay Claim to the North Pole?" *Guardian*, theguardian.com/world/shortcuts/2014/dec/16/why-denmark-thinks-it -can-lay-claim-to-north-pole.

BBC News, 2007. "Russia Ahead in the Arctic 'Gold Rush,'" http://news.bbc.co.uk/2 /hi/in_depth/6925853.stm.

BBC News, 2015. "Arctic Deal Bans North Pole Fishing," bbc.com/news/world-europe -33549606.

Bishop, A., 2010. "Petroleum Potential of the Arctic: Challenges and Solutions," *Oil-field Review*, 22:4.

Blank, S., 2011. *Russia in the Arctic* (US Army War College Press).

Blank, S., 2014. "Enter Asia: The Arctic Heats Up," *World Affairs Journal*, 176:6.

Blank, S., 2014. "The Russian Arctic: Between Economic Development and Accelerating Militarization," *Eurasia Daily Monitor*, 11:199.

Blank, S., 2015. "Russia's New Arctic Base Continues the Militarization of the High North," *Eurasia Daily Monitor*, 12:202.

Bobo, L., 2015. *Russia and the New World Disorder* (Brookings Institution Press).

Borgerson, S., 2008. "Arctic Meltdown," *Foreign Affairs*, 87:2.

Borgerson, S., 2013. "The Coming Arctic Boom," *Foreign Affairs*, 92:4.

Bowers, S., 2015. "BP Ditched Arctic Concerns for Strategic Deal with Russia," *Guardian*, theguardian.com/environment/2015/may/20/bp-ditched-arctic-concerns-for -strategic-deal-with-russia.

BP, 2011. "Rosneft and BP Form Global and Arctic Strategic Alliance," bp.com/en /global/corporate/news-and-insights/press-releases/rosneft-and-bp-form-global -and-arctic-strategic-alliance.html.

Brady, A., 2018. *China as a Great Polar Power* (Cambridge University Press).

Brigham, L., 2010. "Think Again: The Arctic," *Foreign Policy*, 181:71.

Brigham, L., 2014. "The Changing Arctic: New Realities and Players at the Top of the World," *Asia Policy*, 18.

Buchanan, E., 2014. "Consumers, Not Strategists, Are the Winners in the China-Russia Gas Deal," East Asia Forum, eastasiaforum.org/2014/06/19/consumers-not-strat egists-are-the-winners-in-china-russia-gas-deal/.

Bugajski, J., 2008. *Expanding Eurasia: Russia's European Ambitions* (Washington: Center for Strategic and International Studies).

Business New Europe, 2013. "Medvedev's $30bn Giveaway," *Johnson's Russia List*, http://russialist.org/medvedevs-30bn-giveaway.

Byers, M., 2009. *Who Owns the Arctic? Understanding Sovereignty Disputes in the North* (Vancouver, Canada: Douglas & McIntyre).

Chase, S., 2013. "Turf War with Russia Looms over Ottawa's Claim to Arctic Seabed," *Globe and Mail*, theglobeandmail.com/news/politics/turf-war-with-russia-looms-over-ottawas-claim-to-arctic-seabed/article15777123/.

Chazan, G. 2012. "Total Warns against Oil Drilling in Arctic," CNN, https://edition.cnn.com/2012/09/25/business/total-arctic-drilling-warning/index.html.

Chivers, C., 2007. "Russians Plant Flag on the Arctic Seabed," *New York Times*, nytimes.com/2007/08/03/world/europe/03arctic.html?_r=0.

Coffey, L., 2012. "NATO in the Arctic: Challenges and Opportunities," Heritage Foundation, heritage.org/research/reports/2012/06/nato-in-the-arctic-challenges-and-opportunities.

Cohen, A., 2007. "Russia's Race for the Arctic," Heritage Foundation, heritage.org/research/commentary/2007/08/russias-race-for-the-arctic.

Cohen, A., 2007. *Europe's Strategic Dependence on Russian Energy* (Washington: Heritage Foundation).

Colton, T., and others, 2005. "Russia in the Year 2004," *Post-Soviet Affairs*, 21:1.

Conley, H., and Rohloff, C., 2013. *The New Ice Curtain* (Washington: CSIS).

Connolly, R., 2019. "Review of Russia's Strategy for the Development of Marine Activities to 2030," NATO Defense College, ndc.nato.int/research/research.php?icode=618.

Council of the EU and the European Council, 2022. "EU Restrictive Measures in Response to the Crisis in Ukraine," consilium.europa.eu/en/policies/sanctions/ukraine-crisis/.

De Haas, M., 2009. "Medvedev's Security Policy: A Provisional Assessment," *Russian Analytical Digest*, 62:09.

Deng, B., 2016. "The Impact of U.S.-Russian Relations on Chinese-Russian Cooperation in the Arctic," *Russia in Global Affairs*, http://eng.globalaffairs.ru/number/Arctic-Geopolitics-18074.

Dibb, P., 2006. "The Bear Is Back," *American Interest*, 2:2.

Digges, C., 2012. "Russia Announces Enormous Finds of Radioactive Waste and Nuclear Reactors in Arctic Seas," Bellona Foundation, http://bellona.org/news/nuclear-issues/radioactive-waste-and-spent-nuclear-fuel/2012-08-russia-announces-enormous-finds-of-radioactive-waste-and-nuclear-reactors-in-arctic-seas.

Division for Ocean Affairs and the Law of the Sea, Office of Legal Affairs, 2022. "Agreement between the Royal Norwegian Government and the Government of the Union of Soviet Socialist Republics Concerning the Sea Frontier between Norway and the USSR in the Varangerfjord," un.org/depts/los/LEGISLATIONANDTREATIES/PDFFILES/TREATIES/NOR-RUS1957SF.PDF.

Dodds, K., 2013. "The Ilulissat Declaration (2008): The Arctic States, 'Law of the Sea' and the Arctic Ocean," *SAIS Review of International Affairs*, 33:2.

Dodds, K., and Powell, R., 2014. *Polar Geopolitics? Knowledges, Resources and Legal Regimes* (Cheltenham, UK: Edward Elgar Publishing).

Duncan, P., 2007. "'Oligarchs,' Business and Russian Foreign Policy: From El'tsin to Putin," Center for the Study of Economic and Social Change in Europe.

Easter, G., 2008. "The Russian State in the Time of Putin," *Post-Soviet Affairs*, 24:3.

Ebinger, C., 2014. *Offshore Oil and Gas Governance in the Arctic* (Brookings Institution).

Economist Intelligence Unit, 2014. "The Northern Sea Route: Rivalling Suez?" eiu.com /industry/article/591780243/the-northern-sea-route-rivalling-suez/2014-05-02.

Editorial Board, 2007. "Ships, Subs and Missiles," *Economist*, economist.com/node /9622181.

Editorial, *New York Times*, 2015. "As the Arctic Thaws, New Temptations," nytimes .com/2015/08/07/opinion/as-the-arctic-thaws-new-temptations.html?_r=0.

Einstein, N. 2005. "Barents Sea Map," Wikipedia, https://en.wikipedia.org/wiki /Barents_Sea#/media/File:Barents_Sea_map.png.

Emmerson, C., 2010. *The Future History of the Arctic* (New York: PublicAffairs).

Englund, W., 2011. "Exxon Mobil Signs Russian Oil Pact," *Washington Post*, washington post.com/world/exxonmobil-signs-russian-oil-pact/2011/08/30/gIQApIvypJ _story.html.

European Council, 2015. "Russia: EU Prolongs Economic Sanctions by Six Months," press release, consilium.europa.eu/en/press/press-releases/2015/12/21-russia-sanctions/.

European Parliament, 2008. "Communication from the Commission to the European Parliament and the Council: The European Union and the Arctic Region," http://eur-lex.europa.eu/legal-content/EN/ALL/?uri=CELEX%3A52008 DC0763.

European Parliament, 2015. "Russia Is No Longer a Strategic Partner of the EU, Say MEPs," press release, europarl.europa.eu/news/en/news-room/20150604IPR62878 /Russia-is-no-longer-a-strategic-partner-of-the-EU-say-MEPs.

European Union External Action Service, 2016. "EU Launches a New Integrated Policy for the Arctic," https://eeas.europa.eu/headquarters/headquarters-homepage _en/3500/EU%20launches%20a%20new%20integrated%20policy%20for%20 the%20Arctic.

Exner-Pirot, H., 2012. "How Gorbachev Shaped Future Arctic Policy 25 Years Ago," Alaska Dispatch Publishing, adn.com/arctic/article/how-gorbachev-shaped-future -arctic-policy-25-years-ago/2012/10/01/.

Exxon Mobil Corporation, 2014. "Form 10-K Annual Report Pursuant to Section 13 of 15(d) of the Securities Exchange Act of 1934," US Securities and Exchange Commission, sec.gov/Archives/edgar/data/34088/000003408815000013/xom10k2014 .htm.

Eye on the Arctic, 2015. "Russia, Norway Team Up for Joint Exercise in Barents Sea," rcinet.ca/eye-on-the-arctic/2015/03/11/norway-and-russia-join-forces-in-arctic -response-drill/.

Gard, 2015. "New Mandatory Regulations for Vessels Operating in Polar Waters," gard. no/web/updates/content/20872272/new-mandatory-regulations-for-vessels-operating -in-polar-waters-.

Gessen, M., 2012. *The Man without a Face: The Unlikely Rise of Vladimir Putin* (New York: Riverhead Books).

Gideon, R., 2014. "Power to the People: What Will Fuel the Future?" *Foreign Affairs*, 93:3.

Gill, G., 2013. *Symbolism and Regime Change in Russia* (Cambridge University Press).

Gill, G., 2016, "The Basis of Putin's Power," *Russian Politics*, 1.

Gizewski, P., 1993. "Arctic Security after the Thaw: A Post–Cold War Assessment Report of the Panel on Arctic Security," *Aurora Papers*, 17:2.

Godier, K., 2013. "Putin Defends Russia's Unconventional Gas Stance," ROGTEC, rogtecmagazine.com/putin-defends-russias-unconventional-gas-stance/.

Goldman, M., 2008. "Moscow's New Economical Imperialism," *Current History*, 323.

Goldman, M., 2010. *Petrostate: Putin, Power and the New Russia* (Oxford University Press).

Gorbachev, M., 1987. "Speech in Murmansk at the Ceremonial Meeting on the Occasion of the Presentation of the Order of Lenin and the Gold Star to the City of Murmansk," barentsinfo.fi/docs/Gorbachev_speech.pdf.

Gorenburg, D., 2011. "Russia's Arctic Security Strategy," *Russian Analytical Digest*, 96.

Government of Canada, 2013. "Preliminary Information Concerning the Outer Limits of the Continental Shelf of Canada in the Arctic Ocean," un.org/depts/los/clcs _new/submissions_files/preliminary/can_pi_en.pdf.

Government of Canada, 2019. "Submission to the Commission on the Limits of the Continental Shelf," un.org/Depts/los/clcs_new/submissions_files/can1_84_2019 /CDA_ARC_ES_EN_secured.pdf.

Government of Canada, 2022. "Current Operations and Joint Military Exercises List," canada.ca/en/department-national-defence/services/operations/military -operations/current-operations/list.html.

Government of Finland, 1991. "Arctic Environmental Protection Strategy," http:// library.arcticportal.org/1542/1/artic_environment.pdf.

Government of Norway, 2015. "Restrictive Measures against Russia," press release, regjeringen.no/en/aktuelt/Restrictive-measures-against-Russia-/id765896/.

Government of the Russian Federation, 2008. "Principles of the State Policy of the Russian Federation in the Arctic for the Period until 2020 and Beyond," government. ru/media/files/A4qP6brLNJ175I40U0K46x4SsKRHGfUO.pdf.

Government of the Russian Federation, 2009. "National Security Strategy of the Russian Federation to 2020," https://thailand.mid.ru/en/national-security-strategy-of -the-russian-federation.

Government of the Russian Federation, 2010. Prime Minister Vladimir Putin addresses the international forum "The Arctic: Territory of Dialogue," http://archive.premier .gov.ru/eng/events/news/12304/print/.

Government of the Russian Federation, 2013. "Concept of the Foreign Policy of the Russian Federation," https://thailand.mid.ru/en/concept-of-the-foreign-policy-of-russia.

Government of the Russian Federation, 2013. "Strategy for the Development of the Arctic Zone of the Russian Federation and Provision of National Security to 2020," static.government.ru/media/files/2RpSA3sctElhAGn4RN9dHrtzk0A3wZm8.pdf.

Government of the Russian Federation, 2014. "The Military Doctrine of the Russian Federation," rusemb.org.uk/press/2029.

Government of the Russian Federation, 2015. "Maritime Doctrine of the Russian Federation," https://rulaws.ru/acts/Morskaya-doktrina-Rossiyskoy-Federatsii/.

Government of the Russian Federation, 2015. "Partial Revised Submission of the Russian Federation to the Commission on the Limits of the Continental Shelf," un.org/depts/los/clcs_new/submissions_files/rus01_rev15/2015_08_03_Exec_Summary_English.pdf.

Government of the Russian Federation, 2015. "The Russian Federation's National Security Strategy," https://russiamatters.org/node/21421.

Government of the Russian Federation, 2016. "Foreign Policy Concept of the Russian Federation," https://mid.ru/en/foreign_policy/fundamental_documents/1538901/.

Government of the Russian Federation, 2021. "National Security Strategy of the Russian Federation," http://scrf.gov.ru/media/files/file/l4wGRPqJvETSkUTYmhepzRochb1j1jqh.pdf.

Greaves, W., 2016. "Thinking Critically about Security and the Arctic in the Anthropocene," Arctic Institute, thearcticinstitute.org/thinking-critically-about-security-and-the-arctic-in-the-anthropocene/.

Gupta, A., 2009. "Geopolitical Implications of Arctic Meltdown," *Strategic Analysis*, 33:2.

Guschin, A., 2015. "China, Iceland and the Arctic: Iceland Is Playing a Growing Role in China's Arctic Strategy," *Diplomat*, http://thediplomat.com/2015/05/china-iceland-and-the-arctic/.

Haas, M., 2009. "Russia's Arctic Strategy: Challenge to Western Energy Security," *Baltic Rim Economies Review*, 4.

Hamilton, J., 2011. "The Challenges of Deep-Water Arctic Development," *International Journal of Offshore and Polar Engineering*, 21:4.

Hanson, P., and others, 2012. *Putin Again*, Chatham House Report, Royal Institute of International Affairs.

Harding, L., 2010. "Russia and Norway Resolve Arctic Border Dispute," *Guardian*, the guardian.com/world/2010/sep/15/russia-norway-arctic-border-dispute.

Heininen, L., Sergunin, A., and Yarovoy, G., 2014. "Russian Strategies in the Arctic: Avoiding a New Cold War," Valdai Discussion Club, uarctic.org/media/857300/arctic_eng.pdf.

Henderson, J., and Mitrova, T., 2015. *The Political and Commercial Dynamics of Russia's Gas Export Strategy*, Oxford Institute for Energy Studies.

High North News, 2014. "Russia Considers to Establish Arctic Ministry," highnorth news.com/russia-considers-to-establish-arctic-ministry/.

Hoffman, D., 2003. *The Oligarchs: Wealth and Power in the New Russia* (New York: PublicAffairs).

Holter, M., 2016. "Norway Opens Arctic Oil Exploration in Russian Border Area," Bloomberg, bloomberg.com/news/articles/2016-05-18/norway-awards-new-oil -licenses-along-arctic-border-with-russia.

Horensma, P., 1991. *The Soviet Arctic* (New York: Routledge).

Hosa, J., 2018. "Strategy on Ice: Has Russia Already Won the Scramble for the Arc- tic?" European Council on Foreign Relations, https://ecfr.eu/article/commentary _strategy_on_ice_has_russia_already_won_the_scramble_for_the_arct/.

Howard, R., 2010. *The Arctic Gold Rush* (London: Bloomsbury Books).

Huebert, R., 2009. *United States Arctic Policy: The Reluctant Arctic Power*, School of Public Policy, University of Calgary.

International Arctic Science Committee, 2016. "History," https://iassa.org/about-iassa /history.

International Arctic Science Committee, 2016. "Objectives," http://iassa.org/about -iassa/objectives.

Jakobson, L., 2010. "China Prepares for an Ice-Free Arctic," SIPRI, March.

Jensen, D., 2013. "The Kremlin Tries to Roll Back the 'Shale Revolution,'" Institute of Modern Russia, http://imrussia.org/en/economy/524-the-kremlin-tries-to-roll -back-the-shale-revolution.

Keohane, R., 1984. *After Hegemony: Cooperation and Discord in the World Political Econ- omy*, 1st ed. (Princeton University Press).

Keupp, M., 2016. "Five Nations Jockey for Military Influence in Arctic," *National Defense*, nationaldefensemagazine.org/articles/2016/2/29/2016march-five-nations -jockey-for-military-influence-in-arctic.

Kingdom of Denmark, 2011. Strategy for the Arctic 2011–2020, http://library.arcticportal .org/1890/1/DENMARK.pdf. Note: In June 2021, Greenland's self-rule government said it would develop its own foreign and security strategy for the Arctic.

Kingdom of Norway, 2009. Submission to the Commission on the Limits of the Con- tinental Shelf, un.org/depts/los/clcs_new/submissions_files/submission_nor.htm.

Klare, M., 2008. *Rising Powers, Sinking Planet: The New Geopolitics of Energy* (New York: Metropolitan Books).

Klimenko, E., 2016. "Russia's Arctic Security Policy: Still Quiet in the High North," SIPRI Policy Paper 45.

Konyshev, V., and Sergunin, A., 2014. "Is Russia a Revisionist Power in the Arctic?" *Defense and Security Analysis*, 30:4.

Kramer, A., 2014. "Russia Vows to Drill Alone in the Arctic," *Financial Review*, afr.com /news/policy/climate/russia-vows-to-drill-alone-in-arctic-20141029-11e652.

Kramer, A., 2014. "The 'Russification' of Oil Exploration," *New York Times*, nytimes .com/2014/10/30/business/energy-environment/russia-oil-exploration-sanctions .html?_r=0.

Krever, M., 2015. "Norway: We Are Faced with a Different Russia," CNN, http://edition.cnn.com/2015/02/25/world/amanpour-norway-ine-eriksen-soreide/.

Kryshtanovskaya, O., and White, S., 2015. "Inside the Putin Court: A Research Note," *Europe-Asia Studies*, 57:7.

Lackenbauer, P. W., 2016. "Canadian Arctic Security: Russia's Not Coming," news deeply.com/arctic/op-eds/2016/04/14/canadian-arctic-security-russias-not-coming.

Lackenbauer, W., 2010. "Mirror Images? Canada, Russia and the Circumpolar World," *International Journal*, 65:4.

Laruelle, M., 2014. "Continuing Cooperation Patterns with Russia in the Arctic," wilson center.org/publication/continuing-cooperation-patterns-russia-the-arctic-region.

Laruelle, M., 2014. *Russia's Arctic Strategies and the Future of the Far North* (Philadelphia: Routledge).

Le Miere, C., and Mazo, J., 2014. *Arctic Opening: Insecurity and Opportunity* (London: Adelphi Series).

Lucas, E., 2009. *The New Cold War* (London: Bloomsbury Publishing).

Luhn, A., and Macalister, T., 2014. "Russia Signs 30-Year Deal Worth $400bn to Deliver Gas to China," *Guardian*, theguardian.com/world/2014/may/21/russia-30-year-400bn-gas-deal-china.

Mahan, T. A., 1987. *The Influence of Sea Power upon History* (New York: Dover Publications).

Maritime Executive, 2016. "Norway Offers Barents Sea Licenses," maritime-executive.com/article/norway-offers-barents-sea-licenses.

McCannon, J., 1998. *Red Arctic: Polar Exploration and the Myth of the North in the Soviet Union, 1932-1939* (Oxford University Press).

Medvedev, D., 2009. "Go Russia," http://en.kremlin.ru/events/president/news/5413.

Mehdiyeva, N., 2019. "Development Strategy of State Corporation Rosatom to 2030," Russian Studies Series, ndc.nato.int/research/research.php?icode=584.

Mehdiyeva, N., 2018. "Russia's Arctic Papers: The Evolution of Strategic Thinking in the High North," Russian Studies Series, ndc.nato.int/research/research.php?icode=567.

Ministry of Foreign Affairs of the Russian Federation, 2015. Comment by the Information and Press Department on Russia's application for Arctic shelf expansion, mid.ru/foreign_policy/news/-/asset_publisher/cKNonkJE02Bw/content/id/1633205.

Moe, A., Fjærtoft, D., and Øverland, I., 2011. "Space and Timing: Why Was the Barents Sea Delimitation Dispute Resolved in 2010?" *Polar Geography*, 34:3.

Morse, E., 2014. "Welcome to the Revolution: Why Shale Is the Next Shale," *Foreign Affairs*, 93:3.

Moscow Times, 2016. "Russian Government Presents Rosneft Privatization Guidelines," themoscowtimes.com/2016/07/15/russian-government-moving-ahead-with-rosneft-privatization-a54612.

Neef, C., and Schepp, M., 2011. "The Puppet President: Medvedev's Betrayal of Russian Democracy," Spiegel Online, spiegel.de/international/world/the-puppet -president-medvedev-s-betrayal-of-russian-democracy-a-789767.html.

Norwegian Government, 2008. "The Ilulissat Declaration," Danish Ministry of Foreign Affairs, regjeringen.no/globalassets/upload/ud/080525_arctic_ocean_confer ence-_outcome.pdf.

Offshore Technology, 2014. "The Remarkable Decline of Oil Spills in the Baltic Sea: Lessons Learnt?" offshore-technology.com/features/featurelessons-learnt-the -remarkable-decline-of-oil-spills-in-the-baltic-sea-4379564/.

Olcott, M., 2004. *The Energy Dimension in Russian Global Strategy: Vladimir Putin and the Geopolitics of Oil*, http://carnegieendowment.org/files/wp-2005-01_olcott _english1.pdf.

Olenicoff, S., 1972. *Territorial Waters in the Arctic: The Soviet Position*, RAND Corporation, rand.org/content/dam/rand/pubs/reports/2009/R907.pdf.

Oliker, O., 2016. "Unpacking Russia's New National Security Strategy," Center for Strategic and International Studies, csis.org/publication/unpacking-russias-new -national-security-strategy.

Orttung, R., and Wenger, A., 2016. "Explaining Cooperation and Conflict in Marine Boundary Disputes Involving Energy Deposits," *Regional Studies of Russia, Eastern Europe, and Central Asia*, 5:1.

Øverland, I., 2010. "Russia's Arctic Energy Policy," *International Journal*, Autumn.

Oxford Economics, 2014. "The Economic Value of the EU Shipping Industry, 2020," ECSA, https://marine-digital.com/article_eu_shipping_industry.

Parfitt, T., 2007. "Russia Plants Flag on North Pole Seabed," *Guardian*, theguardian .com/world/2007/aug/02/russia.arctic.

Pavlov, A., and Digges, C., 2014. "Russia, Norway Urge Raising of Dumped Soviet-Era Nuclear Subs," Bellona Foundation, http://bellona.org/news/nuclear-issues /2014-04-russia-norway-urge-raising-dumped-soviet-era-nuclear-subs.

Permanent Mission of Canada to the United Nations, 2002. "Notification Regarding the Submission Made by the Russian Federation to the CLCS," un.org/depts/los /clcs_new/submissions_files/rus01/CLCS_01_2001_LOS__CANtext.pdf.

Permanent Mission of Canada to the United Nations, 2014. Response to Continental Shelf Notification, un.org/depts/los/clcs_new/submissions_files/dnk76_14/2014 _12_29_CAN_NV_DNK4_001_en_15-.pdf.

Permanent Mission of Canada to the United Nations, 2015. "Notification Regarding the Revised Partial Submission Made by the Russian Federation to the CLCS," un.org/depts/los/clcs_new/submissions_files/rus01_rev15/2015_30_11_CAN _NV_en.pdf.

Permanent Mission of Denmark to the United Nations, 2001. "Notification Regarding the Submission Made by the Russian Federation to the CLCS," un.org/depts /los/clcs_new/submissions_files/rus01/CLCS_01_2001_LOS__DNKtext.pdf.

Permanent Mission of Denmark to the United Nations, 2015. "Notification Regarding the Revised Partial Submission Made by the Russian Federation to the CLCS," un.org/depts/los/clcs_new/submissions_files/rus01_rev15/2015_10_07_DNK_NV_UN_001_15-00785.pdf.

Permanent Mission of Norway to the United Nations, 2002. "Notification Regarding the Submission Made by the Russian Federation to the CLCS," un.org/depts/los/clcs_new/submissions_files/rus01/CLCS_01_2001_LOS__NORtext.pdf.

Permanent Mission of Norway to the United Nations, 2014. Response to Continental Shelf Notification, un.org/depts/los/clcs_new/submissions_files/dnk76_14/2014_12_17_nor_nv_dnk4_001.pdf.

Permanent Mission of the Russian Federation to the United Nations, 2015. Response to Continental Shelf Notification, un.org/depts/los/clcs_new/submissions_files/dnk76_14/2015_07_21_RUS_NV_NV_001_15-00554.eng.pdf.

Permanent Mission of the United States of America to the United Nations, 2002. "Notification Regarding the Submission Made by the Russian Federation to the CLCS," un.org/depts/los/clcs_new/submissions_files/rus01/CLCS_01_2001_LOS__USAtext.pdf.

Permanent Mission of the United States of America to the United Nations, 2015. "Notification Regarding the Revised Partial Submission Made by the Russian Federation to the CLCS," un.org/depts/los/clcs_new/submissions_files/rus01_rev15/2015_11_02_US_NV_RUS_001_en.pdf.

Perovic, J., Wenger, A., and Orttung, R., 2009. *Russian Energy Power and Foreign Relations: Implications for Conflict and Cooperation* (London: Routledge).

Pettersen, T., 2010. "Russian-Norwegian Naval Exercise in Arctic Waters," *Barents Observer*, http://barentsobserver.com/en/sections/topics/russian-norwegian-naval-exercise-arctic-waters.

Pettersen, T., 2016. "Declining Interest in Use of the Northern Sea Route," *Barents Observer*, https://thebarentsobserver.com/en/industry/2016/03/declining-interest-use-northern-sea-route.

Pinchuk, D., 2013. "Rosneft to Double Oil Flows to China in $270 Billion Deal," Reuters, reuters.com/article/us-rosneft-china-idUSBRE95K08820130621.

Pirani, S., 2010. *Change in Putin's Russia: Power, Money and People* (London: Pluto Press).

Pohler, M., 2009. *Russia's Energy Assets: Security and Foreign Policy Issues* (Hauppauge, NY: Nova Science)

PortNews, 2019. "Draft Strategy for the Development of Russia's Arctic through 2035 to be Presented to Vladimir Putin by Year End," en.portnews.ru/news/288635/.

Poussenkova, N., 2010. "The Global Expansion of Russia's Energy Giants," *Journal of International Affairs*, 63:2.

Putin, V., 2014. "On the Implementation of Russia's State Policy in the Arctic in the Interests of National Security," at the Meeting of the Security Council on State Policy in the Arctic, http://en.kremlin.ru/events/president/news/20845.

Renz, B., 2006. "Putin's Militocracy? An Alternative Interpretation of Siloviki in Contemporary Russian Politics," *Europe-Asia Studies*, 58:6.

Rose, R., 2007. "New Russia Barometer XV: The Climax of the Putin Years" in *Studies in Public Policy* (Glasgow, UK: Centre for the Study of Public Policy).

Ross, C., 2004. *Russian Politics under Putin* (Manchester University Press).

Rossiya Segodnya, 2015. "Patrushev: Arctic Should be an Area of Dialogue, Peace, and Good Neighborliness," arctic.ru/international/20150916/167048.html.

Rossiya Segodnya, 2016. "Russia-US Cooperation within the Arctic Council Remains Successful," http://arctic.ru/international/20160126/276745.html.

Royal Dutch Shell, 2016. "Energy and Innovation," shell.com/global/future-energy /arctic/arctic-technology.html.

Rumer, E., 2007. "Russian Foreign Policy beyond Putin," International Institute for Strategic Studies, Adelphi Paper 390.

Rutland, P., 2015. "Petronation? Oil, Gas and National Identity in Russia," *Post-Soviet Affairs*, 31:1.

Sakwa, R., 2008. "'New Cold War' or Twenty Years' Crisis? Russia and International Politics," *International Affairs*, 84:2.

Sakwa, R., 2014. *Putin and the Oligarch: The Khodorkovsky-Yukos Affair* (London: I.B Tauris & Co.).

Schepp, M., and Traufetter, G., 2009. "Riches at the North Pole: Russia Unveils Aggressive Arctic Plans," spiegel.de/international/world/riches-at-the-north-pole -russia-unveils-aggressive-arctic-plans-a-604338.html.

Schoyen, H., 2011. "The Northern Sea Route versus the Suez Canal: Cases from Bulk Shipping," *Journal of Transport Geography*, 19:4.

Security Council of the Russian Federation, 2020. "Nachalas podgotovka proekta Strategii razvitiya Arkticheskoi zony Rossiiskoi Federatsii i obsepechenia nationalnoi bezopasnosti na period do 2035 goda" (Preparation of the draft strategy for the development of the Arctic Zone of the Russian Federation and National Security for the period up to 2035 has begun), scrf.gov.ru/news/allnews/2737/.

Security Council of the Russian Federation, 2020. "Prezident Rossii utverdil Osnovy gosudarstvennoi politiki Rossiiskoi Federatsii v Arktike na period do 2035" (President of Russia approved the Fundamentals of State Policy of the Russian Federation in the Arctic for the period up to 2035), scrf.gov.ru/news/allnews/2750/.

Shaffer, B., 2009. *Energy Politics* (Philadelphia: University of Pennsylvania Press).

Shaparov, A., 2013. "NATO and a New Agenda for the Arctic," http://eurodialogue .eu/energy-security/NATO-and-a-New-Agenda-for-the-Arctic.

Shearman, P., 2001. "The Sources of Russian Conduct: Understanding Russian Foreign Policy," *Review of International Studies*, 27:2.

Shlapentokh, V., 2006. "Russia as a Newborn Superpower: Putin as the Lord of Oil and Gas," *Johnson's Russia List*, 18.

Smith, K., 2004. *Russian Energy Politics in the Baltics, Poland, and Ukraine: A New Stealth Imperialism?* (Washington: Center for Strategic and International Studies).

Smith-Windsor, B., 2013. "Putting the N back into NATO: A High North Policy Framework for the Atlantic Alliance?" NATO Research Division.

Spiegel International, 2007. "Claim-Jumping the North Pole? Russian Subs Dive to the Arctic Ocean Floor," spiegel.de/international/world/claim-jumping-the-north -pole-russian-subs-dive-to-the-arctic-ocean-floor-a-497774.html.

Sputnik International, 2016. "Russia Confirms Int'l Arctic Projects Thriving Despite Political Situation," http://sputniknews.com/world/20160407/1037653060/arctic -political-situation.html.

Sputnik International, 2016. "US-Russia Cooperation in Arctic Remains Successful—US Envoy for Arctic," http://sputniknews.com/politics/20160126/1033754313/us-russia -actic-cooperation-successful.html.

Staalesen, A. 2013. "First Container Ship on the Northern Sea Route," *Barents Observer*, https://barentsobserver.com/en/arctic/2013/08/first-container-ship-northern -sea-route-21-08.

Staalesen, A., 2016. "What Russia's New Security Strategy Says about Arctic," *Barents Observer*, thebarentsobserver.com/security/2016/01/what-russias-new-security -strategy-says-about-arctic.

Staalesen, A., 2020. "Rosneft Makes New Arctic Discovery, Compares Kara Sea with Gulf of Mexico and Middle East," *Barents Observer*, https://thebarentsobserver.com /en/industry-and-energy/2020/12/rosneft-makes-new-arctic-discovery-compares -kara-sea-gulf-mexico-and.

Stanislaw, J, 2008. "Power Play—Resource Nationalism, the Global Scramble for Energy," Deloitte Center for Energy Solutions.

State Council Information Office of the People's Republic of China, 2018. "China's Arctic Policy," http://english.www.gov.cn/archive/white_paper/2018/01/26/content _281476026660336.htm.

Stevens, P., 2012. *The "Shale Gas Revolution": Developments and Change* (London: Chatham House).

Stimson Analysis, 2013. "Evolution of Arctic Territorial Claims and Agreements: A Timeline (1903-Present)," stimson.org/content/evolution-arctic-territorial-claims -and-agreements-timeline-1903-present.

Stulberg, A., 2007. *Well-Oiled Diplomacy* (State University of New York Press).

Sukhankin, S., 2021. "Russia's LNG Strategy: Foreign Competition and the Role of the Arctic Region," *Eurasia Daily Monitor*, 18:116.

Szászdi, L., 2008. *Russian Civil-Military Relations and the Origins of the Second Chechen War* (Lanham, MD: Rowman & Littlefield).

The Conversation, 2015. "The Truth about Politics and Cartography: Mapping Claims to the Arctic Seabed," http://theconversation.com/the-truth-about-politics-and -cartography-mapping-claims-to-the-arctic-seabed-46043.

The Conversation. 2015. "As the Arctic Melts, the US Needs to Pay Attention," http:// theconversation.com/as-the-arctic-melts-the-us-needs-to-pay-attention-35578

Trenin, D., and Baev, P., 2010. *The Arctic: A View from Moscow* (Moscow: Carnegie Endowment for International Peace).

Tulupov, D., 2013. "Time for Russia and China to Chill Out over the Arctic," russia -direct.org/analysis/time-russia-and-china-chill-out-over-arctic.

Ukaz (decree) 164, "Ob Osnovakh gosudarstvennoi politiki Rossiiskoi Federatsii v Artkike na period do 2035 goda" (On the fundamentals of the state policy of the Russian Federation in the Arctic for the period until 2035), Russian Presidential

Administration, http://static.kremlin.ru/media/events/files/ru/f8ZpjhpAaQ0WB 1zjywN04OgKiI1mAvaM.pdf.

Ukaz Prezidenta no. 296, May 2, 2014. "O sukhoputnykh territoriyakh Arkticheskoi zony Rossiiskoi Federatsii" (On the land territories of the Arctic Zone of the Russian Federation), kremlin.ru/acts/bank/38377.

United Nations, 1958. "Convention on the Territorial Sea and the Contiguous Zone Done at Geneva on 29 April 1958," http://legal.un.org/ilc/texts/instruments /english/conventions/8_1_1958_territorial_sea.pdf.

United Nations General Assembly, December 10, 1982. United Nations Convention on the Law of the Sea, Section 2, Article 4, un.org/depts/los/convention_agreements /texts/unclos/unclos_e.pdf.

US Department of the Interior, 2008. "Circum-Arctic Resource Appraisal: Estimates of Undiscovered Oil and Gas North of the Arctic Circle," US Geological Survey, http://pubs.usgs.gov/fs/2008/3049/fs2008-3049.pdf.

US Government, 2009. "National Security Presidential Directive and Homeland Security Presidential Directive," https://irp.fas.org/offdocs/nspd/nspd-66.htm.

Webb, T., 2011. "BP's Russian Deal with Rosneft Blocked by Court," *Guardian*, the guardian.com/business/2011/mar/24/bp-russian-deal-rosneft-blocked-court.

Wegren, S., and Herspring, D., 2010. *After Putin's Russia* (New York: Rowman and Littlefield Publishers).

White, S., 1993. *After Gorbachev* (Cambridge University Press).

Whitmore, B., 2015. "Why Putin Is Losing," rferl.org/content/why-putin-is-losing /27181633.html.

Wilson, K., 2015. "Modernization or More of the Same in Russia: Was There a 'Thaw' under Medvedev?" *Problems of Post-Communism*, 62:3.

Wilson Rowe, E., and Blakkisrud, H., 2014. "A New Kind of Arctic Power? Russia's Policy Discourses and Diplomatic Practices in the Circumpolar North," *Geopolitics*, 19:1.

Yasman, V., 2007. "Russia: Race to the North Pole," Radio Free Europe/Radio Liberty, rferl.org/content/article/1077849.html.

Yeltsin, B., 1992. "Boris Yeltsin to both Houses of Parliament in Canada," House of Commons Debates, 34th Parliament, 3rd Session (Ottawa: Canadian Government Publishing).

Zagorski, A., 2013. *The Arctic: A New Geopolitical Pivot?* (Moscow: Russia Direct/Russia Beyond the Headlines).

Zysk, K., 2014. "Asian Interests in the Arctic: Risks and Gains for Russia," *Asia Policy*, 18.

INDEX

Transportation routes: air routes, 54;
Arctic great game and, 5–6, 87;
Bering Strait, 33, 87, 144; in interna-
tional waters, 5, 141; Northeast
Passage, 5–6, 85; Northwest Passage,
5, 6, 87, 141, 157; opening of Arctic
region and, 5–7, 85; Suez Canal, 6, 85,
86; Transpolar Sea Route, 5, 6. *See also*
Northern Sea Route
Trenin, Dmitri, 28
Trident Juncture military exercises, 100
Trudeau, Justin, 89, 91, 105
Trump, Donald: Arctic strategy under,
88, 89, 141–45; on icebreaker gap, 141,
143, 156; Putin's relationship with,
141, 144; on US purchase of Green-
land, 141
Trutnev, Yuri, 62, 64
TSR. *See* Transpolar Sea Route

Ukraine: annexation of Crimea by
Russia (2014), vii, viii, 26, 104, 122;
color revolution in, 23; invasion by
Russia (2022), viii, 26, 152, 159–62;
natural gas disputes with Russia, 16
Union of Soviet Socialist Republics
(USSR). *See* Soviet Union
United Nations Convention on the Law
of the Sea (UNCLOS): Arctic Five
support for, 104; EEZs allocated by, 3;
international waters designated by, 3;
legal architecture of, 44, 47, 117–18,
155; maritime zones under, 101, 103;
ratification of, 88–90, 92, 94, 101, 104,
135. *See also* Commission on the
Limits of the Continental Shelf
United Nations Security Council, 16,
29, 72, 160

United States: in Arctic Armageddon
scenario, 153–54; Arctic strategy of,
87–89, 138, 141–45, 162; on Danish
CLCS submissions, 93; offshore
licenses issued by, 107; potential
extended continental shelf claim, 89,
90; on Russian CLCS submissions,
43–44, 46–47; sectoral line principle
rejected by, 33; shale gas production
in, 27; superpower status of, 28, 36;
UNCLOS, failure to ratify, 88–89,
92, 101, 104, 135; US-Russia relations,
25, 36, 137–46, 152. *See also* Arctic
Eight; Arctic Five; Cold War; *specific
leaders*
United States Geological Survey
(USGS), 3–5, 82–84, 108

Valdez oil spill (1989), 107, 127
Varangerfjord agreement (1957),
115–17
Veselov, Igor, 139
Voloshin, Aleksandr, 17
Vostok Oil, 129–30
Voucher privatization, 20

Wealth. *See* Resource wealth
Western relations with Russia. *See*
Russia-West relations
Wheeler, Andrew, 142
White, Stephen, 28
White Sea Canal, 35
World Trade Organization, 25

Yamal LNG project, 130–31, 132*f*
Yeltsin, Boris, 15, 17–21, 38, 39
Yukos, 21, 22
Yumashev, Valentin, 17

Lightning Source UK Ltd.
Milton Keynes UK
UKHW011304010323
417857UK00018B/191

9 780815 738886